Juvenile Justice Systems: Poland-Brazil-Portugal

Lex et Res Publica
Polish Legal and Political Studies
Edited by Anna Jaroń

Volume 18

PETER LANG

Barbara Janusz-Pohl (ed.)

Juvenile Justice Systems: Poland-Brazil-Portugal

PETER LANG

Bibliographic Information published by the Deutsche Nationalbibliothek
The Deutsche Nationalbibliothek lists this publication
in the Deutsche Nationalbibliografie; detailed bibliographic
data is available online at http://dnb.d-nb.de.

Library of Congress Cataloging-in-Publication Data
A CIP catalog record for this book has been applied for at the
Library of Congress.

Cover illustration: Courtesy of Benjamin Ben Chaim

This publication was financially supported by the
Adam Mickiewicz University in Poznań, Poland.

This work has been reviewed by Professor Daniele Vicoli (University of Bologna, Italy).

ISSN 2191-3250
ISBN 978-3-631-85584-3 (Print)
E-ISBN 978-3-631-86205-6 (E-Book)
E-ISBN 978-3-631-86221-6 (EPUB)
DOI 10.3726/b18696

Peter Lang – Berlin · Bern · Bruxelles · New York ·
Oxford · Warszawa · Wien

www.peterlang.com

Table of Contents

Introduction 9

Part I. Analysis of Juvenile Justice Systems: Typologies and Development Perspectives 11
Barbara Janusz-Pohl

1 General remarks 11
2. Welfare model 14
3. Justice model 21
4. Rehabilitative treatment model 25
5. Restorative justice model 29
6. Mixed models: Combinations of welfare and justice, including minimum intervention and elements of restorative justice: Poland, Brazil and Portugal 34

Part II. Juvenile Delinquency: Polish Perspective 41

Chapter 1. Criminal Responsibility of Juveniles in Polish Law 43
Magdalena Kowalewska-Łuku

1. General remarks 43
2. The concepts of a juvenile, a minor and a young offender 44
3. Age limit of criminal responsibility 45
4. Offender age and attribution of guilt 47
5. Prerequisites of the criminal responsibility of juveniles 49
6. Penalty for a juvenile offender 53
7. Conclusion 54

Chapter 2. Juvenile Situation under the 1982 Juvenile Justice Act 59
Konrad Burdziak

1. General remarks: Aims and basic rules of juvenile justice 59
2. Definition of 'Juvenile' 64
3. Definition of 'Antisocial behaviour' 67
4. Definition of 'Punishable act' 70
5. Educational and correctional measures 76
6. Conclusion 80

Chapter 3. Procedural Aspects of Participation of Juvenile Offenders in Criminal Proceedings: General Remarks 85
Szymon Pawelec

1. Introduction 85
2. Juvenile offender as a party to a criminal proceeding 87
3. Juvenile offender as a source of evidence 96
4. Extension of the right to defence principle in the context of juveniles 102

Chapter 4. Procedural Aspects of Participation of Juvenile Offenders in Criminal Proceedings: Selected Specific Institutions 111
Justyna Głębocka

1. General remarks: Formal representation of 'a juvenile' in criminal proceedings 111
2. European measures improving the status of the juvenile offender 115
3. Application of coercive and preventive measures 120

4. Influence of a juvenile offender on the course of the proceedings ... 127

5. Consensual proposals: abbreviation of proceedings ... 130

6. Selected issues related to the extinction of criminal liability . 134

Part III. Juvenile Delinquency: Comparative Perspective – Brazil ... 143
Denise Casanova Villela, Rodrigo da Silva Brandalise

1. General remarks ... 143

2. The historical conception of the socio-educational system in Brazil ... 145

3. Legislation applicable to the Socio-Educational System ... 148

4. Application of the Socio-Educational System ... 151
   4.1. The addressees of socio-educational measures: children and adolescents and the absence of responsibility under criminal law ... 152
   4.2. Procedure for investigating a criminal act ... 155
   4.3. The socio-educational measures ... 161

5. Restorative Justice in the Socio-Educational System ... 165

6. Conclusion ... 170

Part IV. Juvenile Delinquency: Comparative Perspective – Portugal ... 177
Vanessa Pelerigo

1. General remarks ... 177

2. Minors: Law on the protection of children and young people in danger, Child Education and Protection Act, and Extraordinary Criminal Regime for Young Adults ... 179

3. The lack of criminal responsibility due to age ... 183

4. Conclusion ... 187

Introduction

There can be no keener revelation of a society's soul than the way in which it treats its children.

Nelson Mandela

Juvenile justice systems have been of great interest to researchers for years. Although the separation of juvenile criminal responsibility regimes from adult liability regimes took place at the turn of the 19th and 20th centuries and has been undergoing relatively rapid changes, it still remains a dynamic area. On the one hand, modern trends are strongly influenced by international legislation that creates tendency to treat offenders under the age of 18 in a welfare influenced approach. On the other hand, there is the need to strengthen the rules on the responsibility of juveniles when committing the most serious crimes (felonies). The latter is an effect of the brutalisation of social life, technological development and globalisation.

This monograph is one of the results of cooperation between Poland, Brazil and Portugal within the framework of the Evidentiary Axis established in 2019 on the Faculty of Law and Administration at the Adam Mickiewicz University. *Juvenile Justice Systems* outlines options for shaping the juvenile liability models, in the form of model-patterns: welfare model, justice model, rehabilitative treatment model and restorative justice model. The systemic changes that have involved juvenile liability systems over the last 100 years have been highlighted, and particular attention has been drawn to the trend of shaping a mixed model, currently especially so-called '4xD formula.'

This work consists of 4 parts. The first part is devoted to general issues, i.e. model forming variants, while parts 2, 3, and 4 cover the characteristics of three mixed models: the Polish model, the Brazilian model and the Portuguese model, of which the Polish model is the one that is described in a most detailed manner. Its thorough characterization was based on its substantive and procedural aspects. The description of the Polish juvenile justice system is divided into the four chapters contained in Part 2.

The choice of the three models was determined by their common welfare features. The Polish model is the most complex in nature – providing for a number of options where juvenile offenders, as well as young offenders (those who are under the age of 21 when committing a crime and those who are before the age of 24 in the moment of issuing a by the court in the first instance) can be liable for criminal offences under a special juvenile liability regime or juvenile offenders after the age of 15 are liable on general principles applying for the adult. The Brazilian model is a rather welfare model, providing for a specific liability formula for minors under the age of 18. However, this model is currently being reviewed and heavily influenced by the Portuguese model, under which minors after the age of 16 are tried before the court according to the same principles as the adults.

Comparative analysis of the three models allows to capture flaws as well as beneficial aspects of different regulations. More complex models are certainly more appropriate for a full examination of the juvenile's (or young offender's) situation and the application of an adequate sanction's regime, but also entail a risk of arbitrariness. On the contrary, models dominated by rigid rules with a relatively inflexible sanction's regime could put juveniles at risk, especially in the context of the individual's maturity. Therefore, optimization of the juvenile liability model can be achieved by maintaining a balance between three elements: the interests of a particular juvenile, the risks associated with his or her educational and formation process still in progress and the effectiveness of the liability regime. To achieve such optimization, it is crucial to properly identify the benefits and deficiencies of the existing systems. Therefore the purpose of this monograph is to provide the basis for such a systemic analysis.

The authors of this book are distinguished authorities of law: professors and practitioners, affiliated to 5 different research units: the University of Warsaw, University of Szczecin, Adam Mickiewicz University, University of Lisbon, Fundação Escola Superior do Ministério Público do Rio Grande do Sul and Prosecutors of the State of Rio Grande do Sul. This monograph will be of the interest to those wishing to gain an understanding of different Juvenile Justice Systems.

Part I. Analysis of Juvenile Justice Systems: Typologies and Development Perspectives

Barbara Janusz-Pohl

Abstract: This part deals with the issue of models of juvenile responsibility systems. The models shall be treated in an abstract manner as so-called model-patterns, that is, in their extreme (complete) form, so to speak. The model-patterns discussed in this paper are welfare model, justice model, rehabilitative treatment model and restorative treatment one. When juvenile justice systems were beginning to take shape, such model-patterns were occasionally reflected in equally extreme (absolute) forms around the world. Understandable that specific models (model-representations) take rather eclectic forms and share only certain selected characteristics of various abstract models (model-patterns). Polish, Brazilian and Portuguese Juvenile justice system are seen as mixed models.

Keywords: juvenile justice systems, model of juvenile justice systems, comparative systems, welfare system, justice system, rehabilitative treatment system, restorative justice system.

1 General remarks

Juvenile justice evolved from general criminal law, with the evolution being especially dynamic in the 20th century albeit its outcomes varied from region to region and it progressed in waves. The nature of its evolution has already been noticed by the authoritative juristic literature, which has traced the patterns of changes and noted them as separate models of juvenile justice.[1] Moreover, it has been observed that it was juvenile justice, separate from but also closely related to adult criminal justice, that served as a testing ground for new criminal-political conceptions with respect to, for instance, rehabilitation instruments, subsequent

1 See F. Duenkel, 'Juvenile Justice Systems in Europe – Reform developments between justice, welfare and 'new punitiveness,' *Kriminologijos Studijos* 2014/1, p. 31 ff.; F. Duenkel, *(19) (PDF)* 'Juvenile Justice Systems in Europe – Reform developments between justice, welfare and 'new punitiveness'1. Available at: https://www.researchgate.net/publication/291040931_Juvenile_Justice_Systems_in_Europe_-_Reform_developments_between_justice_welfare_and_%27new_punitiveness%271 [access: March 22 2021].

probation measures, greater role of mediation and restitution in connection with the idea of restorative justice.[2]

The need to model juvenile justice along different principles than the responsibility of adult offenders resulted from socio-cultural changes and new trends in psychology and pedagogy. These trends demanded that juveniles be viewed as autonomous. On the one hand, their susceptibility to environmental influence was underscored, while on the other their lack of ability to comprehend the meaning of their actions and accordingly control them, known as the ability of sensible self-determination, was recognized. Attention was drawn to unfinished educational processes and the ongoing personality formation of juveniles. Initially, a crucial role in the emergence of juvenile justice models in the early 20th century is believed to have been played by the so-called positivist school of criminal law. This school preferred the idea of individual prevention to merely general prevention and the classic retributive (justice) function of criminal law. Hence, it can be said that already at the early stages of the rise of juvenile justice models, the ideas of individual and general prevention were in conflict.

This chapter therefore shall describe the key models of juvenile justice. The models shall be treated in an abstract manner as so-called **model-patterns**, that is in their extreme (complete) form, so to speak. When the systems of juvenile justice were beginning to take shape, such model-patterns were occasionally reflected in equally extreme (absolute) forms around the world. Today, however, specific models (**model-representations**) take rather eclectic forms and share only certain selected characteristics of various abstract models (model-patterns).

Although the models of juvenile justice develop autonomously in particular countries, certain unification tendencies and development trends can be seen as well. In the last few decades, these tendencies are encouraged by dynamic changes in criminal-political theories and are driven by the growing impact of standards set by the United Nations, especially those following from the Convention on the Rights of the Child, and others set by the Council of Europe.[3]

---

2 Cf. B. Stańdo-Kawecka, *Prawo karne nieletnich. Od opieki do odpowiedzialności*, Wolters Kluwer, Warsaw 2007, p. 15.

3 Cf. The recommendations of the Council of Europe, in particular the 2003 Recommendation regarding new ways of dealing with juvenile offending (Rec [2003]20) and the 2008 Rules for juvenile offenders subject to sanctions or measures (Rec [2008]11) – see F. Duenkel, 'Juvenile Justice Systems in Europe – Reform developments between justice, welfare and 'new punitiveness.' See F. Bailleau, Y. Crtuyvels (eds.), *La justice pénale des mineurs en Europe. Entre modèle Welfare et inflexions néo-libérales*. Paris 2007, L'Harmattan, pp. 21 ff.

The models of proceedings in juvenile causes can be variously organised. Above all, note must be taken of the criterion of separation of juvenile justice from adult justice, i.e. making the former autonomous of the latter. Furthermore, **formal autonomisation** involves the enactment of special laws for the regulation of the responsibility of juveniles, while **actual autonomisation** makes the rules of juvenile justice autonomous from those applicable to the criminal responsibility of adults without enacting separate laws. Consequently, a formal or actual autonomisation entails the setting up of a procedural model adequate to the autonomous purpose of the proceedings and the way a response is profiled to the violation of criminal law and other instances of antisocial behaviour by a juvenile.

Historically, juvenile justice systems began to develop in the late 19th and early 20th centuries, and in the 1900s with the rise of so-called welfare systems. In them, courts addressed the good of an 'endangered juvenile,' which was considered vitally important. Pure welfare systems, however, began to break down in the second half of the 20th century; besides, mixed systems already then dominated globally and have always been more stable. The middle of the 20th century witnessed rehabilitative tendencies in the criminal policy that were known as 4×D models (diversion, decriminalisation, deinstitutionalisation and due process of law). Towards the end of the 20th century and in the early 21st century, a trend perpetuated by the strong idea of restorative justice gained momentum. Its impact produced so-called 4×R models (responsibility, restitution or reparation, restorative justice and retribution, with the last-mentioned occasionally openly publicised). The relevant literature claims even that 'These so-called "4Rs" have replaced the "4Ds" (diversion, decriminalization, deinstitutionalization and due process).'[4]

The mixed models, most common now, reflect the impact in various proportions though, of such ideas as minimum intervention, education instead of punishment, restorative justice (mainly implemented with the participation of extrajudicial bodies) and the perception of punishment – especially incarceration – as an *ultima ratio* (last resort). For the models of juvenile justice, the

4 F. Duenkel, 'Juvenile Justice Systems in Europe – Reform developments between justice, welfare and 'new punitiveness'…; F. Duenkel, *(19) (PDF)* 'Juvenile Justice Systems in Europe – Reform developments between justice, welfare and 'new punitiveness'1. Available at https://www.researchgate.net/publication/291040931_Juvenile_Justice_Systems_in_Europe_-_Reform_developments_between_justice_welfare_and_%27new_punitiveness%271 [access: March 22 2021].

crucial assumption is that juvenile delinquency is of an ephemeral nature. Statistically, juvenile delinquency shows a strong tendency to wane in early adulthood. In juveniles, moreover, the impact of external factors is seen to be effective. These include environmental factors as well as educational instruments or possibly correctional ones. The punishment of juveniles is thus a last resort and should be an alternative or an option left to the decision of the adjudicating body. It will take into account the degree of the juvenile's intellectual and emotional development, and of the reprehensibility of their behaviour.

It must be made absolutely clear that neither today nor in the past has a uniform model of juvenile justice been developed. In some countries, the administration of justice with respect to bringing juveniles to justice is organised in part or in full within the limits of substantive or procedural criminal law. Whereas in others, separate courts and procedures for juveniles are provided. Countries differ also in the range of responsibility, systems of educational and correctional measures, and possible penal sanctions. In the event juveniles are made to bear criminal responsibility along the principles close to those applied to adult offenders, the age for criminal responsibility varies as well.

This monograph shall describe three systems of responsibility of juvenile offenders and juveniles exhibiting antisocial behaviour: Polish, Brazilian and Portuguese. These are completely different systems, but each to a greater or lesser degree, shows elements of one of the four model-patterns: welfare, justice (including the neo-classical one), rehabilitation and one based on the idea of restorative justice. These four model-patterns, i.e. models considered in abstract (extreme) terms, shall be described below.

2. Welfare model

The rise of this model was stimulated by the output of the so-called positivist school of criminal law which had redefined the function of punishment. A strictly retributive approach to punishment was abandoned, where it was meant as a retribution for evil done and stress was laid on individual prevention.[5] What

---

5 Cf. B. Stańdo-Kawecka, J. Kusztal, 'Procedural Complexity within a Welfare Approach. Country Report Poland' in: M. Panzavolta, D. de Vocht, M. Oosterhout, M. Vanderhallen (eds.), *Interrogating Young Suspects: Procedural Safeguards from a Legal Perspective*, Cambridge-Antwerp-Portland, Intersentia, 2015, pp. 313–368; B. Stańdo-Kawecka, 'Juvenile Justice in Poland' in: F. E. Zimring, M. Langer, D. S. Tanenhaus (eds.), *Juvenile Justice in Global Perspective*, New York, New York University Press, 2015, pp. 291–326; B. Stańdo-Kawecka, 'Poland' in: S. H. Decker, N. Marteache (eds.), *International*

is more, with respect to juvenile delinquency, individual prevention is considered not only prospectively but also retroactively. For it is important for the assessment of the legal situation of an offender not only who the offender was at the time of violating the law and who they are right now, but also what factors shaped them in the past.

Thus, the welfare model adopts a non-deterministic paradigm under which juvenile delinquency is caused by environmental reasons. To combat juvenile delinquency, it is necessary to separate a juvenile from their pathological environment and its detrimental effect on the juvenile's conduct. In this model, an offence committed by a juvenile is grounds for responsibility but does not determine its scope. What is more, in welfare models, a juvenile remains the focus of attention of proceeding bodies when they show an inclination to commit offences, exhibit antisocial behaviour, are educationally neglected or even when only their environment may be considered criminogenic. The child and their needs are the focus of attention while the criminal law response is geared to the enhancement of educational processes and not repressive measures. The purpose of such proceedings is not only to influence the juvenile offender, but also to prevent criminal and antisocial behaviour by taking welfare and educational measures early enough, going even as far as isolating the juvenile from the pathogenic environment if necessary.

Welfare trends moreover, are strongly underpinned by specific pedagogical conceptions, especially those that deal with socially maladjusted children and young persons. When a juvenile has committed an offence, it is in a sense detached from the offender. The proceeding bodies focus their attention on the circumstances of its commission and the preceding psycho-pedagogical situation of the juvenile. This means that the breaching of the norm sanctioned by criminal law is not entertained in the strict sense, but instead the action of the adjudicating body aims at exposing the entire process that led to the commission of the offence or 'pushed' the offender, so to speak, to this behaviour. Hence, the overriding purpose of the proceedings and measures taken is to improve the welfare-educational situation of the offender and not to influence them only in connection with the committed offence. It is worth mentioning that paternalistic judiciary for juveniles was established in the United States in the late 19th and early 20th centuries, with the juvenile court set up in Chicago in 1899 being the first of its kind. This court closely

---

Handbook of Juvenile Justice, ed. II, Switzerland, Springer International Publishing 2017, pp. 345–370.

followed the welfare model as it had broad jurisdiction; its purpose was to act in the best interest of the child, where proceedings before it were informal and the power of judges was fully discretionary.[6]

Crucial for the welfare model, the distinction of the formula of juvenile justice and making its rules autonomous from adult justice was accompanied, not less importantly, by developing an autonomous procedural model. Its level of repressiveness and formality is low while flexibility is high. The welfare model presupposes the establishment of independent proceedings conducted by a special body such as a special juvenile court or an education panel. The role of such bodies is not only to bring offenders to account, but above all to educate juveniles in accordance with the idea 'punishment through education.' Juveniles, in this case, are treated as persons without due care, and co-responsibility for their deeds is attributed in a sense to the actual and legal guardians who have failed in their educational efforts.

As already mentioned, a juvenile offender so perceived is not, in principle, considered an individual capable of bearing criminal responsibility because guilt cannot be laid on them (they are not capable of sensible self-determination). Hence, they cannot apprehend the meaning of their act or control their conduct because they have not learned the model of correct conduct. The impact of the pathological environment, it could be said, has disturbed the process of acquisition of such a model, while harmful stimuli have distorted volitional processes.

In the welfare model, juvenile justice is procedurally tied to the supervision of the entire educational process. This is seen not only in the fact that measures decreed in response to offences are geared to educational aims, but also that responsibility is extended to cover other antisocial behaviour. As a result, the subject matter of proceedings is rather broad. The welfare model makes the child the centre of attention and, what is more, entrusts the proceeding body with responsibility for any necessary action to secure the interest of the child also as far as their legal situation in the course of proceedings is concerned. Consequently, the model does not emphasise procedural safeguards. This approach underpins the doctrine of *parens patriae*,[7] which prevails in

6 See B. Stańdo-Kawecka, *Prawo karne nieletnich…*, pp. 33. ff.

7 See B. Stańdo-Kawecka, *Prawo karne nieletnich…*, pp. 37 ff; B. Stańdo-Kawecka, J. Kusztal, 'Procedural Complexity within a Welfare Approach. Country Report Poland' in: M. Panzavolta, D. de Vocht, M. Oosterhout, M. Vanderhallen (eds.), *Interrogating Young Suspects: Procedural Safeguards from a Legal Perspective*, Cambridge-Antwerp-Portland, Intersentia, 2015, pp. 313–368.

English-speaking countries and which provides for the state to take over the education of, and responsibility for, the child in view of the tutelary failure of their family. The paternalism of the proceeding body makes it possible to lower considerably formalism and widen its discretion. As a rule, juvenile adjudicating bodies enjoy far greater autonomy than criminal courts. When applying educational measures, they make their own findings of fact and law. Moreover, the law provides for wide discretion, following above all from the general clause of the 'good of the child' and consequently determines the direction of proceedings and the kind of decisions made.

At the same time, however, the discretion of adjudicating bodies, seen in the indefinite time for which measures are applied to juveniles, is the most controversial element of welfare systems. Such measures, which are not punishments but are necessary to achieve welfare-educational goals, are not the consequences of an offence committed by a juvenile. Thus, they do not correspond to the gravity of the offence. Instead, educational measures, which in some cases are of the same kind as penal measures, are to be adjusted to the individual traits and personal circumstances of the offender and their environmental situation. In this sense, they are deemed to be the most adequate in terms of a prognosis. The prognosis as to the effectiveness of a measure may, however, be modified, depending on the individual situation of the child. In this sense, educational measures applied in connection with the commission of an offence are highly individualised. The time for which they are applied is adjusted on the fly as it were. Thus, it can be seen that such a system clearly does not respect the principle of equality before the law by differentiating between the legal situations of persons charged with similar offences. The term for which educational measures are applied, which by assumption are to be beneficial to the juvenile involved, depends on the achieving *in concreto* individual educational goals. Paradoxically, this may leave a juvenile in the situation where for committing the same offence as an adult offender, they may be subject to a measure lasting longer while being equally severe. As a rule, welfare-educational measures are applied to juveniles not later than the time of their coming of age. Sometimes, at the final stage of their application, they are converted to penal sanctions.

The critics of the systems that are welfare-oriented in the extreme charge that they are specious to a degree, resulting from too wide a discretion in the choice of measures to be applied to juveniles and procedures to be followed when enforcing such measures, with their educational aspect being often treated *pro forma*.

Juveniles and their legal guardians are, therefore, left to the decision of bodies that they are unable to have effectively revised.[8]

Briefly, in terms of procedure, the welfare model is characterised by (a) broad subject matter of proceedings, (b) weaker safeguards related to the position of the parties, in particular of the juvenile and (c) reduced formalism.

It follows from the earlier findings that the subject matter of proceedings to establish the responsibility of a juvenile in the welfare system goes beyond the question of establishing grounds for responsibility for the offence they have committed. Specifically, the subject matter also encompasses other manifestations of the disturbance of the welfare-educational process seen above all in the juvenile's antisocial behaviour. Hence, the subject matter of such proceedings is quite flexible as it covers not only the violation of legal norms, especially ones sanctioned in criminal law, but also other social norms such as moral ones. Meanwhile, proceeding findings are far more dispersed and inconclusive. In the model under discussion, the subject matter of proceedings encompasses the decision as to the responsibility of the juvenile in connection with the commission of a specific offence. However, the ground for the responsibility is not the attribution – in the legal sense – of the alleged offence to the juvenile, but merely the general finding that the juvenile behaved in a certain way that justifies the need for intervention by the state in the educational-welfare sphere. In some cases, educational measures are applied to prevent the commission of an offence or other breach of social norms, thus, they concern then a merely potential occurrence. Moreover,

8 Inspiring examples in this context can be drawn from an analysis of Canadian juvenile justice system from 80s. An example of a care system still largely remains the Belgian one – see B. Stando-Kawecka, *Prawo karne nieletnich...*, pp. 41–42. In Belgium, the welfare model was based on the doctrine of so-called 'social defence.' On its basis, the primary objective of criminal law is to protect the public from a dangerous offender. Protection consists in the application proportionate to the state of danger of protective measures to offenders; their application is detached from the fault of the offender. In this case, the best interests of the child were crucial and the choice of an adequate measures depended on personal conditions and characteristics, the degree of development of the child, as well as family and environmental conditions. In broader context: D. Wójcik (ed.), K. Buczkowski, J. Czabański, M. Jankowski, 'Wymiar sprawiedliwości wobec nieletnich w wybranych krajach,' *Prawo w Działaniu* 2008/3, pp. 187 ff. and K. Buczkowski, 'Wymiar sprawiedliwości w wobec nieletnich w wybranych krajach,' *Prawo Karne i Kryminologia* 2018, pp. 11 ff. – available at: Minors%20odffenders/ IWS-K.Buczkowski-Wymiar-sprawiedliwości-wobec-nieletnich.pdf, [access: March 22 2021].

the subject matter of proceedings so defined determines the status of the juvenile in the proceedings, preordains legal safeguards and results in a lower level of formalism.

In the procedural welfare model, a juvenile is not a party to proceedings but its centre, even if from the formal point of view their legal position is one of a party. Since it is assumed that the overriding purpose of proceedings is to protect the 'good of the child,' traditional safeguards, which typically protect the position of parties in repressive proceedings, are deemed redundant, with the adjudicating body invariably taking care of the good of the juvenile. The key rule, thus, is that of the adjudicating body acting on one's own motion. Since the antisocial behaviour of the juvenile is viewed in the paternalistic model of responsibility as stemming from their social milieu and family, the procedural aspect of this model does not provide for the trial representation of the juvenile by their actual and legal guardians. The absence of trial safeguards is acutely noticeable in the context of hearing of evidence. Its formality therefore is reduced and is dominated by so-called free production of evidence. The flexible rules of the hearing of evidence lower safeguards for actions taken by limiting to a bare minimum the possibility of disqualifying evidence. Courts or other bodies conducting proceedings as a rule enjoy discretion with respect to actions taken; they are not bound by a rigid legal framework, with the limit of admissibility being set by the purpose of the actions they undertake, i.e. the exercise of welfare-educational functions. When adjudicating, relevant bodies first of all aim at elucidating the circumstances of the case and exposing the motives of the juvenile's conduct, whereas findings concerning the committed offence are of secondary importance. This is so because in the model under discussion, there is no classic attribution of the commission of an offence to the offender, which is a reflection of the assumption about the incapacity of juveniles to bear criminal responsibility along general principles. Therefore, there is no pronouncement of a specifically designated sanction related to the breach of a norm sanctioned in criminal law.

In the context of reduced formalism, it must be noted that the welfare model can be either para-judicial, when the adjudicating body is not a court, or judicial, when it is. The para-judicial variety, obviously, is not found in the jurisdictions where the administration of justice has been entrusted exclusively to courts of law. Importantly, the para-judicial welfare model, in which the adjudicating body has experts who are not lawyers among its members, is even less formal in its work than the judicial welfare model. Nevertheless, in the welfare model, basically regardless of whether the adjudicating body is a court or a para-judicial body, experts in pedagogy, psychology, sexology, medicine (especially paediatrics and psychiatry), rehabilitation and even victimology play a special role even if they participate in proceedings only as expert witnesses and consultants. Furthermore, reduced formalism is reflected in the greater flexibility of proceedings, optionality of procedural forms, absence of strict time limits, in particular those related to the course of proceedings, or certain limitation, or even elimination, of control procedures.

The central feature of the welfare model is the system of educational measures that replaces the system of punishments and penal measures. The replacement follows from the conviction that punishments are not useful educational measures. This has been epitomised by the concept of 'punishment through education,' although there have been more restrictive models, some aspects of which could be adequately described as 'education through punishment.' Measures applied to an offender have formed a broad selection – they belong to educational, welfare, therapeutic or even disciplinary categories. Moreover, the categories are graded with preference given to welfare-educational measures. Disciplinary measures are either custodial or non-custodial, with fines being very rare because from a pedagogical point of view, a fine would be adequate only if a juvenile could pay it out of their own funds.

In today's jurisdictions, the welfare model, even when it is the model ostensibly declared by the legislator, makes concessions to the justice model as well as other models, for instance, rehabilitative or one relying on the idea of restorative justice. Thus, it acquires the characteristics of a mixed model with the dominance of welfare aspects. The system of educational measures is highly flexible, allowing for adjusting the time when a measure is applied and its intensity, depending on the situation and in anticipation of either favourable or unfavourable results. The welfare model comes in many varieties, but its dominating characteristic is an emancipation of a sort – the detachment of juvenile justice from adult justice.[9] In the Polish authoritative juristic literature, the model resembling the welfare model is sometimes called criminological.[10]

Within welfare-orientated models, classified as mixed welfare-justice models, there is also a sub-category of alternating models distinguished. These allow a juvenile justice judge to pronounce alternating sanctions, i.e. to conditionally pronounce criminal sanctions designed for adults and impose typically educational

9 B. Stańdo-Kawecka, J. Kusztal, *Procedural Complexity…*, pp. 313 ff.

10 M. Stanowska, A. Walczak-Żochowska, K. Wierzbowski, 'Uwagi o profilu ustawy o postępowaniu z nieletnimi (zagadnienia materialnoprawne i procesowe),' *Państwo i Prawo* 1983/6, pp. 51 ff.

measures. These are, so to speak, models of last resort and are found in the Polish system of juvenile justice.

3. Justice model

The justice model indicates connections to the classic and neoclassic conceptions of a response to a violation of criminal law. One of such responses is meting out a punishment, being a retribution for the evil done to society. This model holds that it is a duty of the State to ensure a uniform response to a violation of criminal law in proportion to the prohibited act committed. Hence, the justice model is sometimes referred to as the 'criminal law of the act' for simplicity. It draws, therefore, on the idea of substantive legalism, demanding that every violation of a norm sanctioned in criminal law meet with a response from the State proportional to the violated legal interest.

Justice models, with respect to the criminal responsibility of juveniles, are selective as they make offenders answer for the violation of certain criminal law prohibitions, usually the gravest violations of criminal law, in particular felonies, crimes against health and life or crimes with the use of violence, including sexual violence.

In justice models, juvenile justice follows the same or similar rules that are used with respect to adults. Consequently, the subject matter of proceedings is kept relatively narrow, certainly far narrower than that in the welfare model. Crucially, in the justice model, **criminal matters are kept apart from welfare and educational ones.** This makes for the splitting up of the subject matter of juvenile justice into several aspects. One is related to the subject matter itself (criminal responsibility of juveniles is juxtaposed with their responsibility for other violations of law and antisocial behaviour) and another to the person involved (criminally responsible, on analogous principles as those used in respect of adults, are held only those juveniles who have attained a specified age). These models usually stipulate a minimum age that a juvenile must attain to be held criminally responsible. The criteria used for setting such an age limit include their respective maturity or immaturity and subsequent criminal-law competency to be charged with an offence. Specifically, they must have a reasonable understanding of their situation and limits set by criminal law. In other words, they must be capable of sensible self-determination. In this context, it may be noted that jurisdictions in English-speaking countries used to allow a rebuttable presumption that a juvenile below a specific age limit was *doli incapax*.[11]

---

11 Although in practice the presumption had been relatively easy to rebut by state

Statutory age for criminal responsibility in the justice model or the mixed model with the elements of the former varies between different jurisdictions. By way of example, it can be mentioned that in European countries, the minimum age for criminal responsibility varies from 10 (England and Wales, Switzerland, Northern Ireland) to 18 years (Belgium, where the prevailing model is strongly welfare- and restitution-oriented). In the Netherlands, Scotland and Turkey, the age limit in question is 12 years, in France – 13 years, in Austria, Germany, Italy, Spain, Slovakia and Slovenia – 14 years, in Greece and Scandinavian countries – 15 years and in Russia – 16 years.[12]

The justice model in its procedural aspect is patterned on the criminal responsibility of adults: the subject matter of the proceedings involved is analogous (it covers adjudication on the criminal responsibility of a specific person) and the system of trial safeguards is similar, as is the system of penal sanctions. Actually, it is often the same model. Usually, however, the age of an offender makes for the use of additional protective procedures such as an enhanced right to formal defence, protective interviewing, restriction on trial coercive measures and a separate incarceration regime for juvenile offenders or even young offending adults.

In most cases, the system of sanctions decreed in the justice model is identical to or closely resembles that to which adult offenders are subjected. However, the sentencing of juveniles is guided by directives, allowing judges to limit criminal sanctions by their extraordinary mitigation, use of probation measures, or even commutation to correctional measures (autonomous sanctions applied to juvenile offenders and young offending adults that, however, resemble in kind punishments and penal measures to which adult offenders are subjected). In this model, the purpose of juvenile justice is first of all retribution for the offence committed. Present-day justice models, however, also consider punishment as an aspect of 'education through punishment.'

The relevant literature points to the fact that in mixed, justice-welfare systems the attainment by the juvenile of the age for criminal responsibility along

prosecutor, its formal abolition in 1998 was an indication to hold young offenders responsible for their actions. For more, see C. Ball, K. MC Cormac, N. Stone, *Young Offenders: Law, Policy and Practice*, London 2001, pp. 5 ff.

12 Cf. D. Wójcik (ed.), K. Buczkowski, J. Czabański, M. Jankowski, 'Wymiar sprawiedliwości wobec nieletnich w wybranych krajach,' *Prawo w Działaniu* 2008/3, pp. 187 ff. and K. Buczkowski, 'Wymiar sprawiedliwości w wobec nieletnich w wybranych krajach,' *Prawo Karne i Kryminologia* 2018, pp. 11 ff. – available at: Minors%20odffenders/IWS-K.Buczkowski-Wymiar-sprawiedliwości-wobec-nieletnich.pdf [access: March 22 2021].

general principles, does not mean that they will be indeed subjected to identical sanctions as in the case of adults. For in the case of 'younger' juveniles, instead of imprisonment, educational and correctional measures are applied. Depending on the system, they may be applied by a criminal court or even a juvenile court when the system is inclined more towards dispensing justice than providing welfare.

When analysing the justice model, East European jurisdictions (including the Polish system) merit attention as they provide **for the lowering of the age for criminal responsibility pursuant to the Criminal Code in the event a juvenile commits a serious offence.** These are jurisdictions in which the criminal responsibility of juveniles along general principles is conditional, so to speak, and they are brought to account by a criminal court. Furthermore, a trend is observable that affords special treatment to young adults, i.e. adult offenders under 21 (24) years, whereby they are treated less severely than the Criminal Code stipulates.[13]

Further, the justice model in its procedural aspect, may be **uniform**, when juveniles are brought to justice in almost the same manner as adults are, or **non-uniform** where a criminal-law procedural model is applied by a special juvenile court. Most likely by reason of the formalised procedure of bringing persons to justice, it is sometimes referred to as a juridical model.[14]

A juvenile is recognised as a party to proceedings, an individual who is charged with the commission of a specific offence. Thus, as a passive party, they are protected by the right to defence in both the substantive aspect (related to the scope of their rights that they can personally exercise) and a formal one (manifested above all in their right to be represented at trial by defence counsel). Furthermore, a juvenile charged with the violation of a norm sanctioned in criminal law is protected by the presumption of innocence and the rule *in dubio pro reo*, and thus must be treated as not guilty until the proceedings conclude with a final judgment and must be given the benefit of the doubt. The proceedings follow the fair-trial model and the subject matter involved in them is adjudicated by an independent and impartial court.

In contrast to criminal trials of adults, proceedings to determine the criminal responsibility of juveniles are often held *in camera* (without the public) where

13 Cf. D. Wójcik (ed.), K. Buczkowski, J. Czabański, M. Jankowski, *Wymiar sprawiedliwości...*, pp. 187 ff. and K. Buczkowski, *Wymiar sprawiedliwości...*

14 M. Stanowska, A. Walczak-Żochowska, K. Wierzbowski, *Uwagi o profilu ustawy...*, pp. 52 ff.

the hearing of evidence is formalised and moreover, in such cases (1) responsibility rests on the attribution of an act to the offender, (the finding that a juvenile has committed a specific offence and there are no circumstances barring prosecution) and (2) the findings of fact, on which a decision rests, are reached by freely examining the body of evidence by an adjudicating panel (wherein all evidence must be legal and admissible). Specifically, there are rigorous conditions that must be met to make evidence competent and, conversely, there are specific methods of disqualifying incompetent evidence. The procedural safeguards are not uniform in justice models adopted by particular juvenile justice systems and, as such, they reflect considerable differences in adult criminal trial models.

Today, the justice model follows rather the neoclassic trend in criminal law. The trend has begun to shape the models of juvenile justice since the 1970s. Its underlying assumption is that punishment should be an adequate and proportional response to the violation of criminal law, while the good of the convicted person, their reform or education are only of secondary importance. It has stemmed from the rejection of the idea of pure rehabilitation (*see* Sect. 3) or extreme welfare models. Behind the rejection has lain the belief that the good of the convicted person, especially the need to rehabilitate or educate them, should not be considered when pronouncing custodial sentences, thereby relegating a criminological prognosis as to the future conduct of the offender to merely an auxiliary position. Its significance is believed to be lower because it is hardly verifiable, as it refers to future and uncertain events.

With respect to juvenile justice, neoclassic models criticised the rejection of indefinite sanctions and demanded that equality before the law and fundamental procedural safeguards be ensured when both judgments were passed and penal sanctions and measures were executed. It was believed that imprisonment could not be a bridge to rehabilitation. However, a rehabilitative element was an additional aspect of punishment.

One of the major neoclassic conceptions is the 'just-deserts theory' formulated by Andreas von Hirsch.[15] He believes that a deserved punishment has a **prospective character**, i.e. it is future-oriented. On the one hand, it is to be proportional to the degree of guilt and gravity of the offence, on the other, it is to have an individual-preventive impact on the offender to prevent them from relapsing into crime. Additionally, a deserved punishment must take into account their criminal record, specifically whether they were reoffending or not (acted as a recidivist). This conception is a *sui generis* combination of a pure justice model

15 Cf. A. von. Hirsch, *Doing Justice. The Choice of Punishments*, New York, 1980, pp. 10 ff.

and the elements of the rehabilitative model it criticised. The crux of the conception is the equity of punishment seen in its proportionality to the act attributed to the offender, one taking into account the seriousness of harm done or threatened. The other functions of punishment, such as deterrence or rehabilitation, are believed to be supplementary.

It is worth mentioning that neoclassic models made an effort to find adequate sanctions but scorned custodial ones. Hence, penal measures alternative to imprisonment gained in importance and the idea of carrying out punishment more humanely was met with approval. The system of criminal-law means of response was to be effective in terms of individual and general crime prevention, but moderately expensive as well. With this in mind, emphasis was laid on the necessity of separation of an educational impact from a correctional one on a juvenile offender. The authoritative juristic literature refers to this separation as a 'bifurcation of penal policy' for the purpose of building the system of juvenile justice. 'Bifurcation' was seen in a more severe treatment of serious offenders (guilty of crimes against life and health, crimes with violence), especially re-offenders, while affording leniency to offenders guilty of minor offences.[16] In this context, the relevant literature observes that:

> There is a clear tendency in youth justice policy in recent decades to strengthen the justice model by establishing or extending procedural safeguards, also to what may be regarded as welfare measures. This tendency includes a stricter emphasis on the principle of proportionality in the sense of avoiding both sentences and educational measures that are disproportionately harsh.[17]

4. Rehabilitative treatment model

The rehabilitative trend in penal policy, similarly to the welfare trend, has its roots in the positivist school and adopts a prospective approach. Its core element is an individualised impact on the offender aimed at eliminating the characteristics that brought them to commit an offence. Rehabilitation is to bring them back to the bosom of society and induce reform. The chief characteristics of the

---

16 B. Stańdo-Kawecka, *Prawo karne nieletnich…*, pp. 99 ff.; B. Stańdo-Kawecka, 'O koncepcji resocjalizacji w polskiej literaturze naukowej polemicznie,' *Probacja* 2010/1, pp. 108 ff.; B. Stańdo-Kawecka, 'Ruch What works i "nowa resocjalizacja" – nowa perspektywa w polityce karnej?' in: V. Konarska-Wrzosek, J. Lachowski i J. Wójcikiewicz (eds.), *Węzłowe problemy prawa karnego, kryminologii i polityki kryminalnej*, Warsaw, Wolters Kluwer, 2010, pp. 891–907.

17 F. Duenkel, 'Juvenile Justice Systems in Europe'…, p. 39.

trend are thus individuality and correctionalism. Individualised measures focus on morally improving the offender and suppressing the pathological characteristics that follow from either their own imperfections or the detrimental impact of their immediate environment.

When selecting a sanction, the court should so design its impact on the offender to make their return to society possible. Possible measures to select from are quite diverse: therapeutic, psychological-pedagogic and educational (including aspects of vocational training).[18] The manner they are carried out, especially if a custodial punishment is imposed, should, therefore, be constructive by ensuring that an inmate is educated and trained. In the rehabilitative model, preference is given to **indefinite-term sanctions**, meaning that an offender sentenced to a custodial sanction can be released when their rehabilitation is completed. In this aspect then the rehabilitative and welfare trends coincide. In the rehabilitative model, executional aspects grow in importance and traditional penal sanctions are supplemented by probation measures. The impact of rehabilitative trends on juvenile justice systems has paved the way for a broader reception of the idea of probation in respect of adult offenders.

The model in question assumes that an offence is a manifestation of individual pathology. This differs it radically from welfare models, which connect juvenile delinquency to the negative impact of the environment and educational deficiencies. Measures and sanctions decreed in the rehabilitative model correspond to the offender's characteristics and rehabilitation prognosis and not the offence committed. Interestingly, the rehabilitative model is called 'the criminal law of the offender,' as is the welfare model, in contrast to retributive trends, which make use of the concept of 'criminal law of the offence.'[19] The rehabilitative model has given up using the term 'juvenile delinquent' in favour of 'the socially maladjusted juvenile.'[20] Accordingly, the violation of a criminal law norm by a juvenile is viewed as a disruption of the socialisation process that calls for support, as it has been impaired. In sum, the rehabilitative model assumes that measures applied to a juvenile are custom-designed and their choice depends

18 See M. Kalinowski, *Resocjalizacja nieletnich w państwach europejskich i pozaeuropejskich*, Warsaw 2005, pp. 9 ff.

19 Stańdo-Kawecka, *Prawo karne nieletnich...*, p. 61.

20 A. Walczak-Żochowska, 'Modele postępowania z nieletnimi' in: B. Kowalska-Ehrlich, S. Walczak (eds.), *Prawne i pedagogiczne aspekty resocjalizacji nieletnich, Prace Instytutu Profilaktyki Społecznej i Resocjalizacji Uniwersytetu Warszawskiego*, Vol.12, Warsaw 1992, p. 41.

above all on the properties and personal characteristics of the offender, and their criminal-educational prognosis.

Therefore, the choice of a measure is to be prospective because the principal goal of bringing a juvenile to account is their rehabilitation in the future. It must be stressed that while making a criminological prognosis, importance is attached to the probability of relapsing into crime. According to some rehabilitative approaches to juvenile justice, a sanction imposed for an offence should not only correspond to custom-made criminological prognosis, but also make use of custodial measures, with precedence over non-custodial ones, when the incarceration of the offender is conducive to the success of adequate corrective efforts. At the same time, a punishment *per se* is believed to be a totally inadequate rehabilitative measure. It can, however, create conditions conducive to improvement, which justifies its use. In rehabilitative systems, it should be noted, statutory sentencing guidelines are reduced to a bare minimum. The rehabilitative model sometimes takes on medical aspects and perceives crime as a social malady whereby offenders are seen as members of society affected by it and penal institutions – as an organised therapeutic system.

As far as the procedural aspects of the rehabilitative model are concerned, the role of social sciences and medical experts comes to the fore. It is to them that the rehabilitative-therapeutic process has been entrusted. The model in whole or for the most part relies on extrajudicial bodies – the adjudicating body is usually a special panel, with the key role being played by enforcement bodies. The enforcement proceedings is a key stage because rehabilitation, being a long process, needs proper supervision. Furthermore, the system in question is characterised by the broad discretionary powers of the court as well as wide discretion of entities taking part in the rehabilitation process. In particular, enforcement proceedings are flexible and lack excessive formalism, which, however, entails the lowering of trial safeguards with respect to the person subjected to rehabilitation. In addition, a salient procedural feature of the system under discussion is the elaborate probation measures it uses, such as parole and conditional suspension of a sentence. Their application is conditional on the offender's fulfilling certain therapeutic-rehabilitative duties.

The rehabilitative model has various nuances. It is sometimes described as one that does not put in its centre a 'socially maladjusted juvenile' but rather a 'juvenile under threat.' Hence, it takes on a welfare-rehabilitative character. Then, the subject matter of proceedings following this model is broadly marked to cover the cases of a juvenile committing an offence and other deeds violating social norms. The latter violations may serve as grounds for finding the juvenile to be socially maladjusted. The adoption of the **broad subject matter** of proceedings, analogously to the pure welfare model, entails the resignation from the criterion of the offender's ability to apprehend the meaning of their act and control it, believed to be a condition of responsibility. In this variety of the rehabilitative model, welfare law and criminal law are integrated; a mixed variety is also possible that combines the characteristics of the rehabilitative model and elements of criminal responsibility (i.e. a rehabilitative-justice model from which a trend in criminal policy evolved known as 4×D – see below).[21]

Rehabilitative models have been treated as remedies for pure justice models, where a penal sanction is proportional to the gravity of the committed act. Meanwhile, taking into consideration the rehabilitation aspect while sentencing allows the judge to mould the sanction (custodial or non-custodial) so that it suits the need to rehabilitate the offender. In the event a term of imprisonment is imposed, it must be served in correlation with the individual need of rehabilitation. The chief concern should be whether the offender, after they have served the sentence, will not be inclined to reoffend and pose a threat to society. In the rehabilitative model therefore, custodial punishments are imposed on offenders whose criminological prognosis is negative while the probability of relapsing into crime is high.

Purely rehabilitative systems have been criticised for allegedly being at odds with the principle of equality before the law, being *de facto* highly punitive and for petrifying existing social inequalities. As such, they are believed to entrench injustice because reasons for rehabilitation justify a radically different treatment of offenders who committed the same type of offence. Such discrimination has been seen to preserve social, racial, economic and cultural divisions. Furthermore, rehabilitative models have been criticised as extremely arbitrary and conformism-strengthening. This has been observed in the preservation of existing social relations and preferential treatment afforded to privileged social groups. To a degree, radically rehabilitative models have been considered ineffective. Moreover, custodial rehabilitation has raised the rate of imprisonment without conditional suspension, making the costs of the prison system grow. Furthermore, empirical studies have not unambiguously confirmed the benefits of rehabilitative procedures over longer periods of time.[22] For the most part, however, criticism directed at purely rehabilitative systems has concerned their

---

21 In the larger context, see A. Walczak-Żochowska, 'Modele postępowania'..., pp. 40 ff.

22 See A. Kuhn, 'Incarceration rate, Europe versus USA,' *European Jurnal on Criminal Policy and Research,* 1996/3, pp. 60 ff. and B. Stańdo-Kawecka, *Prawo karne nieletnich...*, p. 74.

involuntariness. Meanwhile, it has been shown that rehabilitation is effective only when a therapist and offender cooperate and the autonomous will of the offender is fully respected. It has been observed occasionally that therapeutic-rehabilitative systems are characterised by certain cruelty and the measures used in them resemble in kind severe punishments imposed for indefinite periods, with the offender being left to the mercy of entities conducting and supervising compulsory rehabilitation. Interestingly enough, the purely rehabilitative model of juvenile justice has never been followed in Europe except for Scandinavia.[23]

The rehabilitative model together with the neoclassic justice model have introduced to the models of juvenile justice the idea of 4×D underpinned by diversion, where there is a diversion of juvenile cases from welfare-oriented judicial proceedings to justice ones, but at the same time taking the situation of the offender into account. The 4×D trend involves actual decriminalisation of some offences, i.e. restriction of the criminal responsibility of juveniles and a search for alternative sanctions (deinstitutionalisation). Moreover, it has contributed to the improvement of trial safeguards for juveniles, i.e. 'due process of law.' It is worth mentioning that the 4×D formula has been reflected in the 1985 UN Standard Minimum Rules for the Administration of Juvenile Justice.[24] According to the Rules, 'punishment' is to be conceived as an *ultima ratio* and alternative measures are to be given precedence. As a matter of fact, the idea of diversion has been variously understood in particular jurisdictions.[25] Occasionally, it has encompassed such forms of state response to a committed offence as forgoing judicial proceedings, e.g. discontinuance of proceedings or renouncement of imposing a punishment. In a narrow sense, diversion (later, showing an impact of the ideas of restorative justice) has meant alternative measures related to restitution.

5. Restorative justice model

Restorative justice has advocated a change in the way prosecution of crimes is viewed. Criminal law as a branch of public law is the domain of the State, which

---

23 M. Płatek, 'Współczesne kierunki ewolucji systemów penitencjarnych w krajach skandynawskich' in: B. Hołyst (ed.), *Problemy współczesnej penitencjarystyki w świecie*, Warsaw 1987, pp. 173 ff.

24 B. Stańdo-Kawecka, *Prawo karne nieletnich…*, p. 181; B. Stańdo-Kawecka, 'Restorative Justice in Poland – limitations and prospects for development' in: A. Pitsel i E. Symeonidou-Kastanidou (eds.) *Restorative Justice in Criminal Matters: Towards a New European Perspective*, Athens, Thessaloniki, Sakkoulas Publications, 2013, pp. 313–321.

25 See Stańdo-Kawecka, *Prawo karne nieletnich…*, p. 210.

is thereby authorised to punish those who violate criminal prohibitions in force. Meanwhile, restorative justice in part privatises the ensuing conflict, with an offence being viewed in it above all as an act harming the individual interests of the person wronged. Thus, the restorative paradigm presents an offence as an act directed against a specific person and not society as a whole.[26] In restorative justice, the main purpose of criminal law is to repair damage and redress harm done by an offence. In this sense, similarly to rehabilitative trends, restorative justice focuses on both the 'here and now' and 'future'; that is, it adopts a prospective viewpoint. Consequently, prosecution is reoriented from legalism to opportunism. The departure from legalism of prosecution is defended by the argument that the retributive view of punishment as a repayment due to the offender makes them a passive receiver of an affliction imposed on them. A punishment viewed as a retribution does not by itself bring about the repair of damage and harm done by an offence and even if were to, the offender does not directly take part. Compensating for the damage without the offender participating results in their failure to develop an appropriate attitude. Meanwhile, for individual prevention to be effective, it is vital that the offender personally restitutes and compensates the victim. The representatives of the restorative trend believe that the view of punishment as a retribution does not have a favourable effect on the development of a law-abiding attitude in an offender in the future and nor does it remove the consequences of the evil done.

The adoption of the restorative viewpoint, leading to a partial privatisation of criminal law conflicts, involves the parties themselves in the settlement of conflicts arisen from the violation of criminal law norms. It is necessary therefore to build a specific formal legal framework in order to ensure that the activity of the accused and the aggrieved – the offender and victim – is controlled if only to a minimum degree. This is all the more important as the paradigm of restorative justice recognises the active role not only of the offender, but also the person aggrieved and the entire community. Furthermore, favourable and conciliatory social attitudes need to be developed or the community needs to be persuaded to accept reconciliation and conditions must be created for the repair of social relations disrupted by the offender breaking the law. Society, or more precisely a specific social group, must allow thus for a margin of correction of group members. This means that it should not automatically shun the trespassers of some

26 T. Brooks, 'Punitive restoration,' *Rehabilitating Restorative Justice*, 2015/3, pp. 73–89; J. Braithwaite, *Restorative Justice and Responsive Regulation*, Oxford, Oxford University Press, 2002, p. 69; T. Brooks, *Punishment*, London, Routledge, 2012, pp. 64 ff.

legal or social norms. In this sense restorative justice rests on the assumption that man is capable of improvement.

In the models of juvenile justice moulded under the influence of restorative justice trends – in contrast to welfare models – it is parents and society that engage in the administration of justice as they are in a sense co-responsible for the overcoming of the social and educational problems of the juvenile who has broken the law. Meanwhile, preventing the juvenile from reoffending is viewed as the responsibility of local communities, the family and pedagogues working with the juvenile concerned.

The trend of restorative justice has made a great impact on the models of juvenile justice.[27] Young offenders because of their unfinished education and training, and the fact that their personality is only developing, deserve a second chance even more than adults. They deserve such a choice of measures so that they not only suffer some affliction but also have a chance to participate directly in the restitution and the repair of damage and harm done. Let us notice then that in contrast to the retributive model, the restorative model shifts its focus from punishment to atonement and makes not only the aggrieved person and offender, but also the entire community important stakeholders in ending the conflict caused by the offender's act.

In the restorative justice trend, guilt must be attributed to the offender and the commission of an offence must be ascertained. However, instead of punishment reduced to an adequate retribution, penal sanctions applied must be oriented towards the repair of damage and restoration of the former state (*restitutio in integrum*). The correction of the offender is achieved through the repair of damage and atonement.[28]

Restorative trends have influenced the development of both substantive and procedural criminal law. Their adoption has resulted in the extension of the system of non-custodial sanctions and measures of a compensatory nature and importantly, procedural law has been modified as well. The key modifications have strengthened the role of the person aggrieved in criminal proceedings. In particular, they have been given powers that are important for conclusively

27 J. Dignan, 'Juvenile justice, criminal courts and restorative justice' in: G. Johnstone and D.W. Van Ness (eds.), *Handbook of Restorative Justice*, London, Routledge, 2007, pp. 269 ff.

28 H. Strang, *Victim Participation in a Restorative Justice Process*, Oxford, Oxford Univ. Press 2001, p. 41; R. Weisberg, *'Restorative justice and the danger of "community"', Utah Law Review* 2003, pp. 343– 74.

deciding a criminal case. This, in turn, stimulated the development of consensual institutions: plea bargaining and mediation. There also arose opportunistic reasons for the discontinuance of a criminal trial dependent on the earlier settlement of the conflict between the victim and offender, e.g. so-called restorative discontinuance (*nolle prosequi*).

Against the backdrop of juvenile justice models, the restorative model has given rise in various jurisdictions to supplementary forms with respect to mediation between the offender and victim. These are restorative conferences, family group conferences, community reparative boards and sentencing circles.[29] Restorative justice suggests that the response to youth crime must strike a balance among the needs of victims, offenders, and communities and that each should be actively involved in the justice process to the greatest extent possible.[30]

The supplementary procedures of resolving conflicts between the offender and victim with the participation of a local community are much less formal and highly flexible. It is noted that:

> Such strategies, now being implemented in North America, Australia, New Zealand, and parts of Europe, are one component of a new movement in the 1990s concerned with making criminal and juvenile justice processes less formal, bringing the processes into neighbourhoods, and involving community members in planning and implementation.[31]

It is further noted that: Cases may be referred to victim-offender mediation programs by judges, probation officers, victim advocates, prosecutors, defence attorneys, and law enforcement. In some programs, cases are primarily referred as a diversion from prosecution (assuming that any agreement reached during the mediation session is successfully completed). In other programs, cases are usually referred after a formal admission of guilt has been accepted by the court, with mediation being a candidate. [32]

Three aspects in this context of conference models, in particular, are believed to be beneficial in shortening the distance between the victim and offender, which helps the victim to regain control over the situation:

---

29 G. Bazemore, M. Umbreit, 'A Comparison of Four Restorative Conferencing Models,' *Juvenile Justice Bulletin* 2001 [access: March, 2021] Comparison of Four Restorative Conferencing Models | Office of Juvenile Justice and Delinquency Prevention (ojp.gov).

30 Ibid.

31 Ibid. and the indicated literature.

32 Ibid.

> Supporting the healing process of victims by providing a safe, controlled setting for them to meet and speak with offenders on a strictly voluntary basis. Allowing offenders to learn about the impact of their crimes on the victims and take direct responsibility for their behavior. Providing an opportunity for the victim and offender to develop a mutually acceptable plan that addresses the harm caused by the crime.[33]

It needs to be noted, however, that the use of restorative justice as the sole basis for modelling responsibility gives rise to certain doubts about its effectiveness or even consistency with the principle of equality before the law. For the opportunistic formula gives relatively wide discretion to law enforcement bodies. Specifically, it is observed that its use may end in an excessive privatisation of the criminal trial and occasionally in the so-called secondary victimisation of victims engaged in the procedural resolution of a conflict. Another shortcoming of restorative justice is the fact that its impact is seen in the case of offences that harm a specific person.[34] These shortcomings, however, concern chiefly the design of adult justice systems, while juvenile offenders are much less affected. Nonetheless, restorative justice usually supplements the other justice models and in conjunction forms various mixed models such as justice-restorative, welfare-restorative and rehabilitative-restorative.

The paradigm of restorative justice started a trend to transform and modify the models of juvenile justice based on the idea of diversion. At its heart lay increased opportunism, or an assessment of whether prosecution is at all needed, including the punishing of a juvenile for an offence by a criminal court. At the same time, it added mediations and group conferences to the repertoire of alternative measures, leading to the signing of reparation contracts. The alternative measures applied to juvenile offenders prevented their stigmatisation. Besides extra-trial consensual measures, some welfare-oriented jurisdictions developed alternative juvenile justice bodies such as youth courts.[35] To reiterate, diversion encompasses both judicial and extrajudicial measures to be applied to a juvenile. Their application is supported by an active participation of the juvenile, their family and the local community as well as the victim with respect for the rights

33 Ibid.

34 C. Menkel-Meadow, 'Restorative Justice: What is it and Does it Work' in: *Georgetown Public Law and Legal Theory Research Paper*, No. 1005485, *Annual Review of Law & Social Sciences*, 2007/3, pp. 161–187.

35 J. Butts, J. Buck, M. Coggeshall, 'The impact of teen court on young offenders' in: *Research Raport* 2002, available at: The Impact of Teen Court on Young Offenders. Research Report. | Semantic Scholar [acces: March 22 2021].

and freedoms of the juvenile. Independently of the diversion trends, under the influence of restorative justice, the focus has shifted to restoration. This has been finally conceived as an element of a mixed model of juvenile justice expressed by the 4×R formula: responsibility, restitution (reparation), restorative justice and retribution.

6. Mixed models: Combinations of welfare and justice, including minimum intervention and elements of restorative justice: Poland, Brazil and Portugal

The abstract models of juvenile responsibility systems discussed above do not occur as concrete models in any jurisdiction of today. Those that are followed are thus of a mixed nature. Namely, they combine educational and justice ideas with the elements of rehabilitation and restorative justice. This monograph studies therefore the models of juvenile responsibility in Polish, Brazilian and Portuguese legal systems. What these three models have in common is their clear welfare trait, which in an extreme form is seen in the Brazilian model. It is an example of a mixed welfare-rehabilitation model with some elements of restorative justice. In both Polish and Portuguese models meanwhile, the elements of neo-retributivism can be seen as well. They include the subjection of juvenile offenders, who have attained a specific age, to the regime of criminal responsibility designed for adult offenders. Its justice aspect, however, is always restricted in terms of offence type and offender age.

Furthermore, the choice of means of criminal-law response to be applied is left to the discretion of the court. Specifically, juveniles are made to bear criminal responsibility only for the most serious prohibited acts (felonies) exhaustively enumerated in the penal statute (this is what Polish law provides for in the case of juveniles who are at least 15 years of age at the time of committing a prohibited act). The age limit for holding juveniles criminally responsible differs between Polish and Portuguese law. In the former, criminal responsibility along general principles is extended to offenders aged 17 or more, while in the latter – to those who are 16 years of age. In both systems, the preferential leniency of sanctions, seen in special mitigation of punishment, is applicable to young offenders as well.

The three models under discussion show the clear impact of international standards; in particular, the Convention on the Rights of the Child, approved by the United Nations in 1989 (ratified by Poland, Portugal and Brazil in 1990). With respect to Poland and Portugal, the influence of the European Convention on the Exercise of Children's Rights (1996) is noticeable. Those conventions are highly important as an international legal instrument especially to ensure the exercise of the rights of children under 18 years of age. Their objects are in the best interests of children, to promote their rights, to grant them procedural rights and to facilitate the exercise of these rights by ensuring that children are, themselves or through other persons or bodies, informed and allowed to participate in proceedings affecting them before a judicial authority.

In the Polish system, juveniles under 17, as a rule, are not held criminally responsible for prohibited acts they commit. The Juvenile Justice Act of 1982 applies to such cases and comprehensively regulates matters of the juveniles who commit a prohibited act or display antisocial behaviour (demoralisation). Exceptionally, if certain requirements enumerated in the Polish Criminal Code (1997) are met, a minor who was aged 15 or older when committing a prohibited act can also be held criminally responsible. The age limit of criminal responsibility is linked to a certain assumption that persons aged 17 or older have reached a sufficient level of emotional, intellectual, social and moral development so they can recognize a legal norm and accept full responsibility for their actions. Therefore, taking into account the fact that the age limit of criminal liability set at 17 is a certain compromise presumption, the legislator's making an exception to this presumption, which allows for certain flexibility in adopting an age limit, needs to be recognized as reasonable. This concerns an exceptional exclusion of criminal liability of the offenders who have attained the age of 17 years at the time of committing an offence, but have not yet attained the age of 18 years. In this case the court may apply educational, therapeutic or correctional measures prescribed for juveniles instead of imposing a penalty, if this is deemed appropriate, given the circumstances of the case and the level of mental development of the offender as well as their characteristics and personal circumstances.[36]

When it comes to the application of educational and correctional measures, the concept of a juvenile extends to persons under the age of 21. In the Polish system of juvenile responsibility, a 'young offender' is an offender who, at the time of committing a prohibited act, has not attained the age of 21 years or 24 years at the time of trial in the first-instance court. The status of a young offender has significant consequences for the administration of justice. The goal of a punishment imposed on a young offender is to have an educational effect and the punishment imposed on them may be subject to extraordinary mitigation.

The system prevailing in Poland, although it is founded on the welfare and rehabilitative models, does make rather significant concessions to the justice model, which today is also underpinned by the idea of restorative justice. A

36 See Part II, Chapter 1.

juvenile who is at least 15 years age of may be conditionally subjected to criminal responsibility along general principles with all the trial safeguards enjoyed by adult offenders and in addition, some supplementary procedural advantages relating to interviewing, trial representation and the right to information. Whereas a juvenile who answers for a punishable act or antisocial behaviour before a juvenile court, benefits from a more flexible manner of proceeding.

In Portugal, the responses to juvenile delinquency, as in Poland, vary according to the age of an offender. If the offender is under 12, they will always be treated as a child in danger, and protection measures will be applied. Thus, before the age 12 years, there is no responsibility, so an offender is not to be subject to any sanction or penalty for their actions. Law on the protection of children and young people in danger aims to protect children, as well as promote their education and safety, which may require family support or even an institutional framework to guarantee children's interests. If the offender is between 12 and 16 years old and commits an act defined as a crime, the authorities may apply an educational protective measure stipulated by law (Child Education and Protection Act).[37] If the offender is over 14 years old, this measure may even result in a closed custody regime. Actually, under Portuguese law, juveniles from the age of 16, in general, are considered capable of bearing criminal responsibility. However, there is an Extraordinary Criminal Regime for Young Adults which has been created to be applied (or withdrawn) when young people between 16 and 21 years old are convicted of an act qualified as a crime since they are only on the threshold of maturity. The law says that only a corrective measure may be applied to young offenders up to the age of 21 and provides for specific mitigations of punishment. The Portuguese system is a mixture of a welfare neo-correctional one and some restorative justice elements. In this system, juveniles are subject to regular criminal responsibility from the age of 16, but there is a special protection regime in place for young adults up to 21 years old.

The Brazilian system, in contrast, is known for its extreme welfare. A significant change occurred in the Brazilian system of juvenile responsibility in 2012, owing to the enactment of the Brazilian National Socio-Educational Service System Act.[38] Those who are not subject to criminal responsibility because of their age (they are under eighteen years old) may be subject to the socio-educational and protection measures provided for in the Act. However, when a child under 12 years of age commits an offence only protective measures can be

37 See Part IV.

38 Law No. 12594 / 2012, of January 18, 2012.

applied. The socio-educational measures themselves apply to *adolescents*, who are children between 12 and 18 years old. Despite this age limitation, this particular regime of responsibility can be exceptionally applied to people between 18 and 21 years old. So it is the same practice as that followed in Portugal or Poland: a welfare model with socio-correctional measures and some impact of restorative justice.

As it is clear that the age of 18 years represents the age of criminal responsibility in Brazil, it remains to be explained what treatment is given to those who are under this age. The matter is regulated by a special law (the ECA). It makes an important distinction: a child is a person up to 12 years old and an adolescent – between 12 and 18 years old. This division has consequences for responses to the commission of prohibited acts. In the case of a child, only protective measures can be applied, while in the case of an adolescent socio-educational measures are applicable.

The system adopted by Brazilian legislation has as its primary goal the re-education of the adolescent who has committed an offence. However, it does not pursue this goal with a punitive intention, but keeping in mind the child and adolescent's peculiar condition as people whose development has not finished yet. As a consequence, 'people in development' are treated as subjects (not objects) of responsibility with rights. With the complete protection legally established, children and adolescents began to enjoy the same rights that before had been enjoyed only by adult offenders.[39]

The system of juvenile responsibility currently in place in Brazil is bitterly criticized. In effect, it is necessary to lower the age of criminal responsibility. An increasing number of cruel and violent crimes committed by adolescents, their fast mental development and the practical observation that teenagers are abused by criminal organizations support the idea of lowering the age of criminal responsibility. A proposal for a Constitutional Amendment (No. 4, 2019) has been tabled to reduce the age of criminal responsibility to 16.[40]

One can observe enormous influence of the international standards on the development of the three systems: Polish, Portuguese, and Brazilian. Today, the Polish and Portuguese models create partial criminal responsibility for juveniles when crime is committed. They are similar to the Brazilian one regarding the application of preventive and socio-correctional measures.

39 See Part. III.

40 See Part. IV.

References

Bailleau F., Crtuyvels Y. (eds.), *La justice pénale des mineurs en Europe. Entre modèle Welfare et inflexions néo-libérales*, Paris, L'Harmattan, 2007;

Ball C., MC Cormac K., Stone N., *Young Offenders: Law, Policy and Practice*, London 2001;

Bazemore G., Umbreit M., 'A Comparison of Four Restorative Conferencing Models,' *Juvenile Justice Bulletin* 2001; Available at Comparison of Four Restorative Conferencing Models | Office of Juvenile Justice and Delinquency Prevention (ojp.gov) [access: March 22 2021]

Braithwaite J. *Restorative Justice and Responsive Regulation*, Oxford, Oxford University Press, 2002;

Brooks T., *Punishment*, London, Routledge, 2012;

Brooks T., 'Punitive restoration,' *Rehabilitating Restorative Justice*, 2015/3;

Buczkowski K., 'Wymiar sprawiedliwości w wobec nieletnich w wybranych krajach,' *Prawo Karne i Kryminologia* 2018; Available at Minors%20odffenders/IWS-K.Buczkowski-Wymiar-sprawiedliwości-wobec-nieletnich.pdf [access: March 22 2021];

Butts J., Buck J., Coggeshall M., 'The impact of teen court on young offenders' in: *Research Raport* 2002, available at: The Impact of Teen Court on Young Offenders. Research Report. | Semantic Scholar [acces: March 22 2021];

Dignan J., 'Juvenile justice, criminal courts and restorative justice' in: G. Johnstone and D.W. Van Ness (eds.), *Handbook of Restorative Justice*, London, Routledge, 2007;

Duenkel F., *(19) (PDF)* 'Juvenile Justice Systems in Europe – Reform developments between justice, welfare and 'new punitiveness'1. Available at: https://www.researchgate.net/publication/291040931_Juvenile_Justice_Systems_in_Europe_-_Reform_developments_between_justice_welfare_and_%27new_punitiveness%271 [access: March 22 2021].

Duenkel F., 'Juvenile Justice Systems in Europe – Reform developments between justice, welfare and 'new punitiveness',' *Kriminologijos Studijos* 2014/1;

Kalinowski M.; *Resocjalizacja nieletnich w państwach europejskich i pozaeuropejskich*, Warsaw 2005;

Kuhn A., 'Incarceration rate, Europe versus USA,' *European Journal on Criminal Policy and Research* 1996/3;

Menkel-Meadow C., 'Restorative Justice: What is it and Does it Work' in: *Georgetown Public Law and Legal Theory Research Paper* – No. 1005485, *Annual Review of Law and Social Sciences* 2007/3;

Płatek M., 'Współczesne kierunki ewolucji systemów penitencjarnych w krajach skandynawskich' in: B. Hołyst (ed.), *Problemy współczesnej penitencjarystyki w świecie*, Warsaw 1987;

Stańdo-Kawecka B., *Prawo karne nieletnich. Od opieki do odpowiedzialności*, Warsaw, Woltres Kluwer. 2007;

Stańdo-Kawecka B., Kusztal J., *'Procedural Complexity within a Welfare Approach. Country Report Poland'* in: M. Panzavolta, D. de Vocht, M. Oosterhout, M. Vanderhallen (eds.), *Interrogating Young Suspects: Procedural Safeguards from a Legal Perspective*, Cambridge-Antwerp-Portland, Intersentia, 2015;

Stańdo-Kawecka B., 'Juvenile Justice in Poland' in: F. E. Zimring, M. Langer, D. S. Tanenhaus (eds.), *Juvenile Justice in Global Perspective*, New York, New York University Press, 2015;

Stańdo-Kawecka B., 'O koncepcji resocjalizacji w polskiej literaturze naukowej polemicznie,' *Probacja* 2010/1;

Stańdo-Kawecka B., 'Poland' in: S.H. Decker, N. Marteache (eds.), *International Handbook of Juvenile Justice*, ed. II, Switzerland, Springer International Publishing 2017;

Stańdo-Kawecka B., 'Restorative Justice in Poland - limitations and prospects for development' in: A. Pitsel i E. Symeonidou-Kastanidou (eds.), *Restorative Justice in Criminal Matters: Towards a New European Perspective*, Athens, Thessaloniki, Sakkoulas Publications, 2013;

Stańdo-Kawecka B., 'Ruch What works i "nowa resocjalizacja" - nowa perspektywa w polityce karnej?' in: V. Konarska-Wrzosek, J. Lachowski i J. Wójcikiewicz (eds.), *Węzłowe problemy prawa karnego, kryminologii i polityki kryminalnej*, Warsaw, Wolters Kluwer, 2010;

Stanowska M., Walczak-Żochowska A., Wierzbowski K., 'Uwagi o profilu ustawy o postępowaniu z nieletnimi (zagadnienia materialnoprawne i procesowe),' *Państwo i Prawo* 1983/6;

Strang H., *Victim Participation in a Restorative Justice Process*, Oxford, Oxford Univ. Press 2001;

von. Hirsch A., *Doing Justice. The Choice of Punishments*, New York, 1980;

Weisberg R., 'Restorative justice and the danger of "community",' *Utah Law Review* 2003;

Walczak-Żochowska A., 'Modele postępowania z nieletnimi' in: B. Kowalska-Ehrlich, S. Walczak (eds.), *Prawne i pedagogiczne aspekty resocjalizacji nieletnich, Prace Instytutu Profilaktyki Społecznej i Resocjalizacji Uniwersytetu Warszawskiego*, Warsaw 1992;

Wójcik D. (ed.) K. Buczkowski, J. Czabański, M. Jankowski, 'Wymiar sprawiedliwości wobec nieletnich w wybranych krajach,' *Prawo w Działaniu* 2008/3.

Part II. Juvenile Delinquency: Polish Perspective

Chapter 1. Criminal Responsibility of Juveniles in Polish Law

Magdalena Kowalewska-Łuku

Abstract: The article deals with the issue of criminal responsibility of juveniles in Polish criminal law. Specifically, it analyses the question of the age limit of criminal liability, the meaning of such terms as 'minor,' 'juvenile' and 'adolescent,' and the prerequisites of juvenile criminal responsibility. The article also discusses the problematic relationship between the offender's age and the attribution of guilt and the issues related to the severity of penalty for a juvenile offender.

Keywords: juvenile, minor, young adult offender, age of criminal responsibility, Polish juvenile justice system, age of majority, guilt in criminal law.

1. General remarks

It is a rule in modern legal systems not to hold juveniles criminally responsible.[1] This is justified, naturally, by their emotional, moral, social and intellectual immaturity, preventing them, it is believed, from behaving lawfully at all times. Thus, juveniles, as a rule, cannot be attributed guilt and held criminally responsible.

In Polish criminal law, starting with the 1932 Criminal Code, the age limit of criminal responsibility has always been 17 years. This means that juveniles under 17, as a rule, are not held criminally responsible for prohibited acts they commit. To such cases, the Juvenile Justice Act of 26 October 1982 (hereinafter referred to as Act or JJA) is applied, which comprehensively regulates matters of the juveniles who commit prohibited acts (termed punishable acts in the Act) or exhibit antisocial behaviour.

---

1 Juveniles' criminal responsibility was already absent from the legal systems of ancient states. It is from Ulpian that the following statement comes: damage caused by a child should be seen the same as damage caused by a falling tile, there is no difference between these two incidents – see V. Konarska-Wrzosek, 'Odpowiedzialność/nieodpowiedzialność nieletnich' in: *Nauka o przestępstwie. Zasady odpowiedzialności. System Praw Karnego*, Vol. 3, Warsaw 2017, p. 171.

The Polish Criminal Code allows, however, exceptional responsibility of the juveniles who are aged 15 or older at the time of committing a crime. This responsibility concerns only the most serious prohibited acts and is safeguarded by an array of requirements. To a certain degree, juveniles' responsibility for committing prohibited acts in Polish law is twofold. Provided that certain conditions specified in the current Criminal Code (hereinafter referred to as CrC) are met, above all being aged 15 or older, they may be held criminally responsible for prohibited acts they commit pursuant to the provisions of the CrC. However, in principle, when a juvenile commits a prohibited act, the Juvenile Justice Act applies. This chapter discusses the criminal responsibility that juveniles aged 15 or older can be made to bear under exceptional circumstances.

2. The concepts of a juvenile, a minor and a young offender

Before we get down to reflections about the criminal responsibility of juveniles under Polish criminal law, it is worth setting a clear frame of reference for the reflections by defining the very concept of a juvenile in Polish law and differentiate it from that of a minor and a young offender.

Polish criminal law has no legal definition of a juvenile. The scope of this concept may be, nevertheless, inferred from the CrC, Article 10, Penal-Fiscal Code, Article 5, (hereinafter PFC) and Misdemeanours Code, Article 8, (hereinafter MC). These provisions consistently set the age limit of criminal responsibility and misdemeanour responsibility at 17 years. It is, therefore, a boundary between a mature offender who may be held responsible for their actions and an immature offender, a juvenile, who, as a rule, cannot bear such responsibility. In the aforementioned Codes, a juvenile is actually held to be a person under the age of 17. Therefore, it may be concluded that a juvenile is a person who has not attained 17 years of age. However, this age-related cut-off point defining a juvenile is moved in the JJA. When it comes to prevention and combating antisocial behaviour, it uses the term juvenile to refer to persons under the age of 18 (Article 1 § 2(1) in conjunction with Article 1 § 1(1)). Meanwhile, when it comes to application of educational and correctional measures, the concept of a juvenile is extended to include persons under the age of 21 (Article 1 § 2(1) in conjunction with Article 1 § 1(3)).

Summing up, the concept of a juvenile in Polish law is not clear. In criminal law legislation (CrC, PFC and MC), it is a person under the age of 17 years. In the JJA, it may also be a person under the age of 18, or even under the age of 21, when it comes to applying educational and correctional measures.

The term juvenile must be differentiated from the concept of a minor, which is a civil law concept. Minors denote persons who have not attained the age of 18 years. According to the Civil Code, Article 10 § 1, a person over 18 is of legal age in the light of Polish law. The CrC, however, does feature the concept of a minor as a name for a person under the legal age who is aggrieved by an offence.

Still another concept important for criminal law is that of a young offender. The CrC provides its legal definition: pursuant to Article 115 § 10, a young offender is an offender who at the time of committing a prohibited act has not attained the age of 21 years or the age of 24 years at the time of trial in the first-instance court. The status of a young offender has crucial consequences for the administration of justice. Namely, the dominant goal of a punishment imposed on a young offender is an educational effect (CrC, Article 54 § 1) and the punishment may be subject to extraordinary mitigation (CrC, Article 60 § 1).

The concept of a juvenile is crucial for the discussion in this chapter. It is the term used in the Criminal Code where it is assumed that juveniles, that is persons under the age of 17, as a rule cannot be held criminally responsible.

3. Age limit of criminal responsibility

As pointed out above, the age limit of criminal responsibility under the CrC, Article 10 § 1, is, in principle, 17 years at the time of committing a prohibited act. Exceptionally, pursuant to the CrC, Article 10 § 2, if certain requirements enumerated in this provision are met, a minor who was aged 15 or older when committing a prohibited act can be also held criminally responsible. The age limit of criminal responsibility set in the CrC, Article 10 § 1, is of course an expression of a certain assumption that persons aged 17 or older have reached a sufficient level of emotional, intellectual, social and moral development so they can recognize a legal norm and accept full responsibility for their actions, whereas the same cannot be expected of younger people. It is the cognitive, emotional, social and moral development realized primarily in the socialisation process that determines the acceptance and bearing of responsibility, including criminal responsibility.[2] In consequence, it is the achievement of a certain level of development that determines whether an offender may become an addressee of a

2 See P. Zakrzewski, *Stopniowanie winy w prawie karnym*, Warszaw 2016, pp. 74–75 and T. Kaczmarek, 'Psychologiczne i ustawowe kryteria odróżniania nieletnich od dorosłych w polskim prawie karnym,' *Nowe Prawo*, 1990/1–3, pp. 17–19.

negative assessment of their act, whether they can be attributed guilt and, eventually, whether they can be held criminally responsible.[3]

At the same time, it is quite obvious that the so-called developmental age is not always the same as the so-called birth-certificate age. Moreover, development, including moral development – probably the most important for the issue of responsibility – is a continuum by nature. It is not graduated.[4] For example, one of the researchers of moral development, L. Kohlberg, pointed out that the third and last stage of moral development he identified, the so-called post-conventional morality, may be reached in adolescence or as late as in young adulthood and some people may never reach it.[5] Therefore, taking into account the fact that the age limit of criminal responsibility set in the CrC, Article 10 § 1, at 17 is a certain compromise presumption,[6] the legislator's making an exception to this presumption in the CrC, Article 10 § 2 and § 4, which allows for certain flexibility in adopting an age limit, seems reasonable. Article 10 § 2 stipulates, as already mentioned, as an exceptional possibility, the criminal responsibility of juveniles aged 15 or older. Meanwhile, Article 10 § 4 stipulates an exceptional exclusion of criminal responsibility of the offenders who have attained the age of 17 years at the time of committing an offence, but have not yet attained the age of 18 years. Pursuant to this provision, if an offender commits a prohibited act after turning 17, but before turning 18 years old, the court will apply educational, therapeutic or correctional measures prescribed for juveniles, instead of imposing a penalty, if this is deemed appropriate, given the circumstances of the case and the level of mental development of the offender, their characteristics and personal circumstances.

---

3 See C. Elliott, 'Criminal responsibility and children: a new defence required to acknowledge the absence of capacity and choice,' *The Journal of Criminal Law*, 2003/75, pp. 293–294.

4 See M. Kowalewska-Łukuć, *Wina w prawie karnym*, Warsaw, Wolters Kluwer, 2019, pp. 203–204.

5 See A. Brzezińska, K. Appelt, B. Ziółkowska, 'Psychologia rozwoju człowieka' in: J. Strelau, D. Doliński (eds.), *Psychologia akademicka. Podręcznik*, Vol. 2, Gdansk, 2015, p. 196. See also S. Morse, 'Immaturity and Irresponsibility,' *The Journal of Criminal Law & Criminology*, 1997/1, p. 58.

6 Such a presumption necessarily disregards the findings in the field of psychology concerning individual differences in achieving a specific level of development, including moral development. – see G. Maher, 'Age and Criminal Responsibility,' *Ohio State Journal of Criminal Law*, 2005/2, p. 504.

It needs to be considered whether setting the age limit of criminal responsibility at 17 years is adequate. The majority of jurisdictions set it at 18 years. The Polish Criminal Code, therefore, is a certain exception in this regard.[7] This is partially due to historical reasons. Already the 1932 Criminal Code set the age of criminal responsibility at 17 years. However, it needs to be noted that assuming a 17-year-old offender is no longer a juvenile in criminal law may be challenged by the argument that it is a child that is held criminally responsible. Pursuant to Article 1 of the Convention on the Rights of the Child, ratified by Poland, a child shall be understood as 'every human being below the age of eighteen years unless under the law applicable to the child, majority is attained earlier.' The Constitution of the Republic of Poland also defines a child as a person who is not of legal age, that is a person who has not attained the age of 18 years. It is the persons who have attained the age of 18 years that the Constitution awards the voting right. Attaining the age of 18, as reaching majority, is also a significant cut-off point under other statutes. For example, the Family and Guardianship Code as a rule allows people to enter into marriage after attaining the age of 18. Therefore, certain doubts may arise from the fact that Poland's jurisdiction assumes that only a person aged 18 or older is no longer a child and is mature enough to vote, enter into marriage or buy alcohol, while at the same time a 17-year-old child is mature enough to bear criminal responsibility and, for instance, be sentenced to a prison term.[8] Therefore, the postulate of equalising the lower age limit of criminal responsibility and the age limit of majority, i.e. setting it at 18 years, seems worth considering.[9]

Of course, parallel doubts may concern the possibility, enacted in the CrC, Article 10 § 2, of holding juvenile offenders aged 15 or older criminally responsible. However, it must be noted that this responsibility is safeguarded by an array of conditions, thus it is exceptional responsibility.

4. Offender age and attribution of guilt

The offender's reaching the age indicated in the CrC, Article 10 § 2, i.e. attaining the age of 17 years, is considered as the offender's attaining maturity, allowing

---

7 See V. Konarska-Wrzosek, *Prawny system postępowania z nieletnimi w Polsce*, Warsaw 2013, p. 31.

8 See M. Maraszek, *Dolna granica wieku odpowiedzialności karnej w prawie polskim*, Warsaw 2012, p. 136.

9 See M. Maraszek, *Dolna*..., p. 167, see also C. McDiarmid, 'An Age of Complexity: Children and Criminal Responsibility in Law,' *Youth Justice*, 2013/2, p. 158.

them to be attributed guilt and be held criminally responsible. Thus, maturity defined as attaining a certain age is treated in the Polish criminal law scholarship as one of the prerequisites for attributing guilt, and vice versa: the status of a juvenile is considered a preclusion of this attribution.[10]

The dominant approach to guilt in Polish criminal law is the pure normative theory of guilt. This theory adopts assumptions of finalism which place intentionality and unintentionality on the plane of the act itself, not guilt, which is contemplated as a pure charge against the offender. He or she is charged with the non-observance of a legal norm. If this is possible, in turn, is established on the basis of the offender's sanity, their maturity, awareness of the unlawfulness of the act and normal motivation.

It seems that when agreeing that only a mature offender may be required to obey a legal norm, and that possible criminal responsibility in the event of violating it may be exacted from them, one needs to conclude that being a juvenile is indeed a bar to guilt attribution. It needs to be reiterated that the age limit of criminal responsibility set at 17 years is only a certain presumption that an offender who has not attained this age is not capable of being arraigned or attributed guilt, while offenders over the age of 17 are. Therefore, saying that the offender's being a juvenile and immature cannot be perceived as a bar to guilt is a certain simplification. An offender below the age of 17, as a rule, is not considered an addressee of a charge, i.e. an individual to whom guilt can be attributed, which is not always tantamount to them truly not being able to bear guilt.[11] One cannot rule out a situation in which e.g. a 16-year-old offender is at such a level of emotional, social and moral maturity that it should be objectively stated that from the point of view of the level of their development there are no obstacles to accuse them of committing a prohibited act. However, by reason of the CrC, Article 10 § 1, this is not done. Therefore, it seems far more precise to define maturity as a requirement that determines the possibility of establishing guilt, rather than as a requirement

---

10 See J. Giezek in: J. Giezek (ed.), *Kodeks karny. Część ogólna. Komentarz*, Warsaw 2012, p. 26.

11 See A. Zoll, 'Czy nieletniość jest okolicznością wyłączającą winę?' in: Hofmański, S. Waltoś (eds.), *W kręgu prawa nieletnich. Księga pamiątkowa ku czci Profesor Marianny Korcyl-Wolskiej*, Warsaw, Wolters Kluwer 2009, p. 194; A. Barczak-Oplustil, 'Sporne zagadnienia istoty winy w prawie karnym. Zarys problemu,' *Czasopismo Prawa Karnego i Nauk Penalnych*, 2005/2, p. 80 and P. Zakrzewski, *Stopniowanie...*, p. 317.

for existence of guilt. Analogically, being juvenile should be rather contemplated not as a bar to guilt, but a bar to establishing it. In short, the fact that the offender is a juvenile does not exclude guilt itself at the time the act is committed, but it excludes the possibility of attributing it to the offender.

Therefore, if we cannot presume the existence of guilt at all in the case of a juvenile offender, which, in line with the *nullum crimen sine culpa* principle, is a necessary requirement for deeming a given prohibited act a crime, in consequence, we cannot hold him criminally responsible either.

5. Prerequisites of the criminal responsibility of juveniles

As already mentioned, the CrC, Article 10 § 2, exceptionally allows to hold a juvenile offender as young as 15 criminally responsible. Pursuant to this provision, the provisions of the Criminal Code may apply to juveniles aged 15 or older who commit a prohibited act named in Article 134, Article 148 § 1, 2 or 3, Article 156 § 1 or 3, Article 163 § 1 or 3, Article 166, Article 173 § 1 or 3, Article 197 § 3 or 4, Article 223 § 2, Article 252 § 1 or 2 and Article 280, if deemed appropriate, given the circumstances of the case and the level of mental development of the offender, their characteristics and personal situation. Moreover, an especially important consideration is whether previous attempts at applying educational or correctional measures have been ineffective. This provision enumerates prerequisites for exceptional criminal responsibility of the juvenile, which are:

(1) The juvenile is 15 years old
(2) The juvenile has committed one of the prohibited acts specified in the CrC, Article 134, Article 148 § 1, 2 or 3, Article 156 § 1 or 3, Article 163 § 1 or 3, Article 166, Article 173 § 1 or 3, Article 197 § 3 or 4, Article 223 § 2, Article 252 § 1 or 2 and Article 280
(3) The circumstances of the case, the level of mental development, characteristics and personal situation of the offender justify holding them criminally responsible
(4) Previous attempts at applying educational or correctional measures have failed.

It needs to be emphasized yet again that meeting the above prerequisites only provides conditions for the possibility of a juvenile's criminal responsibility. It is not that each time when they are met, a juvenile must be held criminally responsible for the prohibited act they committed. The prerequisites set out in the CrC,

Article 10 § 2, seem to be worded quite precisely. However, this impression fades after analysing them in more detail.[12]

Most interpretation problems are not caused by the stipulation in the CrC, Article 10 § 2, that the juvenile must attain 15 years of age. Similarly to the age limit of 17 years set out in the CrC, Article 10 § 1, the legislator decided to specify rigidly the age required for exceptional criminal responsibility of a juvenile.[13]

The prerequisite requiring that the juvenile commits a prohibited act specified in the provisions set out in the CrC, Article 10 § 2, seems clear as well, but this is not entirely the case. The provisions listed in this Article name certain serious crimes of the Polish Criminal Code. These are: an attempt on the life of the President of the Republic of Poland (Article 134), homicide in the basic and aggravated forms (Article 148 § 1, 2 and 3), grievous bodily harm, also one aggravated by a consequence involving death and grievous bodily harm (Article 156 § 1 or 3), causing a life-threatening event, also aggravated by a consequence involving death (Article 163 § 1 or 3), hijacking of a ship or an aircraft (Article 166), causing a disaster in traffic, also aggravated by a consequence involving death or grievous bodily harm (Article 173 § 1 or 3), aggravated forms of rape (Article 197 § 3 or 4), aggravated form of assault on a public official (Article 223 § 2), taking a hostage in the basic and aggravated forms (Article 252 § 1 or 2) and armed robbery in the basic and aggravated forms (Article 280).

Łukasz Pohl rightly points out that the CrC, Article 10 § 2, does not enumerate prohibited acts defined in the Polish criminal law scholarship as non-performance forms of criminal cooperation: perpetration involving organisation of a crime (Article 18 § 1 sentence 3), perpetration involving ordering a crime (Article 18 § 1 sentence 4), instigation (Article 18 § 2) and aiding and abetting

---

12 See K. Burdziak, 'Art. 10 § 2 k.k. i Art. 94 u.p.n. z perspektywy Art. 40 ust. 3 konwencji o prawach dziecka, czyli kilka słów na temat odpowiedzialności karnej nieletnich,' *Probacja* 2019/2, p. 40

13 Certain doubts may be raised by the manner of establishing the moment of attaining the age of 15 years required under the CrC, Art. 10 § 2, (and analogically the age of 17 years under Article 10 § 1). It seems that the view about the need to use the *computatio naturalis* formula, i.e. "from moment to moment", is correct. According to this formula, if for example the offender was born on 16 February 2000 at 5 p.m., then he will reach the required age of 15 years on 16 February 2015 at 5.10 p.m. Therefore, under Article 10 § 2 he or she can be held criminally responsible for a prohibited act committed on 16 February 2015 after 5.10 p.m. at the earliest – see M. Nawrocki, 'O sposobie ustalania dolnej granicy wieku odpowiedzialności karnej,' *Państwo i Prawo* 2019/9, p. 91.

(Article 18 § 3). It also fails to mention attempt (Article 13). Therefore, the view of the said author deserves to be concurred with, according to which a juvenile may be held criminally responsible, of course when the remaining prerequisites of Article 10 § 2 are met, only when they commit a given act in the form of performance-involving perpetration and it is an already performed act.[14] It seems that this was not the legislator's intention. This is because in axiological terms, if only for the sake of the justice- and protection-related function of criminal law, it would be difficult to accept that a 15-year-old offender could be held criminally responsible for a homicide (Article 148 § 1), but another 15-year-old offender cooperating with him or her in the organisational role or order-giving capacity, who was a special *spiritus movens* of the homicide, did not bear this responsibility.

One can also ponder how comprehensive the catalogue of prohibited acts for which a juvenile offender can answer under the CrC, Article 10 § 2, in exceptional cases is. It does not include all crimes regulated in the general part of the CrC. It is difficult to see what key the legislator used to place some of the crimes in this catalogue. It is said that the common denominator of the prohibited acts enumerated in the CrC, Article 10 § 2, is the use of violence or causing general danger.[15] If so, then the legislator did not apply this criterion fully consistently. The catalogue includes, for instance, the basic and aggravated types of armed robbery. The basic type of armed robbery is not a crime, but only a summary offence. Yet the catalogue does not include aggravated theft, which is

---

14 See Ł. Pohl, 'Ponownie w sprawie zakresu odpowiedzialności karnej osoby nieletniej według Kodeksu karnego z 1997 r. (zagadnienie form popełnienia czynu zabronionego) – uwagi o metodzie rozwiązania problemu,' *Prawo w Działaniu* 2018/35, pp. 115–119. Ł. Pohl argues that regulated norms that underpin the non-performance forms of criminal cooperation are placed in the CrC, 18 § 1, 2 and 3, respectively, and not in the provisions of the detailed part of the CrC, set out in Article 10 § 2. A similar situation is in the case of attempt. The legal norm was in this case worded in general terms in Article 13 § 1. A different view is presented by A. Zoll who points out that Article 10 § 2 applies to all forms of perpetrating cooperation. However, it cannot be applied in the case of instigation or aiding and abetting to acts specified in the provisions enumerated in Article 10 § 2 – A. Zoll, 'Commentary on Articles 1–52' in: W. Wróbel, A. Zoll (eds.), *Kodeks karny. Część ogólna*, Vol. I. Part I. Warsaw, Wolters Kluwer 2016, Article 10, par. 25. Most criminal law scholars and commentators believe that there are no obstacles to holding a juvenile offender accountable for all forms of perpetrating cooperation under Article 10 § 2 – see A. Grześkowiak, in: A. Grześkowiak, K. Wiak (eds.), *Kodeks karny. Komentarz*, Warsaw 2019, *passim*.

15 See A. Zoll, 'Commentary on Articles 1–52...'

also a summary offence and consists in almost identical violent behaviour by the offender.[16]

The next prerequisite under the CrC, Article 10 § 2, necessary to hold a juvenile criminally responsible, requires that the circumstances of the case, level of mental development of the offender, their characteristics and personal situation be taken into account. Its elements are quite vague, which may cause considerable difficulties in their application to a specific case. This under-defined nature is sometimes justified by the need to personalise proceedings involving juveniles. At the same time, it affects the guarantee function of criminal law in a special area, i.e. juvenile-related criminal law.[17]

Circumstances of the case are considered by jurists and commentators a general category, which includes both personal and material circumstances. They point out that when specifying the scope of the case circumstances that are to decide if a juvenile will be held criminally responsible, the criteria to be used in determining the social harmfulness degree of the act, set out in the CrC, Article 115 § 2, may play an auxiliary role.[18] Circumstances demonstrating the degree of the offender's antisocial behaviour, their possible activity in a criminal gang or their role as an organiser and planner of prohibited acts will be crucial as well.[19]

A slightly better defined criterion listed in the CrC, Article 10 § 2, is the offender's level of development. As already mentioned, it is indeed owing to their ongoing emotional, social and moral development that juvenile offenders, as a rule, do not incur criminal responsibility. This is why the exceptional criminal responsibility under Article 10 § 2 must be made contingent on the level of their development. This level should be high enough to allow to press a charge of not observing a legal norm against the juvenile, and thus attributing guilt to them.

The personal characteristics and situation of the offender are an under-defined concept. It seems correct to identify the offender's personal characteristics with his personality traits such as an inclination to aggressive types of behaviour or, by contrast, submissiveness, and his or her internalised system of values.[20] In turn, the offender's personal situation is believed to be their general circumstances

16 See K. Burdziak, 'Art. 10…,' p. 41.

17 See A. Grześkowiak in: A. Grześkowiak, K. Wiak (eds.), *Kodeks…*

18 See A. Grześkowiak in: A. Grześkowiak, K. Wiak (eds.), *Kodeks…*

19 See A. Zoll, 'Commentary on Articles 1–52…'

20 See Walczak-Żochowska, 'Komentarz do Art. 1–116' in: R. Zawłocki, M. Królikowski (eds.), *Kodeks karny. Część ogólna,* Warsaw, C.H. Beck 2017, *passim.*

that determine his or her position in life and society. They are made up of *inter alia* family-, education-, school- and peer-related environments.

When deciding about the juvenile's exceptional criminal responsibility under the CrC, Article 10 § 2, the court should also take into account the circumstance that previously applied educational and correctional measures have failed. Jurists and commentators and judicial decisions in criminal matters rightly observe that the expression 'especially' used by the legislator when referring to this prerequisite means that it is not absolute and therefore a juvenile to whom educational and correctional measures have not been previously applied can incur criminal responsibility under the CrC, Article 10 § 2.[21]

The court's decision, therefore, about the juvenile's exceptional criminal responsibility under the CrC, Article 10 § 2, should be the product of considering all the prerequisites set out in this provision. At the same time, it needs to be emphasized yet again that satisfying these prerequisites does not necessarily entail the juvenile's obligatory criminal responsibility, but only creates a possibility for them to answer along the principles laid down in the Criminal Code.

6. Penalty for a juvenile offender

The exceptional nature of juveniles' criminal responsibility under the CrC, Article 10 § 2, also entails a number of consequences for the penalty. Two regulations are crucial here: the CrC, Article 10 § 3 and Article 54. Pursuant to the former, the penalty imposed on a juvenile may not exceed two-thirds of the statutory upper limit of the penalty prescribed for a crime attributed to the offender. Moreover, the court may apply extraordinary mitigation of the penalty. The statutory reduction of the penalty to two-thirds of its statutory upper limit and the court's power to mitigate it extraordinarily are consequent upon the lower degree of guilt of a juvenile offender. Guilt, as we already know, may be a charge made against an offender when they are mature enough for committing a prohibited act. Maturity, however, in the case of a juvenile offender is not full. This translates into diminishing their guilt and in consequence into a need to mitigate the penalty, which the legislator expressed in the CrC, Article 10 § 3.[22]

---

21 See M. Maraszek, 'Dolna…,' p. 83 and Judgement of the Supreme Administrative Court of 8 May 1972, III KR 45/72, LEX No. 18479.

22 It may be digressed that even if the regulation laid down in the CrC, Article 10 § 3, was not there, the diminished degree of guilt should be reflected in the penalty, owing to Article 53 § 1 which formulates the principle of guilt limitation. In accordance with

Meanwhile, according to the CrC, Article 54 § 1, when imposing a penalty on a juvenile, the court is to aim primarily at educating them. Moreover, under the CrC, Article 54 § 2, the court cannot sentence a juvenile offender to life imprisonment. The educational aim of the penalty does not mean *per se* that it should be lenient. The Supreme Court has rightly observed that Article 54 § 1 does not eliminate sentencing guidelines specified in Article 53, but places educational reasons first among the directives enumerated therein. For these reasons, the crucial criteria for setting a penalty for a young offender should include the degree of their antisocial behaviour, life style before, and behaviour after, committing the crime, motives and conduct.[23] It is these criteria that seem to be the most strongly associated with the educational aims that the penalty imposed on the juvenile is to achieve. Furthermore, a penalty should be proportional to the degree of social harmfulness of their act, meet the requirements of general and individual prevention and should be limited by the degree of guilt.

The educational aim of the penalty imposed on a juvenile offender corresponds with the prohibition, enacted in the CrC, Article 54 § 2, of sentencing an offender who has not attained the age of 18 years at the time of committing the crime to life imprisonment. Life imprisonment has an eliminating nature. Minor offenders, even those who commit the most serious crimes for which life imprisonment may be imposed, as rightly observed by one appellate court, 'generally do not have a fully developed personality or a fully established system of values adopted in society, they have a less developed mechanism for behaviour control and inhibition, but they have instead a greater inclination to impulsive, including urge-driven, types of behaviour. They are persons not yet established in life who only begin their adaptation in society.'[24] Given the above, sentencing them to life imprisonment would eliminate the existing, at least potentially, possibility of their rehabilitation and re-adaptation.

7. Conclusion

To sum up, the solutions adopted in the Polish legal system concerning the criminal responsibility of juveniles are a certain compromise between a position

---

this provision, the court, imposing a penalty at its own discretion, within the limits prescribed by law, must ensure that its severity does not exceed the degree of guilt.

23 See Decision of the Supreme Court of 4 May 2005, V KK 454/04, LEX No. 149647.

24 Judgement of the Court of Appeal in Cracow of 12 November 2003, II AKa 255/03, LEX No. 148363.

demanding an absolute prohibition of holding juveniles criminally responsible and a position postulating, at times in a distorted way, the primacy of the protective and justice-related function of criminal law. The latter advocates treating juvenile offenders more often as adults in relation to criminal law. On the one hand, Polish law has a rule according to which criminal responsibility cannot be borne by a juvenile, i.e. a person who has not attained the age of 17 years (CrC, Article 10 § 1). To perpetrators of prohibited acts who are under 17 years of age, as a rule, the 1982 Juvenile Justice Act applies, which has enacted a different regime from criminal responsibility. On the other hand, seeing that the most serious crimes may be committed by offenders who are indeed underage though sufficiently mature to have guilt attributed to them, the legislator has provided for the exceptional criminal responsibility of juveniles who were 15 or older at the time of committing the crime (CrC, Article 10 § 2).

This compromise may not be an ideal solution, but it has been functioning in Polish criminal law for decades and has not been seriously challenged, in either criminal law scholarship or judicial decisions. However, the suggestion of raising the age limit of criminal responsibility from 17 to 18 years warrants consideration. This would ward off the criticism that criminal responsibility is laid on people who are considered children (minors) by the legal system and would adjust relevant criminal law regulations to other branches of the law – civil, family or electoral law. Considering such a *de lege ferenda* suggestion seems justified also because there are no reasons, except perhaps for historical ones, that could justify leaving the current age limit at 17 years.

It also seems to be a reasonable suggestion that the CrC, Article 10 § 2, should be amended so that not only does it allow to hold juvenile offenders criminally responsible for carrying out performance-involving forms of criminal cooperation in prohibited acts specified therein, but also so that it allows the criminal responsibility of those offenders who organise such acts and order their execution, instigate, aid and abet them, or attempt to carry them out.[25]

References

Barczak-Oplustil A., 'Sporne zagadnienia istoty winy w prawie karnym. Zarys problemu,' *Czasopismo Prawa Karnego i Nauk Penalnych*, 2005/2;

25 Such a suggestion has actually been made multiple times by Ł. Pohl – see Ł. Pohl, 'Zakres odpowiedzialności karnej nieletniego w Kodeksie karnym z 1997 r. (o konieczności pilnej zmiany Art. 10 § 2 k.k. – problem form popełnienia czynu zabronionego),' *Prawo w Działaniu* 2017/30, pp. 7ff.

Brzezińska A., Appelt K., Ziółkowska B., 'Psychologia rozwoju człowieka' in: Strelau J., Doliński D. (eds.), *Psychologia akademicka. Podręcznik*, Vol. 2, Gdansk, 2015;

Burdziak K., 'Art. 10 § 2 k.k. i Article 94 u.p.n. z perspektywy Article 40 ust. 3 konwencji o prawach dziecka, czyli kilka słów na temat odpowiedzialności karnej nieletnich,' *Probacja* 2019/2;

Elliott C., 'Criminal responsibility and children: a new defence required to acknowledge the absence of capacity and choice,' *The Journal of Criminal Law* 2003/75;

Giezek J., 'Art. 10' in: J. Giezek (ed.), *Kodeks karny. Część ogólna. Komentarz*, Warsaw, Wolters Kluwer 2012;

Kaczmarek T., 'Psychologiczne i ustawowe kryteria odróżniania nieletnich od dorosłych w polskim prawie karnym,' *Nowe Prawo* 1990/1–3;

Grześkowiak A., 'Art. 10' in: A. Grześkowiak, K. Wiak (eds.), *Kodeks karny. Komentarz*, Warsaw 2019;

Konarska-Wrzosek V., 'Odpowiedzialność/nieodpowiedzialność nieletnich' in: *Nauka o przestępstwie. Zasady odpowiedzialności. System Praw Karnego*, Vol. 3, Warsaw 2017;

Konarska-Wrzosek V., *Prawny system postępowania z nieletnimi w Polsce*, Warsaw 2013;

Kowalewska-Łukuć M., *Wina w prawie karnym*, Warsaw, Wolters Kluwer 2019;

Maher G., 'Age and Criminal Responsibility,' *Ohio State Journal of Criminal Law* 2005/2;

Maraszek M., *Dolna granica wieku odpowiedzialności karnej w prawie polskim*, Warsaw 2012;

McDiarmid C., 'An Age of Complexity: Children and Criminal Responsibility in Law,' *Youth Justice* 2013/2;

Morse S., 'Immaturity and Irresponsibility,' *The Journal of Criminal Law & Criminology* 1997/1;

Nawrocki M., 'O sposobie ustalania dolnej granicy wieku odpowiedzialności karnej' *Państwo i Prawo*, 2019/9;

Pohl Ł., 'Ponownie w sprawie zakresu odpowiedzialności karnej osoby nieletniej według Kodeksu karnego z 1997 r. (zagadnienie form po pełnienia czynu zabronionego) – uwagi o metodzie rozwiązania problemu,' *Prawo w Działaniu* 2018/35;

Pohl Ł., 'Zakres odpowiedzialności karnej nieletniego w Kodeksie karnym z 1997 r. (o konieczności pilnej zmiany Article 10 § 2 k.k. – problem form popełnienia czynu zabronionego),' *Prawo w Działaniu* 2017/30;

Walczak-Żochowska A., in: R. Zawłocki, M. Królikowski (eds.), *Kodeks karny. Część ogólna. Komentarz do Article 1–116*, Warsaw, C.H. Beck 2017;

Zakrzewski P., *Stopniowanie winy w prawie karnym*, Warszaw, Wolters Kluwer 2016;

Zoll, A, 'Commentary on Articles 1–52' in: W. Wróbel, A. Zoll (eds.), *Kodeks karny. Część ogólna. Vol. I. Part I,* Warsaw, Wolters Kluwer 2016;

Zoll A., 'Czy nieletniość jest okolicznością wyłączającą winę?' in: P. Hofmański, S. Waltoś (eds.), *W kręgu prawa nieletnich. Księga pamiątkowa ku czci Profesor Marianny Korcyl-Wolskiej*,Warsaw 2009;Judgement of the Supreme Administrative Court of 08 May 1972, III KR 45/72, LEX No. 18479;

Judgement of the Court of Appeal in Cracow of 12 November 2003, II AKa 255/03, LEX No. 148363;

Decision of the Supreme Court of 4 May 2005, V KK 454/04, LEX No. 149647.

Chapter 2. Juvenile Situation under the 1982 Juvenile Justice Act

Konrad Burdziak

Abstract: The publication discusses: 1) aims and basic rules of juvenile justice; 2) the definition of a juvenile and the problems arising in the context of this definition; 3) the concepts of demoralisation and punishable act (as the basis for initiating proceedings); 4) educational and corrective measures that may be adjudicated against the juvenile. The findings presented in the publication were made: 1) by analyzing the normative material relating to the issue under study, and first of all – by analyzing the Juvenile Justice Act of 26 October 1982 (Dz. U. (Journal of Laws) of 2018 item 969 as amended); and – 2) by analyzing views presented in literature. Key findings: 1) The subject-matter of juvenile justice was regulated in Poland in an act completely separate from other acts (an in particular – entirely separate from criminal law acts), to be more specific – in the Juvenile Justice Act. It needs to be emphasized that this Act cut ties with the criminal law past of juvenile justice and its purpose is primarily (if not solely) to assist the juvenile in his return to a normal life. 2) The reasons for interference in the life of the juvenile on the ground of the Act include: a) demoralization understood as 'a psychological and social process which features unfavourable changes in the juvenile's personality and behaviour of an intensified and relatively lasting nature, which is manifested in non-observance of norms and rules of conduct universally applicable to children and young people;' b) a punishable act, which must be understood as a behaviour of the juvenile which meets requirements of a given criminal offence and which typically, when additional elements are satisfied, would be deemed as a crime, a tax offence or a misdemeanour. 3) The Juvenile Justice Act equips the family court with a wide array of measures possible to be applied for a juvenile; measures that are suitable to the achievement of the goal of the child's (juvenile's) welfare.

Keywords: juvenile, age of criminal responsibility, Polish juvenile justice system, anti-social behaviour (ASB), correctional measures, educational measures, punishable act.

1. General remarks: Aims and basic rules of juvenile justice

The subject-matter of juveniles and the issues of juvenile justice were expressly identified by the Polish legislator and regulated in a separate act (apart from the Criminal Code and other statutes), that is in the Juvenile Justice Act.[1] This fact

1 Juvenile Justice Act of 26 October 1982 (Dz. U. (Journal of Laws) of 2018 item 969

clearly points out that the Polish legislator decided to cut the ties (at least partially; see Article 11 of the Criminal Code[2]) with the criminal law past of juvenile justice, which for many years had been regulated in Poland by the 1932 Criminal Code,[3] the 1928 Code of Criminal Procedure[4] and the 1969 Criminal Code.[5]

By separating juvenile justice the legislator decreed that: (1) juvenile justice is not related to the juvenile's criminal responsibility (and in fact it is not related to any responsibility of the juvenile; the proceedings concern the juvenile and are not conducted against him); (2) juvenile justice does not have the nature of a criminal procedure and is not regulated under the Code of Criminal Procedure (it is – at least prima facie – an entirely separate procedure and the juvenile must not be given the status of a suspect or an accused).[6]

---

as amended), hereinafter referred to as JJA or Act.On the Polish criminal code and minors, see P. Daniluk, J. Mieraelńska-Lorencka, 'Responsibility of a Juvenile for a Prohibited Act under Polish Law,' *International & Comparative Law Review / Mezinárodní a Srovnávací Právní Revue*, 2016/2, pp. 99–115. Available at: http://search-1ebscohost-1com-10hkp9id4042a.waw-proxlib.swps.edu.pl/login.aspx?direct=true&db=obo&AN=131170747&lang=pl&site=eds-live. About the forensic aspects on Juvenile Crime in Poland see I. Bembas, 'Forensic Aspects of Juvenile Crime in Poland. From a Juvenile to a Criminal – The Road to Demoralisation,' *Internal Security* 2020/1, pp. 113–23. Available at: http://search-1ebscohost-1com-10hkp9id4042a.waw-proxlib.swps.edu.pl/login.aspx?direct=true&db=obo&AN=146063036&lang=pl&site=eds-live [access: Dec. 17 2020].

2 Act of 6 June 1997 – Criminal Code (Dz. U. (Journal of Laws) of 2020 item 1444 as amended), hereinafter referred to as CrC.

3 Decree of the President of the Republic of 11 July 1932 – Criminal Code (Dz. U. (Journal of Laws) No. 60 item 571).

4 Decree of the President of the Republic of 19 March 1928 – Criminal Code (Dz. U. (Journal of Laws) No. 33 item 313).

5 Act of 19 April 1969 – Criminal Code (Dz. U. (Journal of Laws) No. 12 item 94 as amended). On other European countries see e.g. B. Goldson, *Juvenile Justice in Europe: Past, Present and Future*, Abingdon, Oxon, Routledge 2019, Available at: http://search-1ebscohost-1com-10hkp9id4042a.waw-proxlib.swps.edu.pl/login.aspx?direct=true&db=edsebk&AN=1769982&lang=pl&site=eds-live [access: Dec. 17 2020]. See also F.E. Zimring, M. Langer, D.S. Tanenhaus, *Juvenile Justice in Global Perspective*, New York, NYU Press, 2015 (Youth, Crime, and Justice Series). Available at: http://search-1ebscohost-1com-10hkp9id4042a.waw proxlib.swps.edu.pl/login.aspx?direct=true&db=nlebk&AN=1020812&lang=pl&site=eds-live [access: Dec. 17 2020].

6 This protects the juvenile – at least to a certain degree – against stigmatization. It is only to a certain degree because the terms 'delinquency' or 'punishable act' used by the legislator have clearly negative connotations and may, as a result, constitute a source of the juvenile's stigmatization.

Therefore, the legislator decided that the juvenile is not – simply – a young offender and (solely) the source of danger to society and its essential interests. It has decided that the juvenile is an individual: (1) to whom attention needs to be paid; (2) whose improper behaviour must be responded to; (3) who must not be condemned, punished or isolated from society; and (4) who must be helped by conducing proceedings in his case (and not, let us remember, against him).[7]

The legislator's decision to cut off ties between juvenile justice and responsibility (also criminal responsibility) of juveniles is also, or perhaps primarily, affirmed in the preamble to the Juvenile Justice Act, according to which:

> In pursuit to counteract juvenile delinquency and antisocial behaviour and to create conditions for returning to a normal life for juveniles who have come into conflict with the law or with public policy, and in pursuit to strengthen the welfare and educational function of families and the sense of responsibility of families for raising juveniles to be aware of their duties as members of society, it is enacted as follows.

The preamble also clearly demonstrates that the aim of the Act is not to act against the juveniles, but only to counteract their inappropriate behaviour (juvenile delinquency and antisocial behaviour). It may take the form of prohibited acts (which would be typical of criminal procedure and criminal responsibility) and antisocial behaviour (other socially unacceptable behaviour other than punishable acts). The legislator stresses that the juvenile's inappropriate behaviour must be counteracted. It must be not only eliminated, if it occurs, but also prevented as much as possible. This clearly shows that the legislator does not want

---

7 On the knowledge of risk and protective factors along with information on potential intervention and prevention programs, see e.g. P. Boxer, S.E. Goldstein, 'Treating juvenile offenders: Best practices and emerging critical issues' in: E.L. Grigorenko (ed.), *Handbook of juvenile forensic psychology and psychiatry*, New York, NY, US, Springer Science + Business Media, 2012, p. 323–40. Available at: http://search-1ebscohost-1com-10hkp9id4041b.waw-proxlib.swps.edu.pl/login.aspx?direct=true&db=psyh&AN=2012-11873-021&lang=pl&site=eds-live [access: Dec. 17 2020]; R. Loeber, D.P. Farrington, *Serious and Violent Juvenile Offenders: Risk Factors and Successful Interventions* Vol. 1st paper ed. Thousand Oaks, Calif, SAGE Publications, Inc; 1999. Available at: http://search-1ebscohost-1com-10hkp9id4041b.waw-proxlib.swps.edu.pl/login.aspx?direct=true&db=nlebk&AN=467088&lang=pl&site=eds-live [access: Dec. 17 2020]; M. Basto Pereira, A. da Costa Maia, *Juvenile Delinquency, Crime and Social Marginalization: Social and Political Implications,* Bingley, UK: Emerald Publishing Limited, 2017, (Emerald Points; Vol. First edition). Available at: http://search-1ebscohost-1com-10hkp9id4041b.waw-proxlib.swps.edu.pl/login.aspx?direct=true&db=nlebk&AN=1549783&lang=pl&site=eds-live [access: Dec. 17 2020].

to cause any affliction to the juvenile or cause him to feel such affliction in the course of proceedings in his case; it is rather concerned about providing the juvenile with care and assistance in his continuation of, or return to, a normal life. This is actually affirmed by the next goal enumerated in the preamble to the Juvenile Justice Act, which involves 'creating conditions for the juvenile to return to a normal life,' where the normal life must be understood – let us emphasize – not only as a life that ensures/enables the juvenile's personal development, but also as one which is free of conflicts with society (the legislator emphasizes the importance of raising juveniles who are aware of their obligations as society members).

The preamble to the Juvenile Justice Act is – let us emphasize – crucial here not only from the purely symbolic or informational perspective. The preamble is a key premise that should guide participants in juvenile justice proceedings and according to which they should interpret the regulations of the Juvenile Justice Act. All these participants, especially the family and guardianship court, should therefore act so as to help the juvenile, not to punish them. This, in fact, follows clearly also from two main principles of juvenile justice, in particular from: (1) the principle of the best interest of the child, according to which:

> In a case of a juvenile, one needs to be guided mostly by his best interest, striving to achieve beneficial changes in his personality and behaviour and aiming, if necessary, for parents or a carer to fulfil their obligations towards the juvenile, taking into account the social interest at that (Article 3 § 1 JJA)

(2) the principle of personalisation of procedure, according to which:

> In juvenile justice, the following are taken into account: the juvenile's personality, and his age in particular, his health, degree of mental and physical development, character traits and also his behaviour, reasons for and degree of anti-social behaviour, the nature of the environment and conditions of the juvenile's upbringing (Article 3 § 2 JJA).

In the course of juvenile justice proceedings the family court[8] should, therefore, gather all possible information about the juvenile and their environment and on

---

8 A specialized body operating in the Polish legal system. It is worth noting that: "The specialization of jurisdictions for minors constitutes today a general principle the avoiding of which is extremely exceptional. All reports mention, from a historical point of view, the legislative evolution leading to the progressive specialization in the field of justice for minors. The rare exceptions address the less important offences (for example traffic offences) or some very special ones (such as military offences, terrorist offences, drug trafficking). However, each specialization varies a lot in terms of forms, relevance and importance' (R. Ottenhof, 'Criminal responsibility of minors in national and international legal order,' *Revue internationale de droit pénal*, 2004/1–2 (Vol. 75),

reasons for, and degree of, their antisocial behaviour so as to respond adequately to it in these proceedings, and most of all, to respond in such a way as to ensure the welfare of the juvenile. The welfare should be understood as: (1) achieving beneficial changes in the juvenile's personality and behaviour; (2) creating adequate conditions for the juvenile's appropriate development. The latter sense is the next goal of the Juvenile Justice Act that follows from the preamble.[9] It is formulated thus 'striving to reinforce the care and educational function of families and the sense of responsibility of families for raising juveniles to be aware of their duties as society members.'[10]

To conclude, all the above circumstances clearly show that in the course of juvenile justice, juveniles are treated fully as persons, not as objects. They are treated as an end in itself, not a means to an end, e.g. society's interest or interests essential to society. This is upheld by other provisions of the Act. For example, (1) in juvenile justice, juveniles are given the status of parties to the proceedings (see Article 30 § 1 JJA), (2) they are instructed about their rights and obligations (see Article 32a § 2 JJA), (3) they are often asked for their consent to particular activities (see e.g. Article 32j § 1 JJA). Furthermore, pursuant to Article 19 JJA:

> When interviewing a juvenile, effort must be made to ensure their full freedom of expression. Interviewing of a juvenile should take place in conditions that are similar to natural conditions, in his place of residence if necessary, and the juvenile should not be heard several times with regard to the same circumstances or circumstances already established by other evidence or by evidence that does not raise doubt.[11]

---

pp. 51–74. DOI: 10.3917/ridp.751.0051. Available at: URL: https://www.cairn.info/revue-internationale-de-droit-penal-2004-1-page-51.htm [access: Dec. 17 2020].

9 For more about the preamble to the Juvenile Justice Act, aims and principles of this Act, see V. Konarska-Wrzosek, 'Komentarz do preambuły' in: V. Konarska-Wrzosek, P. Górecki (eds.), *Postępowanie w sprawachnieletnich. Komentarz,* Warsaw 2015, pp. 23–28.

10 The above means that the legislator does not want to take children away from their families or to take over the family's responsibilities. The legislator wants to strengthen the family and make sure that the juvenile has the opportunity to grow up in a properly functioning family (see V. Konarska-Wrzosek, 'Komentarz…,' pp. 27–28).

11 For more, see M. Korcyl-Wolska, *Postępowanie w sprawach nieletnich ma tle standardów europejskich*, Warsaw 2015, pp. 210–211. See P. Banaszak, K. Burdziak, 'Standardy postępowania z nieletnimi – raport z badania' Available at: *Raport z badania 2019*, https://iws.gov.pl/wp-content/uploads/2019/10/IWS_Banaszak-P.-Burdziak-K._Standardy-postępowania-z-nieletnimi-raport-z-badania.pdf, pp. 29 ff. [access: Dec. 17 2020].

2. Definition of 'Juvenile'

As already mentioned in the previous section, pursuant to the Criminal Code a juvenile must be understood – simply – as an offender who at the time of committing the offence was not yet 17 years old.[12] Under the Juvenile Justice Act, the definition of the term 'juvenile' becomes far more complicated. The Act defines a juvenile in a manner from which it may be concluded that in the Polish legal system there are four different groups of individuals (apart from the group distinguished in the Criminal Code) who are considered juveniles. To specify, these are the following groups: (1) offenders who were under the age of 17 when they commit a criminal offence (see Article 10 CrC);[13] (2) persons who, before they attained 18 years of age, demonstrated types of behaviour that evidenced antisocial behaviour, until they reached the age of 18 (Article 1 § 1(1) JJA); (3) persons who committed a punishable act before they attained the age of 17 and after they attained the age of 13 (Article 1 § 1(2);[14] 4) persons under the age of 21 with regard to whom educational or correctional measures are being implemented (Article 1 § 1(3) JJA).

A number of doubts arise in the context of the groups of individuals considered juveniles, among which the following come to the fore: (1) doubts as to the legitimacy of setting age limits, determining whether a given person can be classified as a juvenile; (2) doubt as to how to establish whether the juvenile committed a prohibited act/punishable act before/after he attained a given age.

Note 1. The upper age limit, stipulated in Article 1 § 1(1) JJA, is perfectly reasonable. In Poland, it is the reaching of the age of 18 years that makes one an adult of legal age with full capacity for legal acts (cf. Article 10 and 11 CC[15]). It is at this moment that a person is capable – at least he/she is so assumed – of taking responsibility for himself and their actions. It is also an age limit consistent with the Convention on the Rights of the Child,[16] whose Article 1 says that: 'a *child* means every human being below the age of eighteen years unless under the law applicable to the child, majority is attained earlier.'

---

12 On the age of minors see e.g. McDiarmid C, An Age of Complexity, 'Children and Criminal Responsibility in Law,' *Youth Justice* 2013/2, pp. 145–60, Available at https://doi.org/10.1177/1473225413492056 [access: Dec. 17 2020]; G. Maher, 'Age and Criminal Responsibility,' *Ohio State Journal of Criminal Law* 2005/2, pp. 493–512.

13 Such persons retain their juvenile status also after attaining 17 years of age. Naturally, only in the context of criminal offences committed before reaching the age of 17.

14 Such persons retain their juvenile status also after attaining 17 years of age. Naturally, only in the context of criminal offences committed before reaching the age of 17.

15 Act of 23 April 1964 Civil Code (Dz. U. (Journal of Laws) of 2019 item 1145 as amended), hereinafter referred to as CC.

16 Dz. U. (Journal of Laws) of 1991 No. 120 item 526.

However, certain doubts arise due to the absence of the lower age limit below which it would not be allowed to initiate juvenile justice proceedings with regard to the juvenile's antisocial behaviour. A charge of inconsistency of the Juvenile Justice Act with the Convention on the Rights of the Child may be laid here due to the possibility of initiating juvenile justice proceedings in relation to, for instance, a prohibited act committed by a juvenile regardless of their age at the time of committing this act (this is because juvenile justice proceedings concerning their antisocial behaviour, including that connected to the prohibited act committed by them, may be initiated, at least theoretically, from the very first day he/she is born). Nonetheless, it needs to be highlighted that the Juvenile Justice Act serves to protect the juvenile, to look after him and to help him, and not to prosecute them. Therefore, it is difficult in such a case to preclude the possibility (possibility, not an obligation) of intervening in the life of the juvenile. Indeed, T. Bojarski is right to observe that:

> The act rightly does not specify the lower age limit qualifying for initiation of adequate juvenile justice proceedings due to antisocial behaviour (cf. V. Konarska-Wrzosek in: P. Górecki, V. Konarska-Wrzosek, *Postępowanie w sprawach nieletnich...*, p. 30). It may embrace juveniles under the age of 13. The Act cannot determine the lower age limit as it may be determined by the real needs of counteracting antisocial behaviour by the juvenile and these needs may even concern a child who is a few years old and who needs help.[17]

However, this is, naturally, an issue that is not uniformly assessed in the literature.[18]

Great and, let us add, legitimate doubts arise as to the age limits prescribed in Article 1 § 1(2) JJA. Let us remind that according to the said provision: 'The provisions of the act shall be applied to proceedings in the matter of punishable acts, involving persons who committed such acts after attaining 13 years but before attaining 17 years of age.' It is difficult to find any substantive arguments for placing the lower and upper age limits of the juvenile at 13 and 17 years, respectively. Most probably, these limits result jointly from historical reasons and, to be more specific, from their use in the 1932 Criminal Code.[19] This cannot be

17 T. Bojarski, 'Komentarz do art. 1 u.p.n.' in: T. Bojarski, E. Kruk, E. Skrętowicz (eds.), *Postępowanie w sprawach nieletnich. Komentarz*, Warsaw 2016, p. 49.

18 See in this respect e.g. H. Kołakowska-Przełomiec, D. Wójcik, 'Ustawa z dnia 26 października 1982 r. o postępowaniu w sprawach nieletnich a konwencja praw dziecka,' *Studia Prawnicze* 1992/3–4, pp. 26–27. See P. Banaszak, K. Burdziak, 'Standardy…,' p. 12.

19 Cf. V. Konarska-Wrzosek, 'Komentarz do art. 1 u.p.n. …,' p. 30.

regarded, naturally, as a sufficiently strong case for their use now. At the same time, in the context of the limits, some critical arguments may be raised. They are as follows: (1) the upper and lower age limits of a juvenile set in Article 1 § 1(2) JJA unfoundedly differentiate between the legal position of the juvenile, depending on their reaching a certain age at the time of committing a prohibited act; for example, if a juvenile commits a prohibited act after the age of 13, the proceedings will be carried out in connection to the prohibited act; if the act is committed before he/she attains 13 years of age, proceedings relating to antisocial behaviour will be carried out; (2) the upper and lower age limits stipulated in Article 1(1)(2) JJA may falsify the basis for initiating juvenile justice proceedings (only the prohibited act committed by the juvenile will be the reason for initiating proceedings, yet it is proceedings related to antisocial behaviour that will be carried out); (3) the upper age limit of the juvenile stipulated in Article 1(1)(2) JJA is not consistent with Article 1 of the Convention on the Rights of the Child.

Note 2. In the context of establishing whether the juvenile committed a prohibited act/a punishable act (and what prohibited act/punishable act it was) before or after he/she attained a certain age, a problem arises where the prohibited act committed by the offender lasts longer than one moment or where the offender commits – for example – a few criminal offences in short intervals as part of performing a premeditated act (see Article 12 CrC) and some of their behaviour occurs before/after he/she attains a certain age. It needs to be emphasized, firstly, that there are at least two conceptions in the literature and established line of judicial decisions as to the moment that must be taken in such a situation as the time of committing a criminal offence as defined in Article 6 § 1 CrC. The first conception holds that the entire time of performing an *actus reus* must be assumed as the time of committing an offence. In line with the second conception, only the last moment of performing an *actus reus* must be taken into account.[20] What is more, each of these conceptions is formally (it is one of the possible results of the application of linguistic directives of interpretation) as well as substantively justified (it may be defended on the grounds of functional directives of interpretation). Secondly, it is not clear how to understand expressions such as this in Article 1 § 1(2) JJA: 'with regard to persons who committed such acts after attaining 13 years of age but before attaining 17 years of age.' Doubts may arise as to whether it is a statutory requirement that the offender be of a certain age/not be of a certain age in the entire period considered (eventually) as the time of committing the criminal offence, or whether it is sufficient that he/she has attained a certain age/has not attained a certain age at any moment of performing the *actus reus*, which still falls, naturally, within the period (the time eventually considered as the time of committing the criminal offence).[21]

---

20 See M. Nawrocki, 'Glosa do wyroku Sądu Najwyższego z dnia 14 listopada 2016 r., sig. III KK 273/16,' *Prokuratura i Prawo* 2018/7–8, pp. 276 ff.

21 See P. Banaszak, K. Burdziak, 'Standardy…,' pp. 10–12.

Doubts presented above suggest a need to change the definition of a juvenile in respect of proceedings concerning a punishable act. Standardizing the upper age limit (at the time of committing a prohibited act) may be postulated, below which a given person, the perpetrator of a prohibited act/punishable act, would be treated as a juvenile, with the age limit stipulated in Article 1 § 1(1) JJA, and so may be the removal of the lower age limit stipulated in Article 1 § 1(2) JJA now. This would indeed lead to the adaptation of the Polish legal system to the Convention on the Rights of the Child, according to which: 'The *child* means every human being below the age of eighteen years unless under the law applicable to the child, majority is attained earlier' (Article 1 of the Convention) and at the same time this would remove, at least in part, the doubts that appear in the context of Article 1 § 1(2).

3. Definition of 'Antisocial behaviour'

Antisocial behaviour is one of the primary reasons for intervening in the life of a juvenile stipulated in the Juvenile Justice Act. According to the legislator's will expressed in the preamble to the Act, the object of the act is to counteract antisocial behaviour, that is to eliminate it (when it has already occurred) and prevent it (if it has not occurred yet, but may occur).[22]

The Act includes two different expressions relating to antisocial behaviour: (1) manifestations of antisocial behaviour (see Article 2 JJA) and (2) circumstances evidencing antisocial behaviour (see Article 4 JJA). The former are a basis for undertaking action provided for in the Act and initiating juvenile justice proceedings (see Article 21 § 1 JJA); the latter, in turn, must be established in the course of juvenile justice proceedings in order to apply an educational or correctional measure to the juvenile (see Article 21a JJA). The manifestations of antisocial behaviour must be, therefore, noticeable and must cause concern that something undesirable is happening in the life of the juvenile (this is consistent with its name as manifestation is an external expression of something[23]). The circumstances evidencing antisocial behaviour, as the name suggests, must prove that something undesirable is happening in the juvenile's life – that the juvenile is demoralized.

22 Therefore, the legislator expressly points out that it does not wish to condemn the juvenile, but to help him in a situation that causes concern about his future life.

23 https://sjp.pwn.pl/sjp/przejaw;2510256.html [access: Dec. 17 2020].

In the context of the above, doubts may occur as to the content of Article 4 § 1 JJA (of key significance, let us add, for formulating the definition of antisocial behaviour). It turns out that only the ascertaining of circumstances that evidence antisocial behaviour constitutes a social obligation to counteract the juvenile's improper behaviour appropriately and above all to notify his parents or guardian, school, family court, the police, or another competent organ about it. Therefore, it appears that circumstances evidencing antisocial behaviour must be ascertained practically by any entity before the proceedings concerning the juvenile are instituted. Furthermore, the mere ascertainment of manifestations of antisocial behaviour does not impose any obligations (especially those enumerated above) on the observer. This situation cannot be considered – for obvious reasons – rational. Therefore, it is suggested that Article 4 JJA be amended by giving it the following wording:

> Any person who ascertains manifestations of antisocial behaviour by a juvenile has a social obligation to counteract it in a relevant manner, in particular, to notify the juvenile's parents or guardian, school, the family court, the Police or another competent body about it.

As already suggested, the provision of Article 4 § 1 is key to formulating a new definition of antisocial behaviour. Let us point out that according to the discussed regulation:

> Any person who ascertains circumstances evidencing a juvenile's antisocial behaviour, in particular violation of public policy, commission of a prohibited act, systematic evasion of compulsory education or vocational training, use of alcohol or other intoxicating substances, engaging in prostitution, vagrancy or membership in criminal gangs, has a social obligation to prevent it in a relevant manner, in particular to notify the juvenile's parents or guardian, school, the family court, the Police or another competent body about it.[24]

Article 4 § 1 lists the following circumstances evidencing antisocial behaviour include: (1) violation of public policy; (2) committing a prohibited act; (3) systematic evasion of compulsory education; (4) systematic evasion of vocational education; (5) use of alcohol in order to become intoxicated; (6) use of other intoxicating substances; (7) engaging in prostitution; (8) vagrancy; (9) membership in criminal gangs. The legislator makes it clear that this is a catalogue of

---

24 It is worth pointing out that this order of enumerating the entities that need to be notified clearly shows that the legislator does not wish to punish the juvenile, but provide them with support (see V. Konarska-Wrzosek, 'Komentarz do art. 4 u.p.n. …,' p. 57).

only example circumstances evidencing antisocial behaviour (presumably the most serious ones) by preceding the enumeration with the phrase 'in particular.'

When analysing the above-mentioned circumstances jointly, one may conclude that in order to consider a given behaviour of a juvenile (because it always needs to be a certain specific, observable type of behaviour) as a circumstance evidencing antisocial behaviour, it is necessary that it should be (1) behaviour considered undesirable in the context of juveniles (and thus socially unacceptable); (2) recurring behaviour which extends over a period of time (committing a prohibited act is an exception here, despite the fact that committing a prohibited act does not necessarily mean that a juvenile's behaviour is antisocial); (3) behaviour suggesting the occurrence of undesirable changes in a juvenile's personality. For certain behaviour types the need to identify a certain negative (from the social perspective) mental attitude was indicated *expressis verbis*. For example, (1) a juvenile's alcohol consumption is not enough to ascertain without doubt that we are dealing with a circumstance that proofs antisocial behaviour; it will be necessary to ascertain that a juvenile 'consumes' alcohol regularly (not just once) in order to get intoxicated; (2) it is not enough that the juvenile fails to fulfil the compulsory education obligation; it needs to be ascertained that he/she evades compulsory education and does so systematically.

Therefore, within the meaning of the Juvenile Justice Act, antisocial behaviour may be considered as:

> a psychological and social process which features unfavourable changes in a juvenile's personality and behaviour of an intensive and relatively permanent nature, which is demonstrated in the non-observance of norms and procedures of conduct universally biding on children and young people.[25]

As V. Konarska-Wrzosek and P. Górecki observe:

> This definition captures succinctly the characteristics of antisocial behaviour, saying that it is: (1) a certain process, not a state appearing right away, (2) a process which occurs in a person's head, (3) a process of social significance and associated with the individual's functioning in society, (4) a process entailing unfavourable personality changes, (5) a process manifested on the outside by behaviour flouting norms and rules of procedure adopted in a given society as appropriate and obligatory for minors, (6) an intensive process, not just an incipient one, (7) a fairly persistent process and not one surfacing only for a short while nor manifested in a single reprehensible instance of behaviour.[26]

25 V. Konarska-Wrzosek, 'Komentarz do preambuły…,' p. 26.
26 V. Konarska-Wrzosek, 'Komentarz do preambuły…,' p. 26.

Naturally, in the context of the proposed undeniably ambiguous definition, doubts may arise as to its consistency with the *nullum crimen sine lege* principle (no crime without law).[27] It needs to be emphasized that proceedings provided for in the Juvenile Justice Act do not intend to hold the juvenile criminally responsible, but to provide him with assistance. Therefore, in the context of juvenile justice, maintaining the rules typical of criminal proceedings should not be absolutely required. This issue (including the issue of legitimacy of the legislator's use of the term 'antisocial behaviour' in the Juvenile Justice Act and also its specification by enumerating examples of circumstances evidencing antisocial behaviour[28]) is, however, complex and disputable. In the author's opinion, B. Czarnecka-Dzialuk and D. Wójcik reasonably note that: 'Specification of the definition of antisocial behaviour would strengthen the guarantee functions of the provisions of the Act, but would it not hamper the judge excessively and in consequence, would it not bring more damage than good?'[29]

4. Definition of 'Punishable act'

The Juvenile Justice Act lists a juvenile's committing a punishable act as the second reason for intervening in their life. The legislator does not use the expression prohibited act or offence here, but a completely different term characteristic solely of the Juvenile Justice Act. Let us point out straight away that this term must be deemed inadequate in the situation of the juvenile in the course of

---

27 After all, doubts may be raised by the legislator's mere use of the term 'antisocial behaviour,' which has clearly negative connotations, in the context of the juvenile's behaviour.

28 See for example B. Czarnecka-Dzialuk, K. Drapała, 'Przejawy demoralizacji jako podstawa działań podejmowanych wobec nieletnich przez sądy rodzinne,' *Prawo w Działaniu* 2015/22, pp. 238–275; G. Harasimiak, *Demoralizacja jako podstawowe pojęcie postępowania z nieletnimi. Analiza i wnioski,* Szczecin 2001, pp. 113–234; A. Kania, 'Demoralizacja jako pojęcie kontrowersyjne. Uwagi na tle ustawy o postępowaniu w sprawach nieletnich,' *Studia Prawnicze Katolickiego Uniwersytetu Lubelskiego* 2016/3, pp. 71–91; B. Kowalska-Ehrlich, *Młodzież nieprzystosowana społecznie a prawo*, Warsaw 1988, pp. 17–22; Z. Sienkiewicz, *System sądowych środków wobec nieletnich w prawie polskim,* Wrocław 1989, pp. 84–97; M. Stanowska, A. Walczak-Żochowska, K. Wierzbowski, 'Uwagi o profilu ustawy o postępowaniu z nieletnimi (Zagadnienia materialnoprawne i procesowe),' *Państwo i Prawo* 1983/6, pp. 53–54.

29 B. Czarnecka-Dzialuk, D. Wójcik, 'Dziecko przed organami wymiaru sprawiedliwości' in: *Wokół Praw Dziecka, Part I,* Warsaw 1993; Available at: http://beta.hfhr.pl/wp-content/uploads/2015/10/HFPC_wokol_praw_dziecka.pdf [access: 10.07.19], no page number given. [access: Dec. 17 2020]. See P. Banaszak, K. Burdziak, 'Standardy…,' p. 31.

proceedings conducted pursuant to the JJA. In these proceedings, the juvenile is treated as a person who cannot be held criminally responsible and, what follows, as a person who cannot be prosecuted and sentenced to punishment. The expression 'punishable act' seems to refer to the criminal law past of juvenile justice, thereby contravening the Act's principles laid down in its preamble. Hence, it would be worth considering replacing this expression with a more neutral one, e.g. socially unacceptable act, or refraining altogether from grouping behaviour types such as punishable acts into a separate, independent class, and instead including them simply among circumstances evidencing antisocial behaviour.

A punishable act is defined by the legislator as follows:

> Wherever the Act mentions a *punishable act*, it shall be understood as an act prohibited by statute[30] such as: (a) a crime or tax offence or (b) a misdemeanour specified in Article 50a, Article 51, Article 69, Article 74, Article 76, Article 85, Article 87, Article 119, Article 122, Article 124, Article 133 or Article 143 of the Misdemeanours Code (Article 1 § 2(2) JJA).

Bearing the said definition in mind, it needs to be assumed, that each punishable act is a prohibited act, but not all prohibited acts are punishable acts. It is an obvious conclusion given that according to the will of the legislator itself, a punishable act must be a prohibited act, but at the same time it cannot be any prohibited act; it must be one of the prohibited acts enumerated in a closed catalogue specified in Article 1 § 2(2) JJA. Therefore, a punishable act must be: (1) a criminal offence which may be an element of the structure of a crime; or (2) a criminal offence which may be an element of the structure of a tax offence; or (3) a criminal offence which may be an element of the structure of a misdemeanour, and it must be identified in one of the provisions of the Misdemeanours Code expressly indicated in Article 1 § 2(2)(b) JJA. To be more precise, for an act to be considered a punishable act, it must be a criminal offence specified in a given criminal law provision (*sensu largo*), implementation of which, along with meeting other,

30 It is worth noting that the legislator indicates that it involves an act prohibited by statute, not an act prohibited by a statute in force at the time the act was committed. However, it must emphasized that due to constitutional requirements, including the principle of the democratic state ruled by law (Article 2 of the Constitution of the Republic of Poland of 2 April 1997, Dz. U. (Journal of Laws) No. 78 item 483, hereinafter 'Constitution'), the principle of inherent dignity of the person (Article 30 of the Constitution) or the principle following from Article 42(1) of the Constitution, the above-mentioned expressions must be deemed equivalent as regards the Juvenile Justice Act.

additional requirements, would typically provide a basis for responsibility for a crime, a tax offence or a misdemeanour. Whereas *in concreto*, a punishable act involves such behaviour by a juvenile which constitutes the elements of a given type of a criminal offence and which, typically, meeting additional requirements, would be deemed a crime, tax offence or a misdemeanour.

However, let us add straight away that a punishable act committed by a juvenile before attaining the age of 13 or after attaining the age of 17 will be treated pursuant to the Juvenile Justice Act – simply – as a circumstance evidencing antisocial behaviour of the juvenile demonstrated by the commission of a prohibited act (see Article 4 JJA), thus identically as the commission of prohibited acts by juveniles that do not fall within the definition of a punishable act (this involves other misdemeanours and tax misdemeanours), which may cause certain terminological and factual confusion. However, let us specify that not always when it is impossible to initiate proceedings in a case for a punishable act (also where the act is prosecuted on complaint and the complaint is filed or where the act is prosecuted upon a private accusation, and the initiation of the proceedings is not motivated by public interest or by concern for the education of the juvenile or by protection of the aggrieved party; see Article 22 JJA[31]) will it be possible to

31 The very regulation of Article 22 JJA triggers extreme emotions in the author. Let us point out that according to the discussed regulation: '§ 1. In a case prosecuted on complaint, the family court initiates proceedings in the event of filing the complaint; the proceedings are then conducted ex officio. § 2. In a case for an act prosecuted upon a private accusation, proceedings are initiated if required by public interest or by concern for the juvenile's education or by protection of the aggrieved party; the proceedings are then conducted ex officio.' In the context of Article 22 JJA, the following questions may be asked for which it is difficult, let us add, to give a rational answer: (1) why in a situation where the goal of juvenile justice is education and improvement of the juvenile the filing of a complaint determines initiation of proceedings in the event of the juvenile's committing a prohibited act prosecuted on complaint? (2) why for prohibited acts prosecuted on complaint, which *in abstracto* involve higher social harmfulness than acts prosecuted upon private accusation, is it not possible even as an exception to initiate juvenile justice proceedings when a complaint is not filed (such an exceptional initiation of proceedings is possible for prohibited acts prosecuted upon private accusation)? (3) why for prohibited acts prosecuted upon private accusation initiation of juvenile justice proceedings is possible only in exceptional cases if also in such cases we should care about the juvenile's education and improvement? (4) why for prohibited acts prosecuted upon private accusation initiation of proceedings is determined by public interest, since the dominant aim of juvenile justice is the education and improvement of the juvenile? Due to the aforementioned lack of possibility to give

adjudicate an adequate measure for the juvenile in antisocial behaviour proceedings. Let us remember that the fact of committing a prohibited act or a punishable act will not always evidence a juvenile's antisocial behaviour.

Let us emphasize at the same time, though it should be obvious, that in a situation where a juvenile commits a punishable act after attaining 13 years of age and before attaining 17 years of age, the commission of the act will not be considered at the same time, at least as a rule, a circumstance evidencing antisocial behaviour. This is because if we took a different stand, we would not be able to satisfy the postulate of treating the legislator as a rational legislator. The legislator's irrationality, if a different stand is adopted. Would be seen in 'redundancy of normative information,' involving the legislator's coding identically worded norms in different laws (excessive number of norms is, as we know, an evident praxeological flaw of the legal system which should be avoided each time by a skilful interpretation of the legal text).[32] This would mean that the Juvenile Justice Act would have two norms authorising the family court to initiate juvenile justice proceedings in the event of the juvenile's committing a punishable act when aged between 13 and 17: (1) a norm ordering the family court to initiate juvenile justice proceedings if there is a justifiable suspicion of the existence of circumstances in which the juvenile shows signs of antisocial behaviour; (2) a norm ordering the family court to initiate juvenile justice proceedings if there is a reasonable suspicion of the existence of circumstances in which the juvenile commits a punishable act (see Article 21 § 1 JJA), and at the same time such a solution would entail a deeper substantive justification.

The issue of the relationship between a punishable act and a crime (as well as a tax offence and a misdemeanour) still needs to be considered. Of course, as mentioned above, pursuant to Article 1 § 2(2) JJA a punishable act is such a type of a criminal offence specified in a given criminal law provision (*sensu largo*), implementation of which, while meeting other, additional requirements, would typically provide a basis of responsibility for a crime, a tax offence or a misdemeanour, and *in concreto* – such behaviour of a juvenile which would meet the requirements of a given type of a criminal offence and which typically, while meeting additional requirements, would be considered a crime, a tax offence or a misdemeanour. However, one needs to ponder whether contrary to

---

rational answers to these questions, amending Article 22 JJA or removing it should be considered.

32 See Ł. Pohl, *Prawo karne. Wykład części ogólnej*, Warsaw, Wolters Kluwer 2015, pp. 206–207.

interpretation of 1 § 2(2) JJA, we should not conclude that in order for a punishable act to exist other conditions need to be met, to be more specific – conditions parallel to those necessary for the existence of a crime.

Let us point out that pursuant to Article 1 of the Criminal Code, for a crime to be realized, it is necessary to: (1) recognize a given type of behaviour of a person as an act (see Article 1 § 2 CrC); (2) recognize a given type of behaviour of a person as a criminal offence (see Article 1 § 1 CrC); (3) recognize a given type of behaviour of a person as a non-negligible act of social harmfulness (see Article 1 § 2 CrC); and (4) recognize a given type of behaviour of a person as a culpable act (see Article 1 § 3 CrC). A crime within the meaning of the Polish Criminal Code is, therefore, a person's behaviour which is an act and a criminal offence and a non-negligible socially harmful act and a culpable act. Additionally, as many authors believe, for a crime to exist it is also necessary to deem a given type of behaviour of a person unlawful (which is equivalent to the prohibition under a penalty; see Article 29 CrC).

As mentioned above, it is worth pondering whether for a given type of behaviour of a juvenile to be deemed a punishable act it should meet parallel conditions, that is whether it should be unlawful, reprehensible (non-negligible socially harmful) and culpable or not. Therefore, without a risk of making a major mistake, it may be concluded that it would not be reasonable to initiate proceedings (and to discontinue proceedings already initiated) in a case for a punishable act where: (1) the juvenile meets the requirements of a given type of a criminal offence, acting under justification (a circumstance allowing exception to the prohibition of committing an offence), for example defending one's own life and health, if it causes minor injury to the attacker (the so-called self-defence, see Article 25 CrC); (2) the juvenile meets the requirements of a given criminal offence by displaying a type of behaviour of negligible social harmfulness (for circumstances that need to be taken into account see Article 115 § 1 CrC); (3) the juvenile meets the requirements of a given criminal offence acting in an excusable erroneous belief, for instance, being justifiably convinced that he/she is committing a prohibited act, but acting within the limits of necessity that excludes guilt (see Article 29 CrC). In the above situations one cannot see the need to apply any educational or correctional measures to the juvenile. However, one must ask whether the absence of unlawfulness, reprehensibility or guilt from the behaviour of the juvenile affects the impossibility of concluding that we are dealing with a punishable act or whether it only affects the impossibility of conducting juvenile justice proceedings.

In answer to the above question, it needs to be concluded that the second of the presented alternatives is correct, that is the conclusion that absence of unlawfulness, reprehensibility and fault from the behaviour of the juvenile affects only the impossibility of conducting juvenile justice proceedings. It needs to be emphasized that the issue of meeting the requirement of the juvenile's committing a punishable act is analysed differently from the issue of legitimacy or absence of legitimacy of adjudicating educational or correctional measures for the juvenile. In consequence, it cannot be concluded that the absence of legitimacy to adjudicate a given measure may affect *in concerto* the conclusion that the juvenile did not commit a punishable act (it is necessary to exclude abstract types of behaviour, for which it would not be reasonable to adjudicate any measure, from the concept of a punishable act that does not have any justification either, or at least it does not derive from any provisions of the Act). The following provisions of the Juvenile Justice Act show this: (1) Article 21 § 2 JJA, according to which:

> The family court shall not initiate proceedings or discontinue in whole or in part already initiated proceedings where there is no basis for initiating and conducting them in a specified scope or where the adjudication of educational and correctional measures does not serve any purpose; (2) Article 21a JJA, pursuant to which: Proceedings in the matter of a juvenile aim to establish whether there are circumstances evidencing the juvenile's antisocial behaviour or whether the juvenile has committed a punishable act and also to establish whether it is necessary to apply measures to the juvenile provided for in the Act.

It follows that a punishable act (*in concreto*) must be understood in the end as a type of behaviour by the juvenile which constitutes the *actus reus* of a criminal offence and which, typically, meeting additional requirements, would be deemed a crime, a tax offence or a misdemeanour.

Closing this part of the study, it must be observed that according to the legislator's will the purpose of the Juvenile Justice Act is to counteract criminal activity: to fight crime that has already been perpetrated and to prevent it. Criminal activity is prevented by both responding to an already committed prohibited act, by which the commission of another criminal offence is prevented, and fighting and preventing antisocial behaviour by which the commission of the 'first' criminal offence is prevented. It is not without reason that antisocial behaviour and its prevention are named next to crime prevention; undeniably, antisocial behaviour may be and often is the reason for criminal activity (criminal activity itself may lead to antisocial behaviour or may be associated with antisocial behaviour).[33]

---

33 See V. Konarska-Wrzosek, 'Komentarz do preambuły…,' pp. 24–25.

5. Educational and correctional measures

In principle, two types of measures may be adjudicated with respect to a juvenile: (1) educational measures; (2) correctional measures (actually, a correctional measure as there is only one such measure). The very names of the enumerated measures unambiguously confirm that the legislator decided to reject the criminal law character of proceedings in matters involving a juvenile. Instead, punishments or criminal law measures are replaced in the Act by measures whose names carry connotations of the need to have an impact on the juvenile to the benefit of their behaviour. They are meant as means of their improvement and are not directed against the juvenile. In no case under the Act, therefore, is it about payback for what the juvenile has done or for how he has behaved, nor about general prevention (encouraging other juveniles to act in a socially acceptable way). It is solely about individual prevention when it comes to influencing an individual (in this case a juvenile) so as to convince them to behave in a socially acceptable manner. This is also evidenced by the goals presented by the legislator directly in the Act, i.e. goals of applying individual measures and goals of the manner of their implementation. Therefore, the purpose of applying educational and correctional measures is to educate the juvenile to be an informed and honest citizen, where recommendations of science and pedagogical experience are taken into account (Article 65 § 1 JJA). The way to achieve this goal involves an intention to develop the personality and skills of the juvenile comprehensively and to shape and reinforce in them a socially desirable attitude and the sense of responsibility so that he/she is adequately prepared to perform socially useful work (Article 5 § 2 JJA).

Another matter is that some of the measures provided for in the Juvenile Justice Act are closely related to existing/past criminal law measures provided for in the Criminal Code. An educational measure in the form of a driving ban is a case in point. It seems to be only an inconvenience that the juvenile may experience due to certain previous behaviour. The same can be said of an educational measure in the form of forfeiture of things obtained in connection with the commission of a punishable act. These measures certainly cannot affect the juvenile in an educational/correctional manner, and so they should be given a completely different character in the future (*de lege ferenda* postulate).

The catalogue of educational/correctional measures that can be applied to the juvenile is set out in Article 5 JJA. Pursuant to this provision, the family court may: (1) issue a reprimand; (2) order a specific action to be taken, especially to repair a previously caused damage, to carry out certain works or performances for the benefit of the aggrieved party or local community, to apologise to the aggrieved party, to start education or work, to participate in adequate activities of an educational, therapeutic or training character, to refrain from attending certain circles or places or to refrain from drinking alcohol or other intoxicating substances; (3) establish responsibility-bearing supervision for parents or guardian; (4) establish supervision of a youth organization or another social organization, employer or a trustworthy person who guarantee for the juvenile; (5) establish supervision by a guardian; (6) refer the juvenile to an attendance centre, and also to a community organization or institution working with young people in an educational, therapeutic or training capacity after agreeing the matter with this organization or institution; (7) ban the juvenile from driving a vehicle; (8) order the forfeiture of things obtained in connection with the commission of a punishable act; (9) order that the juvenile be placed in a young people's educational centre or a professional foster family who have been trained in taking care of a minor; (10) order that the juvenile be placed in a young offenders' institution; (11) apply other measures reserved in this act to the jurisdiction of a family court, or apply measures provided for in the Family and Guardianship Code, save for placement in a related foster family, non-professional foster family, family-run foster care, day care facility, care and education facility or regional care and therapy facility.

It needs to be emphasized here that the legislator did not lay down any specific rules for the application of the said measures to the juvenile. Therefore, the family court is given full discretion in this regard, which is naturally entirely reasonable. It must be remembered that according to prime rules of juvenile justice one needs to be guided mostly by the juvenile's welfare by striving to achieve beneficial changes in the juvenile's personality and behaviour. It would be difficult to achieve this goal if decisions were made in an abstract way as to what the court should do in a given case: what measure and for what period should be applied. This would make it impossible to adapt the measure to a specific juvenile and a specific problem he/she is facing, and in consequence, it would also be impossible to ensure in such a case the real welfare of this particular juvenile and to truly achieve beneficial changes in their personality and behaviour. The implementation of another prime rule of procedure would also be prevented in this way, that is the rule of personalisation, according to which, let us restate, in juvenile justice and in terms of application of educational and correctional measures, the juvenile's personality is to be taken into account, in particular their age, health, mental and physical development, character traits, behaviour, and also reasons for and degree of antisocial behaviour, the nature of the environment and conditions of the juvenile's upbringing. After all, the chosen measure should, pursuant to this rule, be adapted to the individual traits and personal circumstances of a specific juvenile, which is impossible, naturally, to achieve by applying an abstractly designed measure.

Therefore, since there are no precise regulations in this regard, the court can: (1) apply any given measure to the juvenile; (2) apply one measure or more than one; (3) apply a given measure for a necessary period of time (it may at the same time change/revoke educational measures if there are educational reasons for it; see Article 79 § 1 JJA).[34] The legislator only stipulates that 'a punishment may only be imposed in cases provided for in the law if other measures cannot ensure the juvenile's rehabilitation' (Article 5 JJA). It is the legislator's clear suggestion that individual measures must be applied proportionally to the situation, i.e. measures which more severely limit the freedoms and rights of a juvenile should not be employed in a situation where the application of less intrusive measures will be sufficient. Of course, the legislator refers in Article 5 JJA only to a punishment which should be applied as a last resort. However, it seems that this postulate must also be directed at all other measures listed in Article 6 JJA. First of all, these measures were set out by the legislator (as it may seem – intentionally) in such an order that measures *in abstracto* more lenient were placed at the beginning, while measures *in abstracto* more serious – towards the end, which may suggest that more lenient measures must be applied first and the more serious ones – as a last resort. Secondly, the legislator said clearly that the family court may order placement of a juvenile in a young offenders' institution (the most severe measure provided for in the Act) when he/she has committed a punishable act referred to in Article 1 § 2(2)(a) JJA. The order must be motivated by the juvenile's high degree of antisocial behaviour and the circumstances and nature of the act, especially where – which is most interesting – other educational measures proved inefficient or are unlikely to bring about the juvenile's rehabilitation (see Article 10 JJA).

At the same time, the law says that the punishment may be imposed only in cases provided for therein. One must note in this context that the legislator

34 However, it needs to be stressed that pursuant to Article 73 § 1 JJA: implementation of measures referred to in Article 6 points 2, 3 and 6 and Articles 7 and 8, and also placement in a juvenile education facility, a professional foster family trained to care for a juvenile, a therapeutic institution which is not a business enterprise or a social welfare home is terminated by law when the juvenile attains the age of 18, and implementation of other measures is terminated when the juvenile reaches the age of 21; if educational measures are applied pursuant to Article 10 § 4 of the Criminal Code or Article 5 § 2 of the Penal-Fiscal Code – implementation is terminated by law when the offender reaches the age of 21.'

decided to introduce Article 94 to the Juvenile Justice Act, questionable from the perspective of the Convention on the Rights of the Child, according to which:

> If the juvenile with respect to whom placement in a young offenders' institution was decreed reaches the age of 18 before the enforcement of the decree starts, the family court shall decide whether to enforce the ordered measure or to refrain from enforcing it and to impose a punishment on the offender.

It is a completely irrational regulation that allows a juvenile to be held criminally responsible (1) by the family court, not the criminal court; (2) without typical criminal proceedings; (3) without having to satisfy specific conditions which should convince the court about the need to impose a punishment (the mere fact of reaching the age of 18 before the enforcement of the ruling starts may turn out sufficient); (4) even if the juvenile is under 13 years of age (sic!). Therefore, this regulation must be urgently removed from the Polish legal system.[35]

However, it must be made clear that the legislator has also enacted many other rational solutions in the Juvenile Justice Act which allow to close proceedings concerning the juvenile in a way that is minimally severe for the juvenile (e.g. by not applying any measures to them or not conducting proceedings according to a 'typical' procedure). These include: (1) an option to refer the case for mediation (see Article 3a JJA) and to discontinue proceedings concerning a juvenile if mediation is successful (the conflict between the juvenile and the aggrieved party is resolved and educational goals for the juvenile have been met); (2) an option to discontinue proceedings in a situation where adjudicating educational or correctional measures does not serve a purpose (see Article 21 JJA); (3) an option to refer the juvenile's case, upon their consent, to the school or a youth, sporting, cultural and educational or other social organization the juvenile belongs to, if the educational measures that a given school or organization has at their disposal are sufficient (see Article 32j JJA); (4) an option not to hold a trial and to make a ruling at a closed hearing if the circumstances and nature of the case, as well as the purpose and selection of educational measures, do not raise doubts (see Article 32l JJA).

Next to the application of educational and correctional measures, the court may also apply the so-called therapeutic measures. Pursuant to Article 12 JJA, there are the following options: (1) to rule that the juvenile be placed in a mental

35 For more, see K. Burdziak, 'Art. 10 § 2 k.k. i art. 94 u.p.n. z perspektywy art. 40 ust. 3 Konwencji o prawach dziecka, czyli kilka słów na temat odpowiedzialności karnej nieletnich,' *Probacja* 2019/2, pp. 37–49.

hospital (or other relevant therapeutic institution) when the juvenile is diagnosed with mental retardation, mental disease or other disturbance of mental activities or with addiction to alcohol or other intoxicating substances; (2) to rule that the juvenile be placed in a youth education facility – if only educational care for the juvenile needs to be ensured; (3) to rule that the juvenile be placed in a social welfare home – if the juvenile is severely mentally retarded and only requires care.

An interesting solution, consistent with the purpose of the Act, striving to strengthen the families' care and educational function and sense of responsibility for raising juveniles to be community members who are aware of their obligations, involves imposing certain obligations on the juvenile's parents. It is entirely justified especially where antisocial behaviour of the juvenile or a prohibited act committed by them have their source in the parents' fulfilling their obligations inappropriately. In such a case the family court may *inter alia* oblige the parents or guardian to improve educational, living or health conditions of the juvenile and to cooperate closely with the school the juvenile attends, a psychological and pedagogical centre or other specialist centres, an employer, a doctor and a therapeutic entity (see Article 7 JJA). Unfortunately, there is no option in the juvenile justice system to impose obligations solely on the juvenile's parents without imposing any obligations on the juvenile him-/herself, even where it would be perfectly sufficient to achieve the goals of these proceedings. In such a case the family court will be obliged to discontinue the proceedings (see Article 21 § 2 JJA).

6. Conclusion

Summing up briefly the above findings, one may contend that:

(1) Juvenile justice is regulated in Poland by a statute completely separate from other statutes (in particular, completely separate from criminal law statutes): the Juvenile Justice Act. Importantly, this Act has cut ties with the criminal law past of juvenile justice and its purpose is primarily (if not solely) to assist the juvenile in their return to a normal life.

(2) The reasons for intervention in the life of a juvenile under the Act include:

  (a) antisocial behaviour understood as a psychological and social process which features unfavourable changes in the juvenile's personality and behaviour of an intensive and relatively lasting nature, which is manifested in the non-observance of norms and rules of conduct universally applicable to children and young people;[36]

(b) a punishable act that must be understood as a type of behaviour by the juvenile constitutes the *actus reus* of a given criminal offence and which typically, when additional conditions are satisfied, would be deemed a crime, a tax offence or a misdemeanour.

(3) The Juvenile Justice Act furnishes the family court with a wide array of measures applicable to a juvenile (not against him!); measures – let us add – that are suitable for achieving the goal of the child's (juvenile's) welfare.

References

Banaszak P., Burdziak K., 'Standardy postępowania z nieletnimi – raport z badania' in: *Raport z badania 2019*, https://iws.gov.pl/wp-content/uploads/2019/10/IWS_Banaszak-P.-Burdziak-K._Standardy-postępowania-z-nieletnimi-raport-z-badania.pdf [access: Dec. 17 2020];

Basto Pereira M., da Costa Maia A., *Juvenile Delinquency, Crime and Social Marginalization: Social and Political Implications*, Bingley, UK, Emerald Publishing Limited; 2017(Emerald Points; 1st edn.). Available at: http://search-1ebscohost-1com-10hkp9id4041b.waw-proxlib.swps.edu.pl/login.aspx?direct=true&db=nlebk&AN=1549783&lang=pl&site=eds-live [access: Dec. 17 2020].

Bembas I., 'Forensic Aspects of Juvenile Crime in Poland. From a Juvenile to a Criminal – The Road to Demoralisation,' *Internal Security* 2020/12(1); Available at: http://search-1ebscohost-1com-10hkp9id4042a.waw-proxlib.swps.edu.pl/login.aspx?direct=true&db=obo&AN=146063036&lang=pl&site=eds-live. [access: Dec. 17 2020].

Bojarski T., 'Komentarz do art. 1 u.p.n.' in: T. Bojarski, E. Kruk, E. Skrętowicz (eds.), *Postępowanie w sprawach nieletnich. Komentarz*, Warsaw 2016;

Boxer P., Goldstein S.E., 'Treating juvenile offenders: Best practices and emerging critical issues' in: Grigorenko E.L.(ed.), *Handbook of juvenile forensic psychology and psychiatry*, New York, NY, US, Springer Science + Business Media; 2012, Available at: http://search-1ebscohost-1com-10hkp9id4041b.waw-proxlib.swps.edu.pl/login.aspx?direct=true&db=psyh&AN=2012-11873-021&lang=pl&site=eds-live [access: Dec. 17 2020];

36 V. Konarska-Wrzosek, 'Komentarz do preambuły…,' p. 26.

Burdziak K., 'Art. 10 § 2 k.k. i art. 94 u.p.n. z perspektywy art. 40 ust. 3 Konwencji o prawach dziecka, czyli kilka słów na temat odpowiedzialności karnej nieletnich,' *Probacja* 2019/2;

Czarnecka-Dzialuk B., Drapała K., 'Przejawy demoralizacji jako podstawa działań podejmowanych wobec nieletnich przez sądy rodzinne,' *Prawo w Działaniu* 2015/22;

Czarnecka-Dzialuk B., Wójcik D., 'Dziecko przed organami wymiaru sprawiedliwości' in: *Wokół Praw Dziecka. Part I,* Warsaw 1993, http://beta. hfhr.pl/wp-content/uploads/2015/10/HFPC_wokol_praw_dziecka.pdf [access: Dec. 17 2020].

Daniluk P., Mieraelńska-Lorencka J., 'Responsibility of a Juvenile for a Prohibited Act under Polish Law,' *International & Comparative Law Review / Mezinárodní a Srovnávací Právní Revue,* 2016/2, Available at: http://search-1ebscohost-1com-10hkp9id4042a.waw-proxlib.swps.edu.pl/login.aspx?direct=true&db=obo&AN=131170747&lang=pl&site=eds-live [access: Dec. 17 2020];

Goldson B., *Juvenile Justice in Europe: Past, Present and Future*, Abingdon, Oxon, Routledge, 2019, Available at: http://search-1ebscohost-1com-10hkp9id4042a.waw-proxlib.swps.edu.pl/login.aspx?direct=true&db=edsebk&AN=1769982&lang=pl&site=eds-live. [access: Dec. 17 2020];

Harasimiak G., *Demoralizacja jako podstawowe pojęcie postępowania z nieletnimi. Analiza i wnioski*, Szczecin 2001;

Kania A., 'Demoralizacja jako pojęcie kontrowersyjne. Uwagi na tle ustawy o postępowaniu w sprawach nieletnich,' *Studia Prawnicze Katolickiego Uniwersytetu Lubelskiego* 2016/3.

Kołakowska-Przełomiec H., Wójcik D., 'Ustawa z dnia 26 października 1982 r. o postępowaniu w sprawach nieletnich a konwencja praw dziecka,' *Studia Prawnicze* 1992/3–4;

Konarska-Wrzosek V., Górecki P., *Postępowanie w sprawach nieletnich. Komentarz*, Warsaw 2015;

Korcyl-Wolska M., *Postępowanie w sprawach nieletnich ma tle standardów europejskich,* Warsaw 2015;

Kowalska-Ehrlich B., *Młodzież nieprzystosowana społecznie a prawo*, Warsaw 1988;

Loeber R., Farrington D.P., 'Serious and Violent Juvenile Offenders' in: *Risk Factors and Successful Interventions*, Vol. 1st paper ed. Thousand Oaks, Calif, SAGE Publications, Inc, 1999, Available at: http://search-1ebscohost-1com-10hkp9id4041b.waw-proxlib.swps.edu.pl/login.aspx?direct=true&db=nlebk&AN=467088&lang=pl&site=eds-live. [access: Dec. 17 2020].

Maher G., 'Age and Criminal Responsibility,' *Ohio State Journal of Criminal Law* 2005/2;

McDiarmid C., 'An Age of Complexity: Children and Criminal Responsibility in Law,' *Youth Justice* 2013/2, https://doi.org/10.1177/1473225413492056 [access: Dec. 17 2020];

Nawrocki M., 'Glosa do wyroku Sądu Najwyższego z dnia 14 listopada 2016 r., sig. III KK 273/16,' *Prokuratura i Prawo* 2018/7–8;

Ottenhof R., 'Criminal responsibility of minors in national and international legal order,' *Revue Internationale de Droit Pénal*, 2004/1–2 (Vol. 75), DOI: 10.3917/ridp.751.0051. URL: https://www.cairn.info/revue-internationale-de-droit-penal-2004-1-page-51.htm [access: Dec. 17 2020];

Pohl Ł., *Prawo karne. Wykład części ogólnej*, Warsaw, Wolters Kluwer 2015;

Sienkiewicz Z., *System sądowych środków wobec nieletnich w prawie polskim*, Wroclaw 1989;

Stanowska M., Walczak-Żochowska A., Wierzbowski K., 'Uwagi o profilu ustawy o postępowaniu z nieletnimi (Zagadnienia materialnoprawne i procesowe),' *Państwo i Prawo* 1983/6;

Zimring F.E., Langer M., Tanenhaus D.S., *Juvenile Justice in Global Perspective*, New York, NYU Press; 2015, (Youth, Crime, and Justice Series). Available at: http://search-1ebscohost-1com-10hkp9id4042a.waw-proxlib.swps.edu.pl/login.aspx?direct=true&db=nlebk&AN=1020812&lang=pl&site=eds-live. [access: Dec. 17 2020]. https://sjp.pwn.pl/sjp/przejaw;2510256.html [access: Dec. 17 2020].

Chapter 3. Procedural Aspects of Participation of Juvenile Offenders in Criminal Proceedings: General Remarks

Szymon Pawelec

Abstract: Under Polish law, if a juvenile commits a punishable act, proceedings are conducted before a family court. However, there are certain exceptions to that rule, which make it possible to conduct criminal proceeding against juvenile before a criminal court. This Chapter discusses the cases where criminal proceeding under the Polish Code of Criminal Procedure may be conducted in case of a juvenile, as well as resulting from this fact consequences for the criminal procedure, together with highlighting some doubts and difficulties in applying relevant provisions of law. It also presents the position of the juvenile acting as a passive party in the proceedings as well as the witness of the criminal proceedings. Finally, it discusses specific entitlements that extend the juvenile's right to defence with a view to improving his legal situation and making it more similar to that which the juvenile would have in proceedings conducted before a family court.

Keywords: juvenile, age of criminal responsibility, Polish juvenile justice system, juvenile as a party to the criminal trial, juvenile as a source of evidence, right to defence.

1. Introduction

Under Polish law, if a juvenile commits a punishable act, the related proceedings are conducted before a family court, in accordance with the Juvenile Justice Act of 26 October 1982 (the 'Act' or 'JJA'), subject to the provisions of the Code of Civil Procedure dealing with care proceedings and the Code of Criminal Procedure ('CCP') in respect of collecting, recording and taking evidence by the police, as well as appointing and acting by the defence lawyer. In exceptional, defined circumstances, a juvenile offender may be subject to the general rules regarding the conduct of criminal procedures under CCP. In such situations, a juvenile is tried before a criminal court, which, however, does not always result in their being held criminally liable.

Thus, the Polish legal system has a twofold approach to conducting court proceedings against a juvenile offender. First of all, where it has been committed by a juvenile of at least 13 years of age and before attaining the age of 17 years, the proceedings are conducted before a family court and they are to determine whether the juvenile has been demoralised or whether they have committed the punishable act, or possibly whether there exists a need to apply specific educational or correctional measures. At the same time, in statutorily defined situations, the system allows criminal proceedings to be conducted, which may also be aimed at holding a juvenile offender criminally liable. Although on multiple levels both ways of proceedings regard the same or similar issues, how they are conducted and the rules that govern them differ and come from various branches of law, which are often contradictory in many respects.

Because of the topics dealt with in this part of the article, the procedure and rules of conducting proceedings involving juvenile offenders under the Juvenile Justice Act have been omitted, and these issues are discussed in Chapter 2 of Part II below. The considerations below regard, above all, the rules of the criminal procedure against juveniles in accordance with CCP; first of all, they present the basis for applying the provisions of procedural criminal law to juveniles, they characterise the status of a juvenile in criminal proceedings, the procedural guarantees and the differences in procedure in the case of a juvenile offender.

At the beginning, it should be pointed out that an analysis of the JJA provisions in terms of the applicability of the Code of Criminal Procedure enables the following four categories of juvenile offenders to be identified: 1) juvenile offenders in respect of whom there exist causes for holding them criminally liable under Art. 10 § 2 CrC, who upon commencement of the proceedings have not attained the age of 18 years; 2) juvenile offender in respect of whom there exist causes for holding them criminally liable under Art. 10 § 2 CrC, who upon commencement of the proceedings are 18 years old or older; 3) juvenile offenders who upon commencement of the proceedings are 18 years old or older; 4) juvenile offenders who remain in a close relationship with an act of an adult person. In the case of all of these categories there are grounds for conducting criminal proceedings on the principles set out in CCP, but only in respect of offenders who upon commencement of the proceedings are 18 years of age or older is criminal procedure obligatory under CCP. JJA provides for differences in criminal proceedings only for category 1 juveniles. The regime of liability under substantive criminal law can be applied to category 1 or 2 juveniles. To category 3 and 4 juveniles, despite the fact that criminal proceedings are conducted on the general principles, the provisions of a substantive character appropriate for juveniles are used, which means, for instance, that under JJA educational or correctional measures are applied towards them. A juvenile is brought before a criminal court by decision of a family court principally only if they belong to category 1; in the case of category

2, 3 or 4 juveniles the prosecutor on their own decides that preliminary proceedings should be instituted, charges brought or an indictment filed with a criminal court. Some interpretational problems may occur in the case of concurrence of categories 1 and 4, which is discussed in more detail further in this Chapter.

What is important and needs to be pointed out clearly is the fact that in the Polish legal system, the decision to apply to a juvenile offender the regime of criminal liability under substantive law is entirely up to a family court, which before making the decision should conduct proceedings to take evidence at least to a minimum extent. The prosecutor's autonomy covers exclusively the ability to apply criminal procedure, with the exclusion of the substantive consequences of such a decision. Such regulation of the family court's competence and the uniqueness of subjecting a juvenile offender to the regime of criminal courts are in line with the general trend observable in West European countries.[1]

At this point, it should be emphasised that both under JJA and CCP, the notion of a 'juvenile' refers to the age at which the juvenile committed a punishable act. Its crossing does not result in the loss of the juvenile status in proceedings – either family ones or – what is more frequent – criminal ones. It should be inferred from the statement that whenever the legislator grants any rights or imposes any obligations on a juvenile, they will remain in force, irrespective of whether they are exercised or fulfilled before or after the juvenile's 17th birthday.[2]

2. Juvenile offender as a party to a criminal proceeding

As mentioned above, in principle, a juvenile offender is tried before a family court under JJA. A proceeding regarding a juvenile is conducted, above all, based

---

1 I. Weijers, A. Nuytiens, J. Christiaens, 'Transfer of Minors to the Criminal Court in Europe: Belgium and the Netherlandss' in: J. Junger-Tas, F. Dünkel (eds.), *Reforming Juvenile Justice*, Dordrecht, Heidelberg, London, New York, Springer, 2009, pp. 106–108.

2 This issue was widely discussed with reference to the no-longer-effective wording of Art. 79 § 1(1) CCP, which granted a 'juvenile' obligatory defence. The discussions focused on whether a juvenile, after their 18th birthday, is still obliged to have a defence counsel or the obligation to have one only applies to the period in which criminal proceedings are conducted until the juvenile comes of age. Now, the legislator has resolved any doubts in this respect by granting obligatory defence to a juvenile that is below the age of 18 years. Another issue is whether the current wording of the provision complies with the EU directives that are in force in Poland, particularly Directive (EU) 2016/800 of the European Parliament and of the Council of 11 May 2016 on procedural safeguards for children who are suspects or accused persons in criminal proceedings.

on the provisions of the Code of Civil Procedure applicable to guardianship matters. Only as regards collecting, preserving and taking evidence by the police and appointing or acting by the defence are the CCP provisions used accordingly, taking account of the changes provided for in JJA. The grounds for such a proceeding (which is conducted not against, but regarding a juvenile) is mainly care for the juvenile's well-being, aimed at bringing about desirable changes in their personality and behaviour, as well as, if needed, making their parents or guardians fulfil their duties towards the juvenile, taking account of public interest. The aim is not to hold a juvenile responsible or to punish them, but to create conditions preventing their demoralisation, to attempt to educate them and to change their social attitude.[3]

The legislator also provides that in certain situations the application of JJA may be insufficient, and the nature of a punishable act or the offender's age situation may call for conducting a criminal proceeding against them on the general principles, applicable to 'adult' offenders. In such situations, a juvenile offender appears not before a family court, but a criminal one.

The exceptions that allow the regulations characteristic of the criminal procedure to be used are set out in Art. 16 § 2, Art. 18 § 1(1) and Art. 18 § 1(2) JJA. However, the application in practice of the provisions regarding juveniles' criminal liability raises a number of doubts.[4] Some of them concern prosecution agencies' competence to decide about the ability to conduct proceedings regarding juveniles in accordance with CCP, in particular in the case of concurrence of prerequisites. Others are to do with the purpose of using the CCP provisions in the cases listed in Art. 18 § 1(2) 2 JJA,[5] as well as the notion of an 'adult' used in Art. 16 § 2 JJA, which is neither defined in the Polish Criminal Code nor in the Juvenile Justice Act or the Code of Criminal Procedure.

The main situation in which criminal procedure is to be used is the exception defined in Art. 18 § 1(1) JJA, which directly refers to the solutions adopted

---

3 Protection and care as the main function of juvenile law is pointed out by A. Grześkowiak, who also emphasises that it is reinforced by the wording of the Convention on the Rights of the Child of 20 Nov 1989, which has been ratified by Poland (Dz. U. (Journal of Laws) 1991 No. 120, item 526). See A. Grześkowiak, *Prawo nieletnich*, Warsaw 2020, p. 8.

4 Cf. A. Herzog, 'Prokurator a odpowiedzialność karna nieletnich,' *Prokuratura i Prawo* 2017/9, p. 133.

5 See Judgement of the Court of Appeal in Białystok II AKa 5/14, Legalis No. 1062552; see also Z. Sienkiewicz in: T. Kaczmarek (ed.), *System Prawa Karnego. Tom 5. Nauka o karze. Sądowy wymiar kary*, ed. 2, Warsaw 2017, pp. 372 ff.

in the Polish substantive criminal law. The criminal procedure may be used in respect of a juvenile if after their 15th birthday, they committed a prohibited act specified in Art. 134, Art. 148 § 1, 2 or 3, Art. 156 § 1 or 3, Art. 163 § 1 or 3, Art. 166, Art. 173 § 1 or 3, Art. 197 § 3 or 4, Art. 223 § 2, Art. 252 § 1 or 2, or in Art. 280 CrC and, at the same time, the circumstances of the case and the degree of the juvenile's development, characteristics and personal conditions support it, and in particular where the previously used educational or correctional measures have proved ineffective. It should be stressed that criminal liability on this basis is always elective and exceptional.[6] First of all, the uniqueness boils down to the types of acts committed by a juvenile aged 15 years or more, which enable them to be held criminally liable. The catalogue referred to in the provision in question is exhaustive,[7] and it mainly contains indictable offences (felonies), but also summary offences (misdemeanours), which are considered by the legislator as serious. As indicated by judicial decisions and the doctrine, the provision, although raising some specific doubts, applies to all punishable forms of crime commission, both stages of crime commission and complicity.[8] The unique

6 A. Grześkowiak, 'A commentary to Art. 10' in: A. Grześkowiak, K. Wiak (eds.), *Kodeks karny. Komentarz*, Warsaw 2021, *passim*. In this respect, the Polish regulations clearly protect a juvenile offender and account for differences in the psychophysical development between a child and an adult, as well as the resultant purposefulness and justifiability of conducting a criminal procedure against a juvenile. In the American legal system, the issue is regulated entirely differently – juvenile courts' rights are significantly limited, a juvenile may frequently be held criminally liable and often the respective decision is made exclusively by the prosecutor, even without hearing the juvenile out. For more, see D.M. Bishop, 'Juvenile Transfer in the United States' in: J. Junger-Tas, F. Dünkel (eds.) *Reforming Juvenile Justice,* Dordrecht Heidelberg London New York, Springr, 2009, p. 91.

7 See, for instance, the ruling of the Court of Appeal in Katowice of 20 October 2016, II AKz 343/16, unpublished.

8 In this manner: A. Grześkowiak, 'A commentary to Art. 10' in: A. Grześkowiak, K. Wiak (eds.), *Kodeks karny…*; also J. Lachowski, V. Konarska-Wrzosek (eds.), *Kodeks karny. Komentarz*, Warsaw 2019, p. 89; differently, however: A. Zoll, W. Wróbel, *Polskie prawo karne. Część ogólna*, Warsaw 2014, p. 331; Ł. Pohl, 'Zakres odpowiedzialności karnej nieletniego w Kodeksie karnym z 1997 r. (o konieczności pilnej zmiany art. 10 § 2 k.k. – problem form popełnienia czynu zabronionego),' *Prawo w Działaniu* 2017/30, pp. 7–18; Ł. Pohl, 'Ponownie w sprawie zakresu odpowiedzialności karnej osoby nieletniej według Kodeksu karnego z 1997 r. (zagadnienie form popełnienia czynu zabronionego) – uwagi o metodzie rozwiązania problemu,' *Prawo w Działaniu* 2018/35, pp. 116 ff.

character of a juvenile's criminal liability also refers to an individual assessment of the circumstances of the case and the degree of the offender's development, characteristics, and personal situation. The electiveness means that irrespective of the existence of the objective prerequisites listed in Art. 10 § 2 CrC, the court may, but does not have to decide to conduct a criminal proceeding against a juvenile. The respective decision is made by a family court, which rules that a proceeding should be continued under JJA or that the offender should appear before a criminal court. In the latter situation, in fact the case is transferred to a prosecutor with a view to carrying out a preparatory proceeding under the CCP provisions.[9]

As mentioned several times already, proceedings regarding a juvenile are in principle conducted by a juvenile court. The decision to institute or conduct a proceeding is made by a family court under Art. 21 § 1 JJA. If during a proceeding there come to light circumstances indicating that a juvenile committed an act in conditions that allow the application of Art. 18 § 1 (1) JJA, the family court determines that the case should be transferred to a prosecutor. The court decision is subject to a complaint (Art. 32k § 1 JJA). Where after the transfer new circumstances are discovered that indicate that there is no need to hold the juvenile criminally liable, the prosecutor will not issue an indictment and will transfer the case to a family court.

It is worth repeating here that, as indicated by the regulations referred to above, the decision on whether a juvenile's case should be referred to a criminal court is always elective in nature and is up to a family court, not prosecution agencies. If a preparatory proceeding is conducted regarding an act listed in Art. 10 § 2 CrC, after determining that the act was probably committed by a juvenile after their 15th birthday, the prosecutor is obliged to transfer the case to a family court, which is the only party authorised to make a decision on the purposefulness of subjecting the offender to the regime of criminal law and applying the criminal procedure to them. The prosecutor is bound by the court decision and this concerns not only the very fact of the case transfer and the obligation to 'accept' it but also a substantive assessment of the grounds for the transfer. Only where new circumstances indicating no grounds for holding a juvenile offender criminally liable come to light (already after the decision on the transfer became valid) does the prosecutor not file an indictment and transfers the case

9 See the Ruling of the Court of Appeal in Warsaw of 25 Feb 2004, II AKA 25/04, *Orzecznictwo Sądów Apelacyjnych* 2005/2, item 13, p. 21; Decision of the Court of Appeal in Cracow of 22 Sep 2007, II AKz 200/07, *Krakowskie Zeszyty Sądowe* 2007/5, item 49.

to a family court. The rationale for the proposed JJA amendment also points out that the repeated transfer of a juvenile's case to a prosecutor is binding on them, but there are no appropriate regulations in this respect.[10] It should be stressed that considering the content of the other prerequisites enabling a juvenile offender to be held criminally liable, the competences of the family court and the prosecutor defined in this manner only regard situations in which a punishable act was committed by a person after they attained the age of 15 years and before their 17th birthday, and the proceeding concerning the case was instituted before their 18th birthday. Where the offender has come of age and has turned 18 years of age, Art. 18 § 1(2) JJA applies, which provides that a case may be tried by a criminal court with respect to juvenile offenders who committed any punishable act (including those committed under the conditions specified in Art. 10 § 2 CrC), if the proceedings regarding the case at the *in personam* stage were instituted after the offender attained the age of 18 years.

Passing on to the second exception to the general rule of the competence of a family court in juvenile cases, one should pay attention to the provision of Art. 18 § 1(2) JJA. It allows the criminal proceeding regulation to be used in the case of a juvenile perpetrator of a punishable act that belongs to the category of crimes or fiscal crimes, where the proceedings were initiated after the offender turned 18 years of age. In such a situation, the proceeding is conducted under CCP, and so the preparatory proceeding is carried out by prosecution agencies, not by a family court. It should be pointed out that Art. 18 § 1(2) JJA has an exclusively procedural character and does not release the criminal court from the obligation to take account of the substantive law principles governed in JJA, especially as regards the directives for ruling specific measures against juveniles.[11] As emphasised by some authors, such a regulatory environment results in a certain inconsistency. 'Thus, after conducting preparatory proceedings in accordance with the Code of Criminal Procedure and filing with a criminal court by a prosecutor an indictment against a juvenile offender who has already turned 18 years of age, the court may only apply towards the offender the educational or correctional measures listed in Art. 6 JJA.'[12] What is more, if an offender is already 21 years

10 The rationale for a 2013 bill on amending the Juvenile Justice Act and certain other acts, Druk No. 1130, p. 11.

11 For instance: the Supreme Court judgement of 3 Sep 1998, V KKN 301/98, "*Biuletyn Informacji Prawnej*" 1999, No. 3, p. 26; similarly, A. Haak-Trzuskawska, H. Haak, *Ustawa o postępowaniu w sprawach nieletnich. Komentarz*, Warsaw 2015, pp. 81 ff.

12 A. Herzog, 'Prokurator a odpowiedzialność karna nieletnich,' *Prokuratura i Prawo* 2017/9, p. 144.

old when the ruling is announced, the court is obliged to discontinue the proceedings under Art. 17 § 1(11) CCP, because a person may only be placed at a correctional facility for young people before they turn 21 years old.[13] Although this does not apply to punishable acts performed in the conditions referred to in Art. 10 § 2 CrC (because the provision of Art. 18 § 1(1) 1 JJA has a substantive law character), the repeal by an amendment in 2014 of the controversial Art. 13 JJA,[14] allowing a sentence to be passed in respect of a juvenile who was 18 years old at the time of the ruling, when imposing a correctional measure would not have been reasonable, raised the question about the expediency of the application of the provisions of criminal procedure towards the offenders detailed in Art. 18 § 1(2) JJA.[15]

The third basis for conducting criminal proceedings against a juvenile, regards a situation in which a juvenile has performed a punishable act together with an adult. This possibility exists where a punishable act by a juvenile is closely linked to an act by an adult, and the juvenile's well-being does not stand in the way of the joint conduct of proceedings by prosecution agencies under CCP. As a general rule, under Art. 16 § 1 JJA, where in a case regarding a punishable act, proceedings were instituted against a juvenile together with an adult, the prosecutor will exclude the juvenile's case and refer it to a family court, which will conduct it under JJC. However, under Art. 16 § 2 JJA, in particularly justified situations, the prosecutor may commence or carry out an investigation also against a juvenile. The doctrine points out the exceptional nature of this basis, which may only apply in cases that are particularly justified by the interests of justice,[16] upon the joint satisfaction of the following two prerequisites: (1) the juvenile's punishable act is closely linked to the adult's act, (2) the juvenile's well-being does not stand in the way of the joint conduct of the case. The literature presents the view that the decision on the matter is made by the prosecutor autonomously.[17] Consequently, prosecutors have been granted the exclusive competence to carry

---

13 Cf. the judgement of the Court of Appeal in Białystok of 29 Apr 2014, II AKa 5/14, Legalis No. 1062552; see also Z. Sienkiewicz in: T. Kaczmarek (ed.), *System Prawa Karnego. Tom 5. Nauka o karze. Sądowy wymiar kary,*Warsaw 2017, pp. 372 ff.

14 See V. Konarska-Wrzosek, *Prawny system postępowania z nieletnimi w Polsce*, Warsaw 2013, p. 137–138 and the bibliography included there.

15 A. Herzog, 'Prokurator a odpowiedzialność karna nieletnich'..., p. 145.

16 A. Haak-Trzuskawska, H. Haak, *Ustawa o postępowaniu w sprawach nieletnich. Komentarz*, Warsaw 2015, a commentary to Art. 16 JJA.

17 P. Górecki, V. Konarska-Wrzosek, *Postępowanie w sprawach nieletnich. Komentarz*, Warsaw 2015, pp. 121–122.

out preparatory proceedings against juveniles under the provisions of criminal procedure. The commencement or conduct of an investigation against a juvenile requires a justification of the satisfaction of the above-mentioned two prerequisites, referred to in sentence 1 Art. 16 § 2 JJA. In such a situation, having completed the preparatory proceedings, the prosecutor, having grounds for supporting the charge, files an indictment against the adult with a criminal court, and excludes the juvenile's case and refers it to a family court. The possibility of filing an indictment against a juvenile requires the existence of another prerequisite in the form of the need to entertain the proceedings jointly. Thus, in the indictment, the prosecutor is obliged to justify not only the satisfaction of the prerequisites that allow preparatory proceedings against the juvenile to be carried out, but also of circumstances that call for the hearing of the case jointly.[18] The judicial decisions indicate that they may regard both considerations of equity and procedural economy. Frequently in cases referred to above, the juvenile's acts are subject to a public hearing anyway, with all its consequences, including the juvenile's participation in the proceedings as a witness, and an assessment of their act necessary to issue a determination against the adult.[19] An exclusion in such cases of the juvenile's case for separate proceedings before a family court does not protect the juvenile against the consequences of the public hearing, but means that the same witnesses need to be called, procedural activities repeated, additional costs borne, and several judge teams occupied, and, what is significant, this increases the risk of subterfuge.[20]

---

18 As indicated by judicial decisions, the circumstances favouring the need to jointly hear a case may regard the closeness of the relationship between the offenders, their similar age, or the juvenile's leading role in the crime. See, for instance, the judgement of the Court of Appeal in Cracow of 27 Mar 2005, II AKa 252/04, *Krakowskie Zesyty Sądowe* 2005/3, item 37; the judgement of the Court of Appeal in Cracow of 9 Sep 1993, II AKr 105/93, *Krakowskie Zesyty Sądowe* 1993/10, item 24; the judgement of the Court of Appeal in Cracow of 17 Jun 2004, II AKA 121/04, *Krakowskie Zesyty Sądowe* 2004/ 8, item 55, p 29. About the requirement to justify the need to hear a case jointly see, for instance, the decision of the Supreme Court of 17 Feb 1984, IV KZ 18/84, *Orzecznictwo Sądu Najwyższego Izby Karnej i Wojkowej* 1984/9–10, item 105; the judgement of the Supreme Court of 9 Jul 1997, V KKN 217/97, *Prokuratura i Prawo. Supplement Orzecznictwo*, 1998/1, item 19.

19 A. Haak-Trzuskawska, H. Haak, *Ustawa o postępowaniu w sprawach nieletnich. Komentarz*, Warsaw 2015, a commentary to Art. 16 JJA.

20 Cf. the judgement of the Court of Appeal in Cracow of 17 Jun 2004, II AKA 121/04, *Krakowskie Zesyty Sądowe* 2004/8, item 55.

Although the justifiability and expediency of the exception in question seem obvious, the prerequisites for its use as designed by the legislator may raise some doubts. The wording of Art. 16 § 1 JJA indicates that the prosecutor may exclude a juvenile's case and refer it to a family court, where proceedings have been instituted against a juvenile. According to the literal interpretation of the provision, a case may only be referred to a family court after charges are brought against a juvenile. It is because it is only from the moment when the passive party to criminal proceedings is created can proceedings against a specific person be said to have been instituted. During the *in rem* phase, proceedings regarding the case are conducted, without identifying the person against whom they are directed. The purpose of Art. 16 § 1 JJA seems to be the confirmation of the principle of conducting proceedings against juvenile offenders according to the rules set out in the Juvenile Justice Act, while its construction necessitates the conduct of preparatory proceedings by prosecution agencies under the Code of Criminal Procedure, only to exclude the juvenile's case and to refer it to a family court after charges have been brought, which is in fact connected with an unnecessary and pointless act of legal procedure.[21] Other issues related to the provision in question are linked to the term 'adult,' which remains undefined under the substantive criminal law, procedural criminal law and juvenile law. Apart from the numerous terms already used to refer to a juvenile,[22] the legislator introduces yet another one, which is not specified in any more detail. At the same time, the term 'adult' may be interpreted in two ways: it may signify the 'adult offender' within the meaning of the Criminal Code, i.e. a person who has attained 17 years of age, but it may also be a person of age within the meaning of the Civil Code, i.e. someone who has attained 18 years of age. It seems that from the point of view of the systemic interpretation, the purposes and principles regulated by the Juvenile Justice Act, the 'adult' referred to in Art. 16 JJA is a person who may be held criminally liable and in respect of whom criminal proceedings are conducted on the general principles, i.e. a person who had attained 17 years of age before they

21 Cf. A. Gaberle, 'O wykładni i stosowaniu art. 16 u.p.n., czyli jak nie należy konstruować przepisów prawnych' in: P. Hofmański, S. Waltoś (eds.), *W kręgu prawa nieletnich. Księga pamiątkowa ku czci Profesor Marianny Korcyl-Wolskiej,* Warsaw 2009, p. 270 and the literature listed there.

22 The difficulties related to the definition of a "juvenile", the multitude of the terms used in substantive criminal law and juvenile law, and, consequently, the multitude of the legal solutions affecting juveniles' legal situation is discussed in the Chapter 'Criminal Responsibility of Juveniles in Polish Law.'

committed a punishable act.[23] It should be pointed out, however, that JJA does not contain such a definition and fails to state explicitly that the said provision refers to such an offender.

At the same time, attention should be drawn to the problems that might occur in the event of concurrence of the grounds for applying the general jurisdiction of a criminal court in a juvenile case. The interpretational doubts regard the prosecutor's competence to decide about conducting criminal proceedings against a juvenile in case of concurrence of the grounds under Art. 18 § 1(1) JJA and Art. 16 § 2 JJA, where the proceedings were instituted before the juvenile turned 18 years of age. Without discussing this issue in any more detail, because this is done in the next Chapter,[24] it should only be mentioned here that the regulations in this respect are imprecise and fail to unambiguously determine the prosecutor's rights in the presented process configuration.

The acknowledgement that criminal proceedings are conducted against a juvenile in accordance with general jurisdiction entails all of the consequences arising from the use of CCP. As a general rule, a juvenile that is a suspect and, subsequently, an accused has the same status as the other passive parties to criminal proceedings. The differences principally occur in the situation where proceedings are conducted before the juvenile turns 18 years of age. It follows from Art. 18 § 2(1) 1 JJA that where criminal proceedings were instituted under Art. 10 § 2 CrC against a juvenile before they attained 18 years of age, there apply the specific provisions characteristic of juvenile proceedings, which extend the procedural guarantees of the accused juvenile.[25] Specific procedural guarantees

---

23 In this way, for instance: T. Bojarski, E. Kruk, E. Skrętowicz, *Postępowanie w sprawach nieletnich. Komentarz*, ed. 5, Warsaw 2016, p. 128; A. Gaberle, M. Korcyl-Wolska, *Komentarz do ustawy o postępowaniu w sprawach nieletnich*, Gdańsk 2002, pp. 100–101; P. Górecki, V. Konarska-Wrzosek, *Postępowanie w sprawach nieletnich. Komentarz*, Warsaw 2015, p. 122; K. Gromek, *Komentarz do ustawy o postępowaniu w sprawach nieletnich*, Warsaw 2001, p. 177; A. Gaberle, 'O wykładni i stosowaniu art. 16 u.p.n., czyli jak nie należy konstruować przepisów prawnych'..., p. 271.

24 See the Subchapter of the following Chapter devoted to the juvenile's impact on the course of criminal proceedings.

25 Art. 18 § 2(1) 1 JJA provides that: "Proceedings in the cases listed in § 1 are conducted in accordance with the provisions of the Code of Criminal Procedure; however, in the cases referred to in: 1) Sec. 1, where the proceedings were instituted before the juvenile attained 18 years of age: a) the preparatory proceedings shall be carried out by a family court, with the provisions of Art. 16 and Art. 32k applied accordingly, b) the juvenile shall have a defence lawyer, c) the juvenile's parents or guardian shall have the rights of a party, d) the provisions of Art. 23–25a, Art. 27, Art. 32, Art. 32f–32h and

of a juvenile accused that extend beyond those enjoyed by an 'adult' are also granted by the very Code of Criminal Procedure. Further on in this Chapter and in the following Chapter, those will become subject to a separate analysis.

In conclusion, it should be pointed out that the evaluation as to the existence of the grounds for conducting criminal proceedings against a juvenile made during the course of the proceedings – both by a family court or a prosecutor – is not binding as to substance for the criminal court hearing. When giving the final ruling, the criminal court may always conclude that in a particular case there were no grounds for applying the substantive criminal provisions and hold that in respect of the juvenile the educational or correctional measures under JJA should be used.[26]

3. Juvenile offender as a source of evidence

In criminal proceedings, any person, irrespective of their age, mental or physical health, may be a witness.[27] It is immaterial whether the person has a full, limited or no capacity to enter into legal transactions.[28] The above complies with the general clauses contained in the UNO's Guidelines on Justice in Matters involving Child Victims and Witnesses of Crime of 22 July 2005, under which every child should be treated as a capable witness, subject to examination, and his or her testimony should not be presumed invalid or untrustworthy by reason of the child's age alone as long as his or her age and maturity allow the giving of intelligible and credible testimony, with or without communication aids and other assistance.[29] The Polish criminal procedure does not include any evidence prohibitions related to juveniles' participation as witnesses.

Art. 32n § 1 shall apply accordingly, e) provisional detention may only be used where placement at a youth detention centre would be insufficient, f) if the court determines that the educational or correctional measures provided for in this Act should be used in respect of the juvenile, it shall rule that they be so used, g) the provisions of Art. 60, 62 and 63 shall apply accordingly".

26 T. Bojarski, E. Kruk, E. Skrętowicz, *Postępowanie w sprawach nieletnich. Komentarz*, ed. 5, Warsaw 2016, p. 189 and the decision of the Court of Appeal in Katowice of 26 Aug 2009, court file No. II AKz 566/09, LEX No. 553816, referred to there.

27 J. Kosonoga, 'Przesłuchanie pokrzywdzonego w trybie art. 185a k.p.k.,' *Prokuratura i Prawo* 2004/1, p. 64.

28 M. Zbrojewska, A. Małolepszy, 'Dziecko jako świadek w procesie karnym,' *Studia Gdańskie*, Vol. XXVIII, p. 106.

29 See Art. 18 of ECOSOC Resolution 2005/20, Guidelines on Justice in Matters involving Child Victims and Witnesses of Crime, the text available at: https://www.un.org/en/ecosoc/docs/2005/resolution%202005-20.pdf [access: Dec. 31 2020].

The criminal procedural provisions relating to a child acting as a witness do not contain any special regulations concerning a witness that is simultaneously a juvenile offender. Undoubtedly, this is a peculiar procedural configuration, as part of which separate proceedings regarding a juvenile are conducted under JJA before a family court, while in respect of the accused, whose act is related to the juvenile's act – a criminal procedure under CCP.[30] A juvenile offender may be a witness in criminal proceedings. Their status is not only determined by the regulations regarding the hearing of juvenile witnesses but also the hearing of the accused in such a capacity in other proceedings regarding complicity in an offence covered by given procedure. No doubt, this is a situation of an obvious conflict of interests – on the one hand, there is the need to ensure the right to defence, including the right to remain silent and not to provide evidence against oneself, on the other hand – to fulfil the procedural obligations on the part of a witness called before a prosecution agency or a court, including the obligation to give evidence and not to hold back the truth.

The criminal procedural regulations governing the issue of hearing juvenile witnesses differentiate various categories of such parties, mainly on the basis of age and the substantive scope of the proceedings in progress. In principle, there are two general categories of juveniles acting as witnesses: 1) juveniles who at the time of the hearing have not attained 15 years of age, 2) juveniles who at the time of the hearing have attained 15 years of age. The procedural differences as to the hearing of juvenile witnesses have been provided for by the legislator mainly with reference to those who have not attained 15 years of age by the time of the hearing. In principle, the other juveniles have the same rights and obligations as other witnesses giving evidence in a criminal case.[31] A broader analysis of

30 The general rule of criminal procedure is substantive connection included in Art. 34 § 1 and 2 CPP. In cases involving juveniles, the rule is that the juvenile's case is excluded for separate proceedings before a family court under JJA, and only in particularly justifiable cases may a juvenile be judged in criminal proceedings conducted under CPP. More on this topic can be found in the remarks on Art. 16 JJA made above, in section 2 of this Chapter.

31 An exception refers to a juvenile victim in crimes committed with violence or an unlawful threat, or specified in Chapters XXIII (crimes against liberty), XXV (crimes against sexual freedom or decency) or XXVI (crimes against family and care) of the Criminal Code, if it is feared that a hearing in normal conditions might have a negative impact on the child's psyche (Art. 185a § 4 CPP), as well as in respect of a juvenile victim of the crime of rape (Art. 197 CrC), exploitation of helplessness, handicap (Art. 198 CrC) or misuse of dependence (Art. 199 CrC) under Art. 185c § 1a CCP.

Art. 185a–185d CCP indicates that, in terms of the procedural status, the legislator differentiates more categories of juvenile witnesses, granting them specific rights depending on their status (a witness or a witness being an injured party) as well as the category of the crimes dealt with in given proceedings. The broadest rights aimed at increasing the protection of a child's psyche have been granted to a juvenile who has also been injured by a crime committed with violence or an unlawful threat or specified in Chapters XXIII (crimes against liberty), XXV (crimes against sexual freedom or decency) or XXVI (crimes against family and care) of the Criminal Code, which is in line with Art. 17 of the UNO's Guidelines. Because of the fact that the issues related to juvenile witnesses are broad and would call for an in-depth discussion that goes beyond the limits of this paper, at this point, only the procedural provisions that relate to a witness who is a juvenile offender should be pointed out. Basically, such a witness is not subject to any special protection because of their age. In Art. 185b § 3 CCP, the legislator explicitly states that the specific conditions of hearing juveniles in criminal cases do not apply to witnesses cooperating in committing the prohibited act which the criminal proceedings regard, or witnesses whose acts are connected with the act the criminal proceedings regard. Thus, it should be assumed that the only rights held by such a witness because of age are those provided for in Art. 171 § 3 and Art. 360 § 1(2) CPP, as well as the regulations related to the prohibition to take an oath before the hearing.

Under Art. 171 § 3 CPP, if the person heard has not attained 15 years of age, acts involving such a person should be, if possible, carried out in the presence of their statutory representative or actual guardian unless the interest of the proceedings stands in the way. It should be emphasised that the specified conditions for hearing a juvenile witness under 15 years of age are not obligatory. The legislator only indicates that if possible, during an act of legal procedure, the current statutory representative or actual guardian should be present. Thus, a failure to fulfil this obligation does not affect the probative value of the act, in particular, it does not turn it into inadmissible evidence, which may not constitute a basis for a settlement by a judicial body.[32] Testimony given by a juvenile may not constitute evidence only if it is proved to have been provided in conditions excluding freedom of expression or contrary to the prohibitions referred to in

32 Decision of the Supreme Court of 26 Nov 2008, IV KK 381/08, *Krakowskie Zeszyty Sądowe* 2009/7–8, item 43.

Art. 171 § 5 CPP,[33] which in fact applies to every witness heard in the course of a criminal case.

The presence of a statutory representative or actual guardian may be inadvisable because of the interest of the proceedings. This refers to a situation in which the person, due to specific procedural configurations, is connected with the act that is the subject of the proceedings.[34] If this is so, it is obvious that participation in the act of legal procedure should be prevented. However, it may also be that the person authorised to attend has no connection with the offence, but their presence nevertheless affects the juvenile's freedom of expression, who may feel more awkward or mentally uncomfortable or even frightened. As indicated by the judicial decisions, in such a situation, a counsellor or a pedagogue may be allowed to be present in the act.[35] The literature points out that each case should be evaluated by the hearing body before commencing the act, e.g. by asking about the relationships and impact of the guardians on the juvenile at the place of their residence or school.[36]

The role of a statutory representative in the course of a hearing has not been specified by the legislator. The doctrine talks about the passive attitude, not only manifesting itself in the very presence[37] but also about active involvement, consisting in questions being asked by the judicial body through the representative or guardian.[38]

With a view to protecting a juvenile witness who has not attained 15 years of age against increased stress or social stigma, for the duration of the hearing the court may conduct the proceedings in the absence of the public. This right is non-compulsory and its exercise depends on the evaluation of a specific case. It is worth mentioning at this point that under JJA proceedings are conducted,

33 A. Sakowicz, 'A commentary to Art. 171 CPP' in: A. Sakowicz (ed.), *Kodeks postępowania karnego. Komentarz*, Warsaw 2020, *passim*.

34 The above should, above all, refer to a situation, where the statutory representative or guardian is a co-perpetrator of the punishable act, but also where the spouse or cohabitant is one. Within this context, see P. Świerk, 'Przesłuchanie małoletniego pokrzywdzonego na podstawie art. 185a k.p.k.,' *Prokuratura i Prawo* 2004/5, p. 155.

35 Decision of the Supreme Court of 26 Nov 2008, IV KK 381/08, *Krakowskie Zeszyty Sądowe*, 2009/7–8, item 43.

36 M. Zbrojewska, A. Małolepszy, 'Dziecko jako świadek w procesie karnym'..., p. 116.

37 T. Grzegorczyk, *Kodeks postępowania karnego i ustawa o świadku koronnym. Komentarz*, Warsaw 2008, p. 211.

38 In this way, R.A. Stefański, 'Zasady przesłuchiwania małoletniego,' *Wojskowy Przegląd Prawniczy* 2004/5, p. 83.

as a matter of principle, in camera. Openness is possible if it is justified by educational reasons. When hearing a juvenile witness-a perpetrator of a punishable act, there should be taken into account the circumstance that the proceedings under JJA regarding the juvenile are conducted in camera. Although in respect of a witness who has not attained the age of 15 years the criminal court may decide to conduct the external principal trial in camera, in the case of an older witness, it has no such right. Thus, a situation occurs in which proceedings under JJA regarding a juvenile are conducted in camera, because of the need to protect the juvenile, while a trial before a criminal court – as part of which related, and often the same issues and circumstances are examined and presented – is open to the public. The judicial decisions rightly indicate that in the case of such a configuration, frequently the reasons for which the juvenile's case should be excluded for separate proceedings under JJA are no longer valid and there are grounds for applying Art. 16 § 2 JJA, which enables a joint hearing of a juvenile's and adult's cases within one trial before a criminal court.[39] Consideration should be given to the issue of whether the lack of the right to hear each juvenile witness in camera in every case, except where it is justified with educational reasons, does not in fact violate the child's protective rights.

When talking about the peculiar status of a witness who is also a juvenile offender, a reference should be made to the regulations that guarantee the right to defence, because the question arises whether in such a situation a juvenile witness may exercise the right to refuse to testify under Art. 182 § 3 CCP. The literal interpretation of the said regulation indicates that the right to refuse to testify is held by a witness who in another pending case is accused of complicity in an offence being tried. This regulation is an expression of the right to defence, which allows avoidance of the situation in which an accused acting as a witness in another case would be obliged to testify and not to hold back the truth as to the circumstances connected with the offence they are accused of. As regards a witness who is a juvenile offender, the following issues should be noted. Firstly, juvenile proceedings are designed in such a way that they are not proceedings against a juvenile; the juvenile is not the accused. This fact alone raises doubts as to the ability to apply the regulation of Art. 182 § 3 CCP. Secondly, the provision explicitly limits its application exclusively to concurrent proceedings, which precludes its use in respect of legally valid proceedings. Thirdly, even if it is assumed that it is applicable to juveniles, one should consider the juvenile's cognitive capability

39 For instance, the judgement of the Court of Appeal in Cracow of 17 Mar 2005, II AKa 252/04, *Krakowskie Zeszyty Sądowe*, 2005/3, item 37.

to make an autonomous, fully conscious decision on whether to make use of the available right. This issue is even of more importance in respect of the right to refuse to answer questions, which is guaranteed under Art. 183 § 1 CPP and which may be even more difficult to understand by a juvenile.

The applicability of the right to refuse to testify by a juvenile offender has been considered by the Polish Supreme Court. Although the literal interpretation of Art. 182 § 3 CCP indicates that it does not apply to such a juvenile, in the judgement of 28 Nov 2003, the view was expressed that both from the functional, guarantee interpretation and the clear analogies between JJA and CCP there arises the ability and the need to extend the right to refuse to testify to a juvenile in respect of whom proceedings are conducted regarding an act that is subject to criminal proceedings.[40] Although the very concept that constituted the basis for such an interpretation by the Supreme Court seems acceptable, some serious doubts arise as to the far-reaching use of analogies and comparison of the status of a 'juvenile' with that of an 'accused.'[41] It should be borne in mind that the purposes of the proceedings regarding the juvenile, their status and the applied measures significantly differ from those specified in the Code of Criminal Procedure and the Criminal Code. Furthermore, the distinctiveness of these two regimes are pointed out explicitly, stressing that a juvenile is not held criminally liable. Without delving into details on this topic, as this would call for a separate discussion, which goes beyond the framework of this paper, consideration should be given to the expansion of the group of the parties entitled under Art. 182 § 3 CCP with juveniles regarding whom proceedings are conducted under JJA in respect of an act subject to criminal procedure.

Irrespective of the above, a certain inconsistency of the legislator, who granted a juvenile witness the right to refuse to testify, should be pointed out. The literature points out that a child witness 'when instructed about the right to refuse

---

40 Judgement of the Supreme Court of 28 Nov 2003, IV KK 14/03, *Krakowskie Zeszyty Sądowe* 2004/4, item 34.

41 The doubts regarding the justifiability of the extension of the scope of applicability of the provision of Art. 182 § 3 CPP contrary to the linguistic interpretation should be even more serious, because both the doctrine and the judicial decisions refuse – with regard to the same provision – to grant the right to refuse to testify to a witness who in other pending proceedings is suspected of complicity in the offence subject to those proceedings (more on this: P. Sowiński, *Prawo świadka do odmowy zeznań w procesie karnym*, Warsaw 2004, p. 75 and the literature given there). On the other hand, it is clear that the procedural status of a suspect is much more similar to that of an accused than a juvenile regarding whom proceedings are conducted under JJA.

to testify, may find it hard to understand their role in the proceedings and the consequences of exercising the right to refuse to testify, and very often, when making the decision on whether to testify, the child will not consider reasonable arguments, but rather their willingness to end the procedural act as fast as possible and to leave the court or prosecution building.'[42] Their cognitive functions, psychophysical capabilities, in particular those connected with analysing the consequences of their decisions, do not enable them to make autonomous decisions on such important matters,[43] although obviously the situation will depend on the child's age and their psychophysical development. It is worth mentioning that the problem has been noticed by the legislator, because when regulating the prohibition to take an oath from a witness who has not attained the age of 17 years, a reference was made to the possibility that a child may not be aware of the consequences of testimony given.

The doubts as to the awareness of the legal consequences and the impact of testimony are even more serious with regard to the use of the right to refuse to answer a question if the answer might expose them or a close person to liability for an offence or a fiscal offence. The granting of this right to a juvenile witness-a perpetrator of a punishable act is imperative and necessary to guarantee them the absolute right to defence and the absence of their obligation to provide evidence against themselves. However, serious doubts are raised by the question whether the right is genuine and may really be exercised by the juvenile. The presence of a statutory representative or the actual guardian might be conducive to its exercise, but it should be remembered that the presence is not obligatory and the ability to make use of assistance provided by a professional attorney in fact is limited – both formally, because of the required interest and right of the body to refuse to admit them, and actually, because of the possible lack of awareness of the need to use such assistance.

4. Extension of the right to defence principle in the context of juveniles

The conduct of criminal proceedings against a juvenile is associated with all of the consequences resulting from applying the procedural criminal law regime to

42 K. Paszek, K. Pawelec, 'Prawo małoletniego do odmowy złożenia zeznań,' *Prokuratura i Prawo* 2008/12, p. 122.

43 A different position was expressed in the judgement of the Supreme Court of 19 Feb 2003, I KZP 48/02, *Orzecznictwo Sądu Najwyższego Izby Karnej i Wojskowej* 2003/3–4.

such a perpetrator of a punishable act. In such proceedings, the institutions of the criminal procedure are, as a matter of principle, used in the same way as in respect of other accused persons. However, it should be stressed that a situation in which a juvenile is legally liable like an adult may only be justified with special circumstances. Furthermore, in some cases, the legislator granted the juvenile specific entitlements that extend their right to defence with a view to improving their legal situation and making it more similar to that which the juvenile would have in proceedings conducted under JJA. However, not all of the grounds for conducting criminal proceedings against a juvenile are connected with extending their rights during the proceedings. Additionally, not all juveniles have received such guarantees.

Under Art. 18 § 2(1) JJA, the additional rights were only granted to juveniles against whom proceedings are instituted before they attain the age of 18 years. The extension of the procedural guarantees only applies to juveniles who at the moment of the institution of proceedings have not come of age within the meaning of the Civil Code, but also only to those who are subject to criminal proceedings, because they committed the punishable act referred to in Art. 10 § 2 CrC. The provision extending the rights of the accused in criminal proceedings does not apply to a juvenile subject to proceedings before a criminal court conducted under the second prerequisite under Art. 18 § 1(2) JJA, i.e. a juvenile who committed a punishable act and the proceedings were instituted after they attained the age of 18 years. The prerequisite for conducting criminal proceedings regulated in Art. 16 § 2 JJA (an act by a juvenile in close connection with an act by an adult) also does not constitute grounds for extending the scope of the procedural guarantees of the accused.

Art. 18 § 2(1) JJA introduces the institutions known to JJA into criminal procedure. The justification for such a solution is, firstly, that proceedings before a criminal court should not basically differ from proceedings that would be conducted under JJA, if the exception enabling the offender to be criminally liable had not been applied, and, secondly, that the criminal court should have at its disposal a broader scope of criminal measures to choose from to enable educational and correctional functions to be performed.

First of all, the legislator indicated that preparatory proceedings should be carried out by a family court, not prosecution agencies. At the same time, however, there apply the regulations imposing the obligation to refer the case to a prosecutor in the event of fulfilment of the prerequisites under Art. 10 § 2 CrC, as well as those regulating the jurisdiction of the family court and the prosecutor if a punishable act was performed by a juvenile together with an adult. The said regulations mean in fact that preparatory proceedings – after establishing circumstances that allow the decision to be made to apply the criminal procedure to the case – are not conducted by a family court, but by a prosecutor in the form of an investigation, subject to the differences specified in Art. 18 § 2(1) JJA. Consequently, the juvenile involved must have a defence lawyer; additionally, their parent or guardian has been granted the right of a party to the proceedings. It should be stressed that, as opposed to the obligatory defence under Art. 79 § 1(1) CCP, the defence granted under Art. 18 § 2(1) JJA is granted for the entire duration of the proceedings, not only until the juvenile comes of age.[44]

The possibility of a parent or guardian acting as a party means that the family court is obliged to notify the relevant person of the institution of the proceedings and also about their completion if the closing ruling has not been served on them.[45] The right to appear in the capacity of a party obligates the court to notify such a party about the dates and times of the hearings.[46] The judicial decisions indicate that, contrary to the obligatory defence referred to above, 'the right to participate in criminal proceedings in the capacity of a party held by the parents under Art. 18 § 2(1)(c) JJA expires upon the attainment by the accused of the age of 18 years.'[47]

Furthermore, in criminal proceedings there apply special JJA provisions regarding community interviews (Art. 24 JJA), observation of the juvenile with a view to issuing a comprehensive diagnosis of their personality, to which the civil procedure provisions (Art. 25 JJA) apply accordingly, as well as a psychiatric assessment of the juvenile (Art. 25a JJA). Differences are also provided for as to the use of coercive measures – the rule is that the offender should be placed at a youth detention centre; provisional detention may only be used in exceptional circumstances.[48]

---

44 As indicated by the Supreme Court in its judgement of 19 Feb 2019, the provision of Art. 18 § 2(1b) JJA 'has a *lex specialis* character in relation to the provisions of CCP, and so the obligatory character of defence would not cease also upon the attainment by the accused of the age of 18 years.' Judgement of the Supreme Court of 19 Feb 2019, III KS 1/19, Legalis No. 1883228.

45 The court may also inform the school attended by the juvenile, the relevant public or social institution, or a local government unit, in particular, the county family assistance centre competent in respect of the juvenile's place of residence (Art. 18 § 2(1) JJA in connection with Art. 23 § 2 JJA).

46 Judgement of the Court of Appeal in Katowice of 20 Oct 2016, II AKa 343/16, *Orzecznictwo Sądu Apelacyjnego w Katowicach*, 2016/4, item 1.

47 Judgement of the Court of Appeal in Katowice of 13 Jan 2011, II AKa 443/10, *Orzecznictwo Sądu Apelacyjnego w Katowicach*, 2011/1, item 3.

48 More about coercive measures and preventive measures in the next Chapter.

In criminal proceedings conducted against a juvenile in respect of whom the proceedings were instituted before they attained 18 years of age also there apply other rules regarding interrogation, as well as detention and possible placement at a police youth home. Here, a discussion is needed of, above all, the conditions of the juvenile's interrogation, because the coercive and preventive measures will be examined in detail in the further part of this paper.

The provision of Art. 32f JJA introduces the obligation to interrogate a juvenile by the police in the presence of a third party related to the accused juvenile. In principle, this should be the parents who have parental responsibility, or the juvenile's guardian or defence lawyer. Where, however, it is impossible to ensure their presence, the prosecution agency is obliged to call the person close to the juvenile that they identified, a school representative, a family assistant, a foster care coordinator or a representative of a social organisation whose statutory tasks include exerting educational impact on juveniles or helping their social rehabilitation. As indicated by the literature, the order of the above persons is not accidental. The interrogation of a juvenile in the presence of people other than their parents, guardian or defence lawyer is only possible if their presence during the act cannot be arranged; in such a situation, the first person to be called is the person of age close to the juvenile designated by them.[49] The legislator also stresses that during hearing out of the juvenile, efforts should be made to ensure that they are free to express themselves fully. The juvenile should be heard out in conditions similar to natural ones, possibly at their place of residence, and steps should be taken to avoid hearing the juvenile out repeatedly as to the same circumstances or circumstances already established by means of other evidence and which do not raise any doubt (Art. 19 JJA). The said regulations are obviously aimed at protecting the juvenile against negative psychological consequences of the conducted proceedings. However, the file research study analysing proceedings involving juveniles aged 15–16 years carried out in the years 2004–2008 showed that the juveniles subjected to criminal proceedings were much more exposed to various forms of abuse on the part of prosecution agencies than adult accused persons. Frequently, juveniles were treated like adults, in many cases the provisions referred to above that extend the scope of the procedural guarantees were not applied, e.g. by not allowing the juvenile's parents to attend their interrogation, misusing provisional detention or not taking into account Art. 19

---

49 In this way: A. Haak-Trzuskowska, H. Haak, *Ustawa o postępowaniu w sprawach nieletnich. Komentarz*, Warsaw 2015, a commentary to Art. 32f JJA.

JJA during the interrogation.[50] No doubt, such practice should be regarded as undesirable.

In conclusion of this discussion it should be mentioned that in the case of juveniles involved in proceedings instituted before they attained the age of 18 years there also apply the provisions of JJA regarding the costs of proceedings, which, in principle, are charged to the parents or guardians, as well as those regarding the limiting of external openness. As a rule, court proceedings are conducted in camera, unless their openness is justifiable with educational purposes. When issuing the final settlement, the criminal court – recognising such justifiability – may apply in respect of the juvenile the educational or correctional measures provided for in JJA.

It should be stressed that irrespective of the rights granted under Art. 18 § 2(1) JJA, the very Code of Criminal Procedure introduces specific regulations that extend the scope of the procedural guarantees of the juvenile accused. The provisions apply to all juveniles involved in criminal proceedings in the capacity of a passive party, regardless of the grounds on which they were referred to a criminal court.

First of all, the legislator provides for obligatory defence in respect of every accused person who has not attained the age of 18 years, and it should be emphasised that the obligation to have a defence lawyer ceases upon the attainment by the juvenile of the age of 18 years, irrespective of the stage of the process at which it occurs.[51] Prior to the amendment of 2013,[52] obligatory defence was required for every juvenile, with the term 'juvenile' interpreted in accordance with JJA, and it was connected with the commission of a punishable act by a juvenile, which meant that obligatory defence was provided for the entire duration of the proceedings, even where the accused came of age during their course. Regardless of the civil law grounds for attaining majority, it should be emphasised that the obligatory defence referred to in Art. 79 § 1(1) CPP sets out the criterion of age, not the attainment of maturity, and so it was granted to every accused person who has not attained the age of 18 years, irrespective of whether the person has

50 A. Więcek-Durańska, 'Odpowiedzialność nieletnich za czyny z art. 10 § 2 k.k. przed sądem rodzinnym i przed sądem karnym – wybrane zagadnienia,' *Prawo w Działaniu*, 2013/16, p. 196.

51 Judgement of the Supreme Court of 19 Feb 2019, III KS 1/19, Legalis No. 1883228.

52 The Act of 27 Sep 2013 Amending the Act – the Code of Criminal Procedure and Certain Other Acts, Dz. U. (Journal of Laws) 2013, item 1247, entry into force: 1 Jul 2015.

or has not acquired the capacity to enter into legal transactions under any special regulations.

Apart from the obligatory participation of a defence lawyer, the Code of Criminal Procedure also provides for the participation in the proceedings of the juvenile's statutory representative or actual guardian, which, in principle, should be conducive to protecting their rights and interests during the proceedings (Art. 76 CPP). The issue of a juvenile's representative is discussed in the following Chapter; here, it should only be mentioned.

Irrespective of the above regulations, the legislator provided for the optional possibility of conducting the main trial in camera, where at least one of the accused persons is juvenile, which makes the position of such an accused analogous to that of a juvenile witness. As opposed to the latter, however, in the case of a juvenile, the possibility of closing the trial to the public is not only applicable to the part of the judicial proceedings, but also to the entire main trial. The closing of the proceedings to the public is optional, and the decisions in this respect and with regard to the scope of the closure are made by the court trying the case, taking account of all circumstances, the impact of the proceedings on the juvenile, the educational purposes and the ability to enable the juvenile to return to the society as fast as possible.[53] Juvenile proceedings under JJA are, as a rule, conducted in camera (Art. 32n § 1 JJA). It should be stressed that until the juvenile attains the age of 18 years, where criminal proceedings are conducted because the juvenile committed the act under Art. 10 § 2 CrC, the proceedings are obligatorily conducted in camera, because of the obligation to apply in such situations the provision of Art. 32n § 1 JJA also in criminal proceedings.

References

Bishop D.M., 'Juvenile Transfer in the United States' in: Junger-Tas J., Dünkel F. (eds.), *Reforming Juvenile Justice*, Dordrecht Heidelberg London New York, Springer, 2009;

Bojarski T., Kruk E., Skrętowicz E., *Postępowanie w sprawach nieletnich. Komentarz*, ed. 5, Warsaw 2016;

Haak-Trzuskawska A., Haak H., *Ustawa o postępowaniu w sprawach nieletnich. Komentarz*, Warsaw 2015;

53 Cf. B. Wójcicka, 'Podstawy wyłączenia jawności rozprawy,' *Acta Universitatis Lodziensis. Folia Iuridica* 1988/35, pp. 54–55.

Herzog A., 'Prokurator a odpowiedzialność karna nieletnich,' *Prokuratura i Prawo* 2017/9;

Gaberle A., 'O wykładni i stosowaniu art. 16 u.p.n., czyli jak nie należy konstruować przepisów prawnych' in: Hofmański P., Waltoś S. (eds.), *W kręgu prawa nieletnich. Księga pamiątkowa ku czci Profesor Marianny Korcyl-Wolskiej*, Warsaw 2009;

Górecki P., Konarska-Wrzosek V., *Postępowanie w sprawach nieletnich. Komentarz*, Warsaw 2015;

Gromek K., *Komentarz do ustawy o postępowaniu w sprawach nieletnich*, Warsaw 2001;

Grzegorczyk T., *Kodeks postępowania karnego i ustawa o świadku koronnym. Komentarz*, Warsaw 2008;

Grześkowiak A., Wiak K., *Kodeks karny. Komentarz*, Ed. 7, Warsaw 2021;

Grześkowiak A., *Prawo nieletnich*, Warsaw 2020;

Kaczmarek T. (ed.), *System Prawa Karnego. Tom 5. Nauka o karze. Sądowy wymiar kary*, ed. 2, Warsaw 2017;

Konarska-Wrzosek V., *Prawny system postępowania z nieletnimi w Polsce*, Warsaw 2013;

Kosonoga J., 'Przesłuchanie pokrzywdzonego w trybie art. 185a k.p.k.,' *Prokuratura i Prawo* 2004/1;

Lachowski J., Konarska-Wrzosek V. (eds.), *Kodeks karny. Komentarz*, Warsaw 2019;

Paszek K., Pawelec K., 'Prawo małoletniego do odmowy złożenia zeznań,' *Prokuratura i Prawo* 2008/12;

Pohl Ł., 'Zakres odpowiedzialności karnej nieletniego w Kodeksie karnym z 1997 r. (o konieczności pilnej zmiany art. 10 § 2 k.k. – problem form popełnienia czynu zabronionego),' *Prawo w Działaniu* 2017/30;

Pohl Ł., 'Ponownie w sprawie zakresu odpowiedzialności karnej osoby nieletniej według Kodeksu karnego z 1997 r. (zagadnienie form popełnienia czynu zabronionego) – uwagi o metodzie rozwiązania problemu,' *Prawo w Działaniu* 2018/35;

Sakowicz A. in: Sakwicz A. (ed.), *Kodeks postępowania karnego. Komentarz*, Warsaw 2020;

Sowiński P., *Prawo świadka do odmowy zeznań w procesie karnym*, Warsaw 2004;

Stefański R.A., 'Zasady przesłuchiwania małoletniego,' *Wojskowy Przegląd Prawniczy* 2004/5;

Świerk P., 'Przesłuchanie małoletniego pokrzywdzonego na podstawie art. 185a k.p.k.,' *Prokuratura i Prawo* 2004/5;

Weijers I., Nuytiens A., Christiaens J., 'Transfer of Minors to the Criminal Court in Europe: Belgium and the Netherlandss' in: Junger-Tas J., Dünkel F. (eds.), *Reforming Juvenile Justice*, Dordrecht, Heidelberg, London, New York, Springer, 2009;

Więcek-Durańska A., 'Odpowiedzialność nieletnich za czyny z art. 10 § 2 k.k. przed sądem rodzinnym i przed sądem karnym – wybrane zagadnienia,' *Prawo w Działaniu* 2013/16;

Wójcicka B., 'Podstawy wyłączenia jawności rozprawy,' *Acta Universitatis Lodziensis. Folia Iuridica* 1988/35;

Zbrojewska M., Małolepszy A., 'Dziecko jako świadek w procesie karnym,' *Studia Gdańskie*, Vol. XXVIII;

Zoll A., W. Wróbel, *Polskie prawo karne. Część ogólna*, Warsaw 2014;

Decision of the Supreme Court of 17 Feb 1984, IV KZ 18/84, *Orzecznictwo Sądu Najwyższego Izby Karnej i Wojskowej* 1984/9–10, item 105;

Judgement of the Court of Appeal in Cracow of 9 Sep 1993, II AKr 105/93, *Krakowskie Zeszyty Sądowe* 1993/10, item 24;

Judgement of the Supreme Court of 9 Jul 1997, V KKN 217/97, *Prokuratura i Prawo. Suplement orzecznictwo* 1998/1, item 19;

Judgement of the Supreme Court of 3 Sep 1998, V KKN 301/98, *Biuletyn Informacji Prawnej* 1999/3, p. 26;

Judgement of the Supreme Court of 19 Feb 2003, I KZP 48/02, *Orzecznictwo Sądu Najwyższego Izby Karnej i Wojskowej* 2003/3–4;

Judgement of the Supreme Court of 28 Nov 2003, IV KK 14/03, *Krakowskie Zeszyty Sądowe* 2004/4, item 34;

Ruling of the Court of Appeal in Warsaw of 25 Feb 2004, II AKA 25/04, *Orzecznictwo Sądów Apelacyjnych*, 2005/2, item 13;

Judgement of the Court of Appeal in Cracow of 17 Jun 2004, II AKA 121/04, *Krakowskie Zeszyty Sądowe* 2004/8, item 55;

Judgement of the Court of Appeal in Cracow of 17 Mar 2005, II AKa 252/04, *Krakowskie Zeszyty Sądowe* 2005/3, item 37;

Decision of the Court of Appeal in Cracow of 22 Sep 2007, II AKz 200/07, *Krakowskie Zeszyty Sądowe* 2007/5, item 49;

Decision of the Supreme Court of 26 Nov 2008, IV KK 381/08, *Krakowskie Zeszyty Sądowe* 2009/7–8, item 43;

Decision of the Court of Appeal in Katowice of 26 Aug 2009, II AKz 566/09, LEX No. 553816;

Judgement of the Court of Appeal in Katowice of 13 Jan 2011, II AKa 443/10, *Orzecznitwo Sądu Apelacyjnego w Katowicach* 2011/1, item 3;

Judgement of the Court of Appeal in Białystok of 29 Apr 2014, II AKa 5/14, Legalis No. 1062552;

Judgement of the Court of Appeal in Katowice of 20 Oct 2016, II AKa 343/16, *Orzecznitwo Sądu Apelacyjnego w Katowicach* 2016/4, item 1;

Judgement of the Supreme Court of 19 Feb 2019, III KS 1/19, Legalis No. 1883228;

ECOSOC Resolution 2005/20, Guidelines on Justice in Matters involving Child Victims and Witnesses of Crime, the text available at: https://www.un.org/en/ecosoc/docs/2005/resolution%202005-20.pdf [access: Dec 31 2020];

Directive (EU) 2016/800 of the European Parliament and of the Council of 11 May 2016 on procedural safeguards for children who are suspects or accused persons in criminal proceedings;

Convention on the Rights of the Child of 20 Nov 1989, which has been ratified by Poland, Dz. U. (Journal of Laws) 1991 No. 120, item 526.

Chapter 4. Procedural Aspects of Participation of Juvenile Offenders in Criminal Proceedings: Selected Specific Institutions

Justyna Głębocka

Abstract: Discussing in more depth the cases of conducting criminal proceedings before the criminal court in the case of juvenile, this Chapter presents a number of polish legal institutions allowing to treat a juvenile offender differently than an adult accused. It indicates the rights of the juvenile's guardians in the criminal procedure, differences in the use of coercive and preventive measures and also consensual methods of terminating the proceeding conducted against juvenile, emphasising at the same time some of doubts, that may occur in the course of a trail. The impact of the appearance of a juvenile offender on the already initiated proceeding before law enforcement authorities was discussed in detail. Also, the European legislative solutions aimed at improving the legal situation of a juvenile against whom the criminal proceeding is conducted, were pointed out. Finally, some problems and doubts regarding the extinction of criminal liability in case of a juvenile and the inability to conduct the proceeding after he turns 21, were discussed.

Keywords: juvenile, Polish system of juvenile responsibility, formal representation of juvenile, European law on children and minors, international and European standards, consensual proposals, legal actions of juveniles, coercive measures versus juveniles, preventive measures versus juveniles.

1. General remarks: Formal representation of 'a juvenile' in criminal proceedings

The topic of representation of a juvenile in criminal proceedings is not only related to criminal law and procedure, but also to civil law.

Representation of a juvenile offender is regulated in Art. 76 CPP, under which if the accused is a juvenile, their legal representative or the person in whose custody they are, may undertake any act of legal procedure for their benefit, in particular, seek review, submit motions and appoint a defence lawyer.

First, a discussion is needed of the term 'juvenile,' as used in the provision referred to above, because it is not defined in CPP. Therefore, it is necessary to look for it in other parliamentary acts. It follows from the Polish substantive criminal law that a juvenile is a person who has not attained the age of 17 years. Considering the fact that a juvenile may be held criminally liable for specific acts, enumerated in the parliamentary act, after they attain the age of 15 years, it should be borne in mind that a juvenile in criminal proceedings is a person who committed a specific punishable act while being from 15 to 17 years old. Such a person is regarded as a 'juvenile' within the meaning of the Criminal Code, irrespective of when the criminal proceedings are taking place. A broader conceptual scope is provided by JJA, under which a 'juvenile' is a person who committed a punishable act after turning 13 years of age, but before attaining 17 years of age. However, irrespectively of the age range adopted in the parliamentary acts referred to above, especially its lower limit, the possibility of a juvenile being a passive party to criminal proceedings results from special regulations, specifying the grounds for holding a juvenile criminally liable, which were discussed more broadly in the previous Chapter. It should be stressed that in every case the adoption of the juvenile status in criminal proceedings is contingent on the age at the moment of the act; such an accused will remain to be regarded as a juvenile throughout the criminal proceedings against them.[1]

However, the notion of a 'juvenile' should be interpreted differently in respect of representation and participation in criminal proceedings by a statutory representative. The systemic and teleological interpretations indicate that after a juvenile has come of age within the meaning of the Civil Code (i.e., in principle, upon the attainment of the age of 18 years), despite the continued juvenile status, the right to represent them by their representative in legal proceedings expires under Art. 76 CCP.[2]

More parties are authorised to represent a juvenile accused in criminal proceedings than under civil law. Thus, apart from statutory representation within the meaning of family and guardianship law, which may be exercised by a parent,[3] a probation officer[4] or a guardian,[5] a juvenile may also be represented by a person under whose care the accused remains, a so-called 'actual guardian.'

---

1 D. Drajewicz, 'A commentary to Art. 76' in: D. Drajewicz (ed.), *Kodeks postępowania karnego. Komentarz. Art. 1–424*, Vol. I, Warsaw 2020, *passim*.

2 T. Grzegorczyk, *Kodeks Postępowania Karnego. Komentarz do art. 1–467*, Vol. I, Warsaw, 2014, p. 338.

3 See Art. 98 § 1 of the Family and Guardianship Code.

4 See Art. 99 § 1 of the Family and Guardianship Code.

5 See Art. 94 § 3 of the Family and Guardianship Code.

Without delving into formal and legal aspects associated with statutory representation, a few words about an actual guardian are in order. Unlike a representative of a juvenile aggrieved party, a representative of a juvenile accused party does not have to take care of the juvenile all the time; it is sufficient if their care is actual in nature – it may be transient, not comprehensive and indivisible.[6] The legislator does not require that guardianship should be formally established by a court or other competent authority; there is also no need to prove the legal right to act on the juvenile's behalf. The decision on whether an actual guardian may participate in criminal proceedings is made by the agency conducting the proceedings, which may carry out additional proceedings to take evidence to that end.

Where there are more persons authorised to represent a given juvenile, each of them retains their right, and the performance of a specific act by one of them does not preclude its performance by another authorised representative. In the event of a divergence of opinion between individual representatives of a juvenile, the one that is most in line with the interests of the accused is effective, which is determined by the family court under Art. 97 § 2 of the Family and Guardianship Code.

Attention should be drawn here to the fact that neither parent may represent an accused juvenile in criminal proceedings if the other parent has the status of the aggrieved party.[7] Under no circumstances may that also be a person who is a juvenile's co-defendant in the proceedings.[8]

A representative of a juvenile acting under Art. 76 CCP may perform any acts of legal procedure, however exclusively for the benefit of the accused. The directional character of the acts carried out by the representative remains concordant with the acts by the defence lawyer; the representative may also, just like the defence lawyer, select them autonomously and independently.[9] Thus, a representative may not perform any acts to the detriment of the accused, even if they have requested it themselves. Each act performed in violation of the obligation

---

6 In this context, see the Decision of the Supreme Court of 27 May 1997, V KKN 248/96, *Orzecznictwo Sądu Najwyższego Izny Karnej i Wojskowej* 1997/9–10, item 77.

7 See Art. 98 § 2(2) and § 3 of the Family and Guardianship Code, under which neither parent can represent their child in legal acts between the child and the other parent or their spouse, including in court proceedings or before another state authority.

8 T. Grzegorczyk, J. Tylman, *Polskie postępowanie karne*, ed. 8, Warsaw 2011, p. 367.

9 More broadly, see P. Mazur, W. Nowak, 'Sytuacja prawna opiekuna oskarżonego ubezwłasnowolnionego całkowicie w polskim postępowaniu karnym przed sądem pierwszej instancji,' *Ruch Prawniczy, Ekonomiczny i Socjologiczny* 2007/1, pp. 91–92.

should be regarded as ineffective, as if it had been undertaken by an unauthorised person[10] or as inadmissible,[11] and the criteria determining whether an act was performed for the benefit or to the detriment of the accused should be objective, not subjective.[12] In the proceedings, the party acts alongside, not instead of the accused. The granting of the right to represent to a legal representative or guardian does not deprive the juvenile of the right of autonomous participation in the criminal proceedings. The legislator assumes that because a juvenile may be held criminally liable, there are no grounds to limit them in their right of defence.[13]

Importantly, a representative of an accused acting under Art. 76 CCP is the only party authorised to establish a defence counsel for a juvenile who has not attained the age of 18 years. This is because the act is a civil law act and if it is undertaken by an accused who has turned 13 years old, for its validity it requires confirmation by their statutory representative.[14]

To finish off these deliberations, it is worth pointing out that the presence of a close person acting as a representative during proceedings involving a juvenile constitutes an important and relevant guarantee aspect, which strengthens the child's sense of security and their trust in judicial authorities. It enables the

---

10 See e.g. J. Bratoszewski in: J. Bratoszewski, L. Gardocki, Z. Gostyński, S.M. Przyjemski, R.A. Stefański, S. Zabłocki (eds.), *Kodeks postępowania karnego. Komentarz*, Vol. II, Warsaw 2003, p. 388; T. Grzegorczyk, J. Tylman, *Polskie postępowanie karne*, ed. 8, Warsaw 2011, p. 367.

11 In this manner: R. Koper [w:] K. Marszał, J. Zagrodnik (eds.), *Proces karny*, Warsaw 2013, p. 161. See also the judgment of the Supreme Court of 19 Mar 1997, IV KKN 326/96, *Orzecznictwo Sądu Najwyższego Izny Karnej i Wojskowej* 1997/7–8, item 64, judgment of the Court of Appeal in Katowice of 24 Mar 2005, II AKa 4/05, *Krakowskie Zeszyty Sądowe* 2005/7–8, item 139.

12 K. Witkowska, 'Strony procesowe i ich reprezentanci w postępowaniu przygotowawczym,' *Prokuratura i Prawo*, 2012/9, p. 114.

13 P. Czarnecki, 'Status nieletniego w postępowaniu w sprawach nieletnich,' *Przegląd Sądowy* 2016/9, p. 54.

14 In this manner: J. Gurgul, 'A gloss to the Supreme Court judgment of 28 Aug 2002, court file No. II KKN 368/00,' Prokuratura i Prawo 2004/ 4, p. 116. However, it is worth pointing out that A. Bojańczyk believes that from the primacy of will and procedural sovereignty, as well as the historical interpretation there follows the right of an accused juvenile to withdraw appointment of a defence lawyer effected by their statutory representative under Art. 76 CCP. See A. Bojańczyk, 'Czy nieletni lub ubezwłasnowolniony mandant może cofnąć upoważnienie do obrony udzielone przez przedstawiciela ustawowego lub osobę, pod której pieczą pozostaje?,' *Palestra* 2011/7–8, pp. 180–181.

juvenile's rights to be exercised more effectively and allows the juvenile to better understand their legal position.[15]

2. European measures improving the status of the juvenile offender

The standards of juvenile proceedings are not only set by acts of internal law, but also those of international law – Poland, being a member of the European Union and numerous international organisations that are fighting for the fundamental human rights, is a party to binding international acts. Under the Polish Constitution, a ratified international agreement becomes part of the country's legal order and is, in principle, applicable directly. What is more, if this follows from an agreement that establishes an international organisation and that has been ratified by the Republic of Poland, any laws made by such an organisation are directly applicable and take precedence in the event of a conflict with the country's parliamentary acts.[16] Apart from international agreements, of significance are also guidelines, instructions, indications or recommendations of specific international entities, which although have no direct binding effect, exert an influence as a peculiar model of behaviour and serve as an indication in the legislative process.[17]

It should be emphasised that, in respect of juveniles, first of all, the general legal acts that regulate human rights apply, followed by special regulations dealing explicitly with children's rights. The legal acts that regulate the fundamental human rights and children's rights call for a special, in-depth analysis, which goes beyond the framework of this publication;[18] here, the author would like to draw attention, above all, to documents with the European reach, which deal with children's rights, pointing out their principal assumptions within the context of conducting criminal proceedings against juvenile offenders.

---

15 Fore more on this, see T. Liefaard, U. Kilkelly, 'Child-Friendly Justice. Past, present and future' in: B. Goldson (ed.), *Juvenile Justice in Europe: past, present and future*, Routledge Taylor & Francis Group, 2019, p. 63.

16 See Art. 91 of the Constitution of the Republic of Poland.

17 P.J. Jaros, M. Michalak, *Prawa Dziecka. Dokumenty Organizacji Narodów Zjednoczonych*… p. 11.

18 On the development of international legislation with regard to children's rights see B. Goldson, 'Reading the Present and Mapping the Future(s) of Juvenile Justice in Europe. Complexities and Challenges' in: B. Goldson (ed.), *Juvenile Justice in Europe: past, present and future*, Routledge Taylor & Francis Group, 2019, pp. 210–214.

When analysing the European measures that set the standards of conduct in juvenile law cases, the following EU legal acts addressed to Poland should be listed: (1) Recommendation Rec(2003)20 of the Committee of Ministers of the Council of Europe to member states concerning new ways of dealing with juvenile delinquency and the role of juvenile justice of 24 September 2003,[19] (2) European Parliament resolution of 21 June 2007 on juvenile delinquency, the role of women, the family and society of 21 June 2007,[20] (3) Recommendation CM/Rec(2008)11 of the Committee of Ministers of the Council of Europe to member states on the European Rules for juvenile offenders subject to sanctions or measures of 5 November 2008 regarding penalties and alternative measures used in respect of juvenile offenders, referred to as the European Rules on juvenile offenders subject to sanctions or measures,[21] (4) Guidelines of the Committee of Ministers of the Council of Europe on child-friendly justice of 17 November 2010,[22] (5) Directive of the European Parliament and of the Council of 11 May

---

19 Recommendation Rec(2003)20 of the Committee of Ministers of the Council of Europe to member states concerning new ways of dealing with juvenile delinquency and the role of juvenile justice adopted by the Committee of Ministers on 24 September 2003 on 24 September 2003 at the 853th meeting of the Ministers' Deputies. P.J. Jaros, *Prawa Dziecka. Dokumenty Rady Europy*, Warsaw 2012, pp. 516–522; Available at: https://brpd.gov.pl/sites/default/files/prawa_dziecka_dokumenty_rady_europy.pdf [access Jan 9 2020]. More about this document: F. Dünkel, 'Young People's Rights: The Role of the Council of Europe' in: J. Junger-Tas, F. Dünkel (eds.) *Reforming Juvenile Justice*, Dordrecht-Heidelberg-London -New York, Springer, 2009, pp. 33–34.

20 European Parliament resolution of 21 June 2007 on juvenile delinquency, the role of women, the family and society (2007/2011(INI)), OJ C 146E, 12.6.2008, Vol. 51, pp. 344–353. Available at: https://www.europarl.europa.eu/sides/getDoc.do?pubRef=-//EP//TEXT+TA+P6-TA-2007-0283+0+DOC+XML+V0//EN [access: Jan 9 2020].

21 Recommendation CM/Rec(2008)11 of the Committee of Ministers of the Council of Europe to member states on the European Rules for juvenile offenders subject to sanctions or measures adopted by the Committee of Ministers on 5 November 2008 at the 1040th meeting of the Ministers' Deputies. P.J. Jaros, *Prawa Dziecka. Dokumenty Rady Europy*, Warsaw 2012, pp. 555–587, text available at: https://brpd.gov.pl/sites/default/files/prawa_dziecka_dokumenty_rady_europy.pdf [access: 9 Jan 2020]. More about this document: F. Dünkel, 'Young People's Rights: The Role of the Council of Europe…,' pp. 34–44.

22 Guidelines of the Committee of Ministers of the Council of Europe on child-friendly justice adopted by the Committee of Ministers on 17 November 2010 at the 1098th meeting of the Ministers' Deputies. Available at: https://rm.coe.int/CoERMPublicCommonSearchServices/DisplayDCTMContent?documentId=09000016806b7c62 [access Jan 9 2020].

2016 on procedural safeguards for children who are suspects or accused persons in criminal proceedings.[23]

All of the above legal acts indicate the need to ensure that juvenile offenders have rights that together will guarantee just and fair court proceedings, taking account of the child's welfare and their cognitive capabilities resulting from their age, as well as physical and mental development. Without going into a detailed discussion of all of the issues dealt with by the documents referred to above, attention should be drawn to the principal tendencies that should be implemented by the member states. The main focus should be placed on the Guidelines of the Committee of Ministers of the Council of Europe on child-friendly justice of 2010 (the Guidelines) and the Directive (EU) of the European Parliament and of the Council of 2016 on procedural safeguards for children who are suspects or accused persons in criminal proceedings, which should have been implemented by the member states by 11 June 2019 (Directive 2016/800). It should be stressed that Directive 2016/800 only refers directly to criminal procedure, not to any juvenile proceedings conducted by other courts. What is more, its performance should take account of the provisions of Directive 2013/48/EU of the European Parliament and of the Council of 22 October 2013 on the right of access to a lawyer in criminal proceedings and in European arrest warrant proceedings, and on the right to have a third party informed upon deprivation of liberty and to communicate with third persons and with consular authorities while deprived of liberty.[24]

Principally, the standards improving the juvenile offender's status come down to the need to ensure procedures that will take account of the child's welfare and strengthen their procedural position, which because of their age and psychophysical development may be more endangered than in the case of an adult. Naturally, no aspect of a juvenile offender's situation may be less favourable than

23 Directive (EU) 2016/800 of the European Parliament and of the Council of 11 May 2016 on procedural safeguards for children who are suspects or accused persons in criminal proceedings, OJ L 132, 21.5.2016, v. 59, p. 1–20. The deadline for the implementation of this Directive expired on 11 June 2019. Available at: https://eur-lex.europa.eu/legal-content/EN/TXT/?uri=CELEX%3A32016L0800 [access: Jan 9 2020].

24 Directive 2013/48/EU of the European Parliament and of the Council of 22 October 2013 on the right of access to a lawyer in criminal proceedings and in European arrest warrant proceedings, and on the right to have a third party informed upon deprivation of liberty and to communicate with third persons and with consular authorities while deprived of liberty (OJ L 294, 6.11.2013, p. 1). Available at: https://eur-lex.europa.eu/legal-content/EN/TXT/?uri=celex%3A32013L0048 [access: Jan 9 2020].

that of an adult offender, which means that the scope of the rights and guarantees should be at least the same. The EU authorities point out that a child should be perceived and treated as a person with full rights, and they should also be entitled to exercise all their rights in a manner that takes account of their ability to express their opinion, and the circumstances of the case. The juvenile offender must have the right to be heard and present their opinions, which also entails the need to make such statements adequately important, taking account of the child's maturity and any communication problems, so that the child's participation in the proceedings and their use of their rights should have a genuine and real impact on the proceedings.

Above all, attention is drawn to the need to safeguard the right to information; with respect to juveniles, it is important that all instructions and information should be conveyed intelligibly and in a manner adapted to the age and the ability to comprehend.[25] To this end, it is suggested that persons working in the justice system, but also lawyers and legal advisers, should have an opportunity to undergo appropriate training in this respect.[26] The need is also stressed to prepare special information leaflets and educational material that might help juveniles to understand their procedural position, as well as their rights and duties.[27] Within this context, special emphasis is placed on the right to formal defence, including defence at the cost to the state, imposing on the member states the obligation to grant obligatory defence to a juvenile offender. Professional assistance should be available from the first possible moment,[28] and the defence lawyer's participation

---

25 The European Court of Human Rights in Strasbourg points out that: "However, 'effective participation' in this context presupposes that the accused has a broad understanding of the nature of the trial process and of what is at stake for him or her, including the significance of any penalty which may be imposed." See ECHR judgment of 15 June 2004 on S.C. v. UK, appl. No. 60958/00, item 29.

26 This issue is also pointed out with reference to the American justice system. See R.D. Hodge, 'Assessment in Juvenile Justice Systems' in: R.D. Hodge, N.G. Guerra, P. Boxer (eds.), *Treating the Juvenile Offender,* New York, London, The Guilford Press, 2008, p. 71.

27 Critically about the actual exercise of the right to information and suggestions regarding its genuine implementation see J. Doek, 'The UN Convention on the Rights of the Child' in: J. Junger-Tas, F. Dünkel (eds.), *Reforming Juvenile Justice*, Dordrecht-Heidelberg-London-New York, Springer, 2009, pp. 25 ff.

28 Art. 6(3) of Directive 2016/800 provides that the ability to take advantage of a lawyer's assistance should be ensured from whichever of the following points in time is the earliest: a) before they are questioned by the police or by another law enforcement or judicial authority; b) upon the carrying out by investigating or other competent authorities

should be effective; first of all, the child should be able to meet with the lawyer in private and be ensured confidentiality of their communication. The lawyer's participation must comply with procedures under national law, provided that such procedures do not prejudice the effective exercise or essence of the right concerned. There is some doubt as to the conformity with Directive (EU) 2016/800 and Directive 2013/48/EU of the provisions of the Polish CCP which allow activities to be carried out despite the defence lawyer's excused absence or which do not provide for the lawyer's obligatory participation in each successive activity of the suspect's interrogation, and not only the first one.[29]

As regards juvenile offenders, it is also necessary to ensure, as part of the proceedings, that they are able to inform their parents or guardians about the conducted proceedings and that such adults are able to accompany their child during any acts. In principle, both parents and children should receive information from law enforcement authorities directly. This should mean in practice that notifying the parents or guardians should not replace notifying the child.

Criminal proceedings against a child should always be treated as a matter of urgency and with due diligence. Court hearings involving children should be adapted to children's tempo and their ability to concentrate: regular breaks should be scheduled and questionings should not last too long. In order to facilitate children's participation to the fullest extent of their cognitive ability and to support their emotional balance, efforts should be made to limit any disturbance of court hearings to the minimum. In principle, hearings should be held in the absence of the public with a view to protecting the privacy of children.

Directive 2016/800 also stresses that each child should be subject to an individual assessment, taking into account their personality and maturity, their economic, social and family background, and the possible need to treat a given child

---

of an investigative or other evidence-gathering act in accordance with point (c) of paragraph 4; c) without undue delay after deprivation of liberty; d) where they have been summoned to appear before a court having jurisdiction in criminal matters, in due time before they appear before that court.

29 For more, see Opinion of the Criminal Law Codification Committee on the implementation in Polish law of Directive 2013/48/EU of the European Parliament and of the Council of 22 October 2013 on the right of access to a lawyer in criminal proceedings and in European arrest warrant proceedings, and on the right to have a third party informed upon deprivation of liberty and to communicate with third persons and with consular authorities while deprived of liberty, pp. 3–4. The Opinion is available at: https://www.gov.pl/web/sprawiedliwosc/opinie-komisji-kodyfikacyjnej-prawa-karnego [access: Jan 14 2020].

in a special way.[30] The use of solutions alternative to a trial should be encouraged, such as mediation, preventive programmes (instead of court mechanisms) and alternative dispute resolution methods, in every situation in which they are conducive to the child's welfare.[31] The implementation of measures connected with deprivation of liberty should ensure special treatment for juveniles, consisting, for instance, in separating them from adults, ensuring their physical and mental development, the ability to learn and train, and the effective and regular exercise of their right to family life.

As can be seen, the standards referred to in the directives and recommendations of the European Union authorities are mainly designed to make sure that juvenile offenders have the right to a fair trial, with the right of the defence being its most important aspect. National legislation should not only take account of the minimum standards provided for accused adults, but above all create conditions that allow genuine and real exercise of the right of defence by juveniles, adapted to their age and psychophysical development. In this context, some specific gaps – both legislative and practical – can be observed.[32]

3. Application of coercive and preventive measures

Subjecting a juvenile offender to the regime of a criminal court means that the provisions of criminal procedure will be applied to them. Thus, as a rule, law

---

30 The need to take account of differences in assessing juveniles' behaviour is stressed particularly in psychology and psychiatry, indicating that because of various stages of development of children and youth aged 10–20 years, it is extremely important to maintain a developmental perspective when evaluating antisocial behaviours. See R.D. Hodge, 'Assessment in Juvenile…,' p. 60.

31 At present, it is emphasised that 'The introduction of educational sanctions involving restitution, social training or educational courses, community service orders and other so-called intermediate sanctions is indicative of a strong movement for more constructive and educational response to juvenile delinquency.' See F. Dünkel, I. Pruin, 'Community Sanctions and the Sanctioning Practice in Juvenile Justice Systems in Europe' in: J. Junger-Tas, F. Dünkel (eds.), *Reforming Juvenile Justice*, Dordrecht-Heidelberg-London-New York, Springer, 2009, p 184.

32 In this context, see K. Wiśniewska, M. Wolny, 'Mój prawnik Moje prawa. Dostęp dzieci do pomocy obrońcy' in: *Raport Krajowy – Polska*, Warsaw 2017, pp. 20 ff. On obstacles in implementing soft law regarding juveniles by the member states see E. Bell, 'Juvenile (in)Justice and Neoliberal Austerity in the European Union' in: B. Goldson (ed.), Juvenile Justice in Europe: past, present and future, Routledge Taylor & Francis Group 2019, pp. 136–141.

enforcement authorities may apply to a juvenile coercive measures, including preventive measures, on the terms set out in CCP. However, similarly to procedural safeguards, also in the case of coercive measures, the legislator provides for the use of certain institutions known to JJA in respect of a specific group of juvenile offenders against whom criminal proceedings are conducted. This means that in specific situations the criminal court is obliged to apply some of the JJA provisions accordingly, not those of CCP.

With respect to the coercive measures under JJA, there are the following three groups of juvenile offenders: 1) juveniles who committed a punishable act referred to in Art. 10 § 2 CrC in respect of whom proceedings were instituted before they reached the age of 18 years, 2) juvenile offenders who remain in a close relationship with an act of an adult person, 3) the other juvenile offenders in respect of whom criminal proceedings are conducted. Differences as to the use of coercive measures are provided for with respect to the first and second group. In any other situation, it is possible to apply towards a juvenile offender any of the full range of the coercive measures known to the Code of Criminal Procedure, in particular apprehension and any of the available preventive measures, including provisional detention.

As it follows from Art. 18 § 2(1) JJA, a juvenile offender in respect of whom proceedings are conducted under Art. 10 § 2 CrC that were instituted before the juvenile attained the age of 18 years should be treated like a juvenile subject to proceedings under JJA. Thus, a juvenile should be subject to apprehension under JJA, and any deprivation of liberty should principally consist in detention at a police youth home, and possibly a subsequent placement at a youth detention centre. Provisional detention may only be applied if placement in a youth detention centre would be insufficient, which explicitly establishes the primacy of educational and corrective institutions over the coercive measures applicable to adults. However, not all grounds for apprehension provided for in JJA are applicable to the criminal process.

In the course of criminal proceedings, a juvenile may be apprehended under JJA with a view to placing them in a police youth home, if this is necessary because of the circumstances of the case (Art. 32g § 1 JJA), or where an order has been issued to place a juvenile in a police youth home for a time necessary to perform specified procedural acts, not exceeding 48 hours (Art. 32h § 3 JJA). Apprehension is thus an act aimed at placing a juvenile in a police youth home.

The grounds for apprehending a juvenile is a reasonable suspicion that they committed a punishable act, as well as the existence of a well-founded fear that they may go into hiding or try to cover up traces of the act, or when the juvenile's identity cannot be determined. In every situation, the apprehension needs to be justified with the need to apply the measure, because of the circumstances of the case. The grounds for apprehending and placing a juvenile in a police youth home are in fact the same as the ground for placing them in a youth detention centre, the difference being that placement in such a centre may only be effected in connection with a suspicion of commission of a punishable act constituting a crime or a fiscal crime, with the exception of a petty crime; however, it should be pointed out that in practice in respect of petty crimes, usually placement in a police youth home will not be justified with the need because of the circumstances of the case.[33]

The rights of an apprehended juvenile are similar to those of a juvenile apprehended under CCP. Immediately after apprehension, the juvenile should be informed about the reasons for the apprehension, their right to receive assistance from a lawyer, to remain silent or not to answer specific questions. and to complain about acts that violate their rights. A juvenile should be questioned promptly. At their request, they should be allowed to contact their parent or guardian or a lawyer. Irrespective of the above, the juvenile's parents or guardian should be informed of the apprehension and instructed about the rights held by the apprehended juvenile. In respect of the questioning the respective provisions regarding the questioning of juveniles should be applied; above all, it should be conducted in the presence of the parents or a guardian.

The duration of the detention has been regulated similarly to detention in the criminal process. Promptly after the apprehension, not later than during 24 hours, the police are obliged to inform a family court about the apprehension. Within 48 hours of the notification, the family court is obliged to issue and announce to the juvenile its order to place them in a youth detention centre.[34]

The grounds for placing a child in a youth detention centre are set out in Art. 27 JJA. In principle, the possibility to place a juvenile in a youth detention centre is connected with the obligatory prerequisites of procedural nature, which

---

33 A. Haak-Trzuskowska, H. Haak, *Ustawa o postępowaniu w sprawach nieletnich. Komentarz*, Warsaw 2015, comments to Art. 32g JJA, *passim*.

34 Under Art. 18 § 2(1) JJA, in criminal proceedings the provisional measures detailed in Art. 26 JJA, i.e. a provisional placement in a youth educational centre, with a professional foster family or in a treatment facility, do not apply. This means that a family court may at best place the juvenile taken into custody at a youth detention centre. Also, the family court may not use the preventive measures known to CPP, because the only party entitled to use them during preparatory proceedings is the prosecutor, and during the trial – the criminal court, which might order such a measure to be used after the case has been referred to it.

are similar to those for the application of provisional detention, because they are related to safeguarding the proper procedure by preventing or making it difficult for the juvenile to go into hiding or to cover up traces, or when it is impossible to determine their identity. The measure may be used if there are grounds for ordering the measure in the form of placing the juvenile in a corrective facility, which is a solution analogous to provisional detention, which is, in principle, not used if it can be expected that in the final decision the accused will not be sentenced to the penalty of an absolute deprivation of liberty.[35]

What is important is that JJA provides for the possibility of placement in a youth detention centre, which is a temporary measure of coercion used during proceedings, before a legally valid confirmation that a punishable act was performed, also exclusively on the basis that the juvenile is accused of the commission of a serious punishable act. In such a situation, there is no need for the existence of the procedural prerequisites in the form of the going of the offender into hiding, his covering up of traces of the act or where the juvenile's identity cannot be determined. The institution is analogous to that referred to in Art. 258 § 2 CCP. Attention should be drawn to the fact that it is regarded in the doctrine as controversial and the possibility of using it as an independent basis for provisional detention has been discussed in the literature on many occasions.[36]

It should be underlined that the scope of cases that allow an offender to be placed in a youth detention centre without the need for the existence of any additional prerequisites of a genuinely procedural nature corresponds to the scope of the cases which might involve criminal liability before a criminal court. This means that in all criminal proceedings in which a juvenile is tried under Art. 18 § 2(1) JJA and in which the JJA provisions in question apply, placement in a

35 Art. 259 § 2 CCP: 'Provisional detention shall not be applied when the facts of the case permit presumption that the court will sentence the accused to the penalty of deprivation of liberty with conditional suspension of its execution, or to a milder penalty, or that the term of provisional detention would exceed the expected sentence of deprivation of liberty without a conditional suspension.' Art. 259 § 3 CCP: 'Provisional detention cannot be imposed, if the offence carries the penalty of deprivation of liberty not exceeding one year.'

36 See e.g. M. Warchoł, 'Domniemania przy tymczasowym aresztowaniu' in: T. Grzegorczyk (ed.), *Funkcje procesu karnego. Księga jubileuszowa Profesora Janusza Tylmana*, Warsaw 2011, p. 277; M. Drewicz, 'A gloss to the Supreme Court judgment of 19 Jan 2012, court file No. I KZP 18/11,' *Czasopismo Prawa Karnego i Nauk Penalnych* 2012/3, pp. 165 ff.; S. Waltoś, P. Hofmański, *Proces karny. Zarys systemu*, Warsaw 2008, p. 430.

youth detention centre is possible exclusively on the grounds that the juvenile is accused of a serious punishable act referred to in Art. 27 § 2 JJA.

Considering the observations made so far, it is important to note the interpretational doubts regarding the competence of individual authorities to use during criminal proceedings the coercive measures listed in JJA. It seems obvious that until a case is referred to criminal procedural law enforcement agencies, the decision as to whether a given measure under JJA should be applied is up to a family court. A problem arises where a case is subject to the regime of criminal procedure. The disposition of Art. 18 § 2(1d) JJA requires that specific provisions of the Juvenile Justice Act should be used, including those regulating apprehension, placement in a police youth home or a youth detention centre, respectively. Without delving into dogmatic considerations about appropriate application of legal regulations,[37] it should be emphasised that such legislative practice creates specific interpretational issues. As regards the regulations in question, reasonable doubt might arise as to who may apply a specific coercive measure in respect of a juvenile subject to criminal procedure. The literal interpretation of the regulations indicates the exclusive competence of the family court to order that a juvenile be placed in a police youth home under Art. 32h § 1(2) JJA (for the time needed to perform specific procedural acts, not longer than 48 hours) or in a youth detention centre. However, subjecting a case to the regime of criminal procedure might indicate that the decision as to the application of a measure limiting the freedom of the accused should be made by a criminal court, especially considering the fact that direct application of the JJA provisions results in an unclear situation as to the jurisdiction of the police and the prosecutor. The substantive scope of the cases subject to criminal procedure indicates the mandatory character of the form of the investigation conducted by a prosecutor, while the regulations governing the institution of apprehension, placement in a police youth home or youth detention centre grant the police the right to refer the case to a family court. The direct application of the regulations in criminal procedure would mean that the prosecutor, who conducts preparatory proceedings, may not motion for the use of a specific coercive measure in respect of a

37 See e.g. J. Nowacki, '"Odpowiednie" stosowanie przepisów prawa,' *Państwo i Prawo* 1964/3, p. 374; Z. Siwik, '"Odpowiednie" stosowanie przepisów kodeksu karnego w prawie karnym skarbowym,' *Przegląd Prawa i Administracji*, Vol. XXIII, Wroclaw 1987, p. 97; M. Hauser, 'Odpowiednie stosowanie przepisów prawa – uwagi porządkujące,' *Przegląd Prawa i Administracji*, Vol. LXV, Wroclaw 2005, p. 151; L. Morawski, *Wykładnia w orzecznictwie sądów. Komentarz*, Toruń 2002, p. 300.

juvenile, although this right is held by the police, which is subordinate to the prosecutor. The lack of appropriate regulations that would resolve this issue indicates that it must be assumed that a family court is the only competent authority to exercise control over a juvenile's apprehension and to decide whether they should be placed in a police youth home under Art. 32h § 1(2) or in a youth detention centre.

It should also be stressed that JJA – as opposed to CCP – does not grant the right of interlocutory appeal against apprehension, only indicating that its application is supervised by the family court. However, it should be emphasised that the regulations governing the supervisory powers of the family court in this respect are not applicable in criminal proceedings. Moreover, also the disposition enabling an appeal to be lodged against the decision to place a juvenile in a youth detention centre specified in Art. 29 JJA is not listed among the regulations that have an appropriate application in criminal procedure, which indicates that perhaps also this procedural act may not be subject to appeal in the situations in question. It should be assumed that only placement in a police youth home by a family court for the time needed to perform specific procedural acts, not exceeding 48 hours, may be appealed against where criminal proceedings are conducted against a juvenile. This phenomenon should be evaluated critically and appropriate changes should be proposed to be made to shape the position of a juvenile offender analogously to that of an adult detained or accused in respect of whom specific coercive measures are used.

Furthermore, as regards competence, also the provisions regarding the application procedure for provisional detention under Art. 18 § 2(1e) JJA, i.e. when placement in a youth detention centre is insufficient, are unclear. Where criminal proceedings are conducted by a prosecutor after the case has been transferred by a family court, the situation is obvious and does not call for any in-depth analysis. However, the issue is debatable with regard to a situation where, under Art. 18 § 2(1a) JJA preparatory proceedings are conducted under the Code of Criminal Procedure by a family court. If a case is referred by a prosecutor to a family court, the prosecutor becomes a party to it instead of the investigating authority. At the same time, under Art. 250 CCP, the only party authorised to motion for provisional detention is the prosecutor. In the doctrine, it is disputable who may use the measure in such a situation – the family court[38] conducting the

38 E.g. P. Górecki, S. Stachowiak, *Ustawa o postępowaniu w sprawach nieletnich*, ed. 5, Warsaw 2010, pp. 79 ff.

preparatory proceedings or the criminal court.[39] The general rules connected with the application of preventive measures favour the granting of this power only to the criminal court, which means that the possibility of using provisional detention in respect of a juvenile where placing them in a youth detention centre would be insufficient is only possible when the family court admitted the expediency of conducting criminal procedure against the juvenile and referred the case to be tried by a prosecutor in the form of an investigation.

Certain institutions known to JJA as regards coercive measures may be used also to the second group of juvenile offenders against whom a criminal proceeding is conducted – juvenile offenders who remain in a close relationship with an act of an adult person. In the case of conducting the investigation pursuant to Art. 16 § 2 JJA, the family court may apply, at the prosecutor's request, the measures referred to in Art. 26 JJA (provisional supervision of a youth organization or other social organization or workplace, supervision of a probation officer or other trustworthy person, provisional placement in a youth educational centre or professional foster family, application of therapeutic and educational measures: placement in a psychiatric hospital or other appropriate treatment facility, in a youth care centre or nursing home) and Art. 27 JJA (youth detention centre). In this case, however, the legislator directly regulated the competences of individual bodies – the prosecutor and the family court, leaving no broader ambiguities in this respect. Summarising, the differences provided for in the Juvenile Justice Act as regards coercive measures only regard juveniles who committed the punishable act detailed in Art. 10 § 2 CrC and whose proceedings commenced before they reached the age of 18 years and juveniles against whom the criminal procedure is conducted under Art. 16 § 2 JJA. However, the use of the explicitly mentioned institutions from the JJA does not exclude the possibility of applying preventive measures regulated in the Code of Criminal Procedure (e.g. police supervision or a ban on leaving the country), since in both cases indicated above, the provisions of the criminal procedure apply first. In every other case where a juvenile offender is a passive party to criminal proceedings there apply the general rules of using coercive measures known to the Code of Criminal Procedure. CPP does not introduce any differences in this respect due to the criterion of age.

39 In this manner: e.g. W. Grzeszczyk, 'Właściwość sądu do stosowania tymczasowego aresztowania wobec nieletniego,' *Prokuratura i Prawo* 2002/7–8, pp. 137 ff.

4. Influence of a juvenile offender on the course of the proceedings

In principle, the commission of a punishable act by a juvenile results in the need to apply in respect of them the provisions of the Juvenile Justice Act, which regulates the procedure to be used before the family court in such a situation. Where the perpetrator of a punishable act was caught in the commission of the offence or immediately afterwards, the evaluation of the situation is simple and does not call for any closer analysis. The police – because usually it is the police who are notified of the event – apprehend the juvenile and hand them over to a family court, which institutes proceedings in respect of the juvenile under Art. 21 JJA. More consideration is needed in situations, where criminal proceedings are in progress and during their course circumstances come to light that indicate that the act was performed by a juvenile.

Under Art. 303 CCP, if there is good reason to suspect that an offence has been committed, an order to institute an investigation is issued – either *ex officio* or upon receiving a notice of an offence – in which the act in question is described and its legal classification is set out. The evidentiary process carried out in the course of the investigation are aimed, among other things, at discovering the offender. If, as a result of the process, it turns out that the offender is juvenile, the prosecution agencies, in principle in most cases, are obliged to refer the case to a family court to be conducted under the provisions of the Juvenile Justice Act. However, during the proceedings circumstances may come to light constituting a reason for the case to be conducted by a criminal court under CCP.

If a conducted investigation regards one of the crimes listed in Art. 10 § 2 CrC, the juvenile case is not transferred to a criminal court automatically. If it is discovered that the offender is juvenile, the prosecutor is obliged to refer the case to a family court, which then determines – as the only authority competent in this respect – if there are grounds for holding the juvenile criminally liable under the same rules as adult offenders. The family court, on the basis of the evidential material collected so far and its own preparatory proceedings, may make one of the following decisions: 1) to conduct the case under JJA (despite determination of the commission of an act under Art. 10 § 2 CrC, no other necessary prerequisites are met or a further evidentiary process indicates that the act, after all, is not an act under Art. 10 § 2 CrC), 2) to discontinue the proceedings (e.g. because the juvenile did not commit the act or another negative procedural prerequisite under

Art. 17 CCP is met[40]), 3) to refer the case to a prosecutor for an investigation in respect of the juvenile to be conducted. In the latter case, the prosecutor again conducts proceedings in respect of the case, and subsequently, after performing the necessary investigative activities, makes a decision to discontinue the proceedings or to file an indictment, or to refer the case back to the family court, if during the proceedings circumstances indicating the lack of any grounds for holding the juvenile criminally liable are disclosed.

The situation is different where during proceedings instituted in respect of any other punishable act it comes to light that a juvenile committed it together with an adult. In such a situation, it is the prosecutor who autonomously evaluates the circumstances of the case and makes a decision under Art. 16 JJA whether to transfer the juvenile's case to a family court or there exist grounds under CCP for a joint conduct of the preparatory proceedings for the juvenile and the adult together. Subsequently, after concluding the investigation or inquiry, the prosecutor refers the juvenile's case to a family court, files an indictment in the adult's case, or – if joint proceedings are necessary – refers the case with an indictment to the court having the jurisdiction in accordance with the provisions of CCP, which then tries the juvenile's case under JJA. In such a situation, the proceedings are governed by the provisions of criminal procedure, while the JJA regulations of the substantive law nature are binding.

The third prerequisite indicating the need to use the provisions of the Code of Criminal Procedure concerns cases in respect of acts committed by juveniles where proceedings were commenced after they attained the age of 18 years (Art. 18 § 1(2) 2 JJA). If during the preparatory proceedings law enforcement authorities establish that at the moment of the commission of the punishable act the offender was juvenile, they continue the proceedings under the provisions of CCP. In such a case, the family court has no competence. Two issues should be pointed out. Firstly, as regards the prerequisite of the reaching of the age of 18 years by the juvenile, the deciding factor is the moment when charges are brought against them – the conduct of proceedings at the *in rem* stage has no importance in this respect. Secondly, just like in the previously analysed situation, the provision of Art. 18 § 1(2) JJA has an exclusively procedural character and does not constitute any grounds for applying any measures or penalties in

40 The application of the provisions of criminal procedure results from the adoption of the grounds for holding a juvenile criminally liable under Art. 10 § 2 CrC – in such a situation the family court is obliged to conduct preparatory proceedings under CCP (Art. 18 § 2(1a) JJA).

respect of the juvenile under criminal legislation; the only applicable measures are those provided for in JJA, i.e. the educational and corrective measures set out in Art. 6 JJA, which may, however, be used only until the offender reaches the age of 21 years. After that date, the only decision that the criminal court may make is to discontinue the proceedings under Art. 17 § 1(11) CCP.[41]

Most interpretational difficulties regard an evaluation of cases in which the prerequisites from Art. 16 § 2 and Art. 18 § 1(1) JJA concur. Where during criminal proceedings there comes to light that a juvenile committed an act under Art. 10 § 2 CrC, however not on their own, but in a close relationship with an adult, the important question arises as to the prosecutor's competence to decide on the further fate of the proceedings with regard to the juvenile. The complications in this respect result, above all, from the reference in Art. 18 § 2(1)(a) JJA to respective application of Art. 16 JJA. Views have been expressed in the literature and judicial decisions that in such a procedural configuration the prosecutor may autonomously – without the need to refer the case to a family court – decide to conduct proceedings against the juvenile, and then on the need to try it together with the case of the adult and to file an indictment with a court in respect of the two offenders.[42] This interpretation is said to be supported principally by procedural economy. It is worth mentioning, however, that the doctrine also includes opposite views. Referring to the systemic and teleological interpretations, as well as the safeguarding nature of the provision of Art. 32k JJA granting the right of interlocutory appeal against the decision of the family court to refer the case to a prosecutor, attention is drawn to the fact that in such a procedural arrangement the prosecutor should not acquire the right of interlocutory appeal in the case of a juvenile regarding an act under Art. 10 § 2 CrC, without the family court.[43] Because of the existing interpretational problems, it would be reasonable for the legislator to define the rights of the prosecutor and the family court in the situation in question.

---

41 More on this further on in this Chapter, in the section on the expiry of criminal responsibility.

42 See K. Gromek, *Komentarz do ustawy o postępowaniu w sprawach nieletnich*, Warsaw 2001, p. 202; A. Gaberle, 'O wykładni i stosowaniu art. 16 u.p.n., czyli jak nie należy konstruować przepisów prawnych' in: P. Hofmański, S. Waltoś (eds.), *W kręgu prawa nieletnich. Księga pamiątkowa ku czci Profesor Marianny Korcyl-Wolskiej*, Warsaw 2009, p. 276. See also the judgment of the Supreme Court of 14 Dec 2007, IV KK 285/07, Legalis No. 162856.

43 A. Herzog, 'Prokurator a odpowiedzialność karna nieletnich,' *Prokuratura i Prawo* 2017/9, p. 143.

5. Consensual proposals: abbreviation of proceedings

Based on the Polish Code of Criminal Procedure, certain consensual manners of finishing criminal proceedings may be defined, which in fact come down to the passing of a judgment of conviction and the imposing of penalties or punitive measures agreed with the accused, without conducting the evidentiary process. The institutions that allow the shortening of proceedings consensually include: 1) the prosecutor's motion to pass a judgment of conviction under Art. 335 § 1 CCP, 2) the prosecutor's motion to pass a judgment of conviction under Art. 335 § 2 CCP, 3) a motion by the accused to pass a judgment of conviction without conducting evidentiary proceedings under Art. 338a CCP, 4) a motion by the accused to pass a judgment of conviction without conducting evidentiary proceedings, a so-called 'voluntary submission to punishment' under Art. 387 CPP. The Juvenile Justice Act lacks any analogous legal solutions that would allow proceedings conducted by a family court in respect of a juvenile to be shortened, which seems to be an obvious consequence of the goals of such proceedings (education of the juvenile, their welfare and not holding them liable), their subject (collection of data about the juvenile, their educational, health and living conditions), as well as the nature of the educational and corrective measures that may be imposed.

The issue that, however, calls for a more detailed analysis regards the possibility of making use of the consensual modes referred to in the Code of Criminal Procedure in respect of juveniles against whom criminal proceedings are conducted on the basis of the above-mentioned exceptions under Art. 16 § 2, Art. 18 § 1(1) and Art. 18 § 1(2) JJA.

In the situations listed above, the subjecting of a juvenile to the regime of criminal procedure is consistently connected with the need to apply the provisions of the Code of Criminal Procedure during proceedings. As mentioned a number of times already, only the exception referred to in Art. 18 § 1(1) JJA has substantive law results in the form of the need to apply the provisions of the Criminal Code. The other cases have a procedural nature and do not affect the applicability of the substantive law provisions of the Juvenile Justice Act. This means, with regard to the issues in question, that in the event of the exception referred to in Art. 16 § 2 and 18 §(1)(2) JJA the criminal court trying the case rules on the basis of the JJA provisions about educational and corrective measures. The literature points out that the above results in the inability to make use of the consensual procedures, because the precisely formulated prerequisites for their admissibility refer to the passing of a judgment of conviction and imposition of a specific penalty or punitive measure, the ordering of forfeiture or a compensatory measure, i.e. the penalties or measures known to criminal law and criminal liability. The arguments in the literature in favour of the possibility of using the consensual procedures in respect of juveniles were based on the no-longer-binding provision of Art. 13 JJA, which enabled a corrective measure to be 'replaced' with a penalty or a punitive measure.[44] At present, because of the lack of any grounds for imposing on a juvenile a penalty instead of an educational or corrective measure in the situation at hand, any deliberations on the subject should be regarded as immaterial. Thus, the view should be divided that the duty to impose on a juvenile one of the measures referred to in the Juvenile Justice Act precludes the possibility of applying any of the consensual procedures. There are also some other problems that may raise doubts as to the possibility of applying a consensual procedure in respect of a juvenile, especially with regard to the exception under Art. 18 § 1(1) JJA, which has a substantive law character and enables the regime of criminal liability to be used in respect of such an offender.

Some of the doctrine representatives believe that the reason for the prohibition to make use of consensual conclusion of proceedings against juveniles is a defect in a declaration of will made by a juvenile, because of their lack of discernment resulting from their psychophysical development connected with age, also where they have a defence lawyer, as the will in respect of the expression of the consent to the conclusion of the proceedings without conducting evidentiary proceedings and to the imposition of a specific penalty or punitive measure must be expressed by the accused personally.[45] According to this view, in every case where proceedings are conducted in respect of a person who has not come of age and does not have a full capacity to enter into legal transactions it is not possible to effectively make a declaration of will with regard to a consensual conclusion of proceedings. It should, however, be pointed out that on many occasions in judicial practice a juvenile with no capacity to enter into legal translations has been regarded as having the right to make effective declarations of will during criminal proceedings; a mention should be made, for instance, of the right to refuse to testify or to answer a question asked as part of a questioning. Although the concerns as to the real ability of a juvenile to assess the legal

44 Cf. A. Choroszewski, P. Starzyński, 'Konsensualne zakończenie postępowania w przedmiocie odpowiedzialności prawnej nieletniego' in: C. Kulesza (ed.), *Ocena funkcjonowania porozumień procesowych w praktyce wymiaru sprawiedliwości*, Warsaw 2009, p. 293.

45 In this manner: A. Choroszewski, P. Starzyński, 'Konsensualne zakończenie postępowania…,' p. 290.

implications of the declarations of will made by them should be shared, there are no distinct legal grounds for refusing to grant such a right to an accused juvenile. Consequently, it should be accepted that a declaration of will expressing the consent to a conviction without conducting a trial or a motion to pass a judgment of conviction without conducting evidentiary proceedings may be submitted by any accused, including a juvenile one without a full capacity to enter into legal transactions within the meaning of the provisions of the Civil Code.[46] Because of the above concerns, the court, when making a decision on the motion for a consensual procedure should evaluate the psychophysical development of the accused within the context of their capability to make the decision consciously.[47]

However, irrespective of the above considerations regarding the capability to enter into legal transactions, attention should be drawn to the aspect of admissibility of holding a juvenile criminally liable under Art. 10 § 2 CrC. As follows from the said provision, the possibility of treating a juvenile who has committed one of the acts listed in it and who has reached the age of 15 years, but not 17 years, as an adult, in respect of whom the Criminal Code applies, is connected with an evaluation of the circumstances of the case and the level of development of the offender, their characteristics and personal conditions, in particular the effectiveness to date of the educational or corrective measures imposed on them. Such an evaluation is performed, first of all, by a family court, which decides on referring the case to a prosecutor under Art. 32k § 1 JJA. This, however, does not release the criminal court from the duty to carry out its own assessment of the

---

46 See D. Nowocień, 'Instytucja "dobrowolnego poddania się karze" w kodeksie postępowania karnego z 1997 r.' in: L. Bogunia (ed.), *Nowa kodyfikacja prawa karnego*, Vol. VII, Wroclaw 2001, p. 220; see also R.A. Stefański, 'Skazanie bez rozprawy w znowelizowanym kodeksie postępowania karnego,' *Prokuratura i Prawo* 2003/6, p. 24; see also S. Steinborn, *Porozumienia w polskim procesie karnym. Skazanie bez rozprawy i dobrowolne poddanie się odpowiedzialności karnej*, Cracow, Wolters Kluwer 2005, p. 242.

47 A similar attitude is expressed as to the possibility of making such declarations of will by the accused in respect of whom there are met the conditions for obligatory defence referred to in Art. 79 § 1(2) (the accused is deaf, mute or blind), Art. 79 § 1(3) (there is good reason to doubt whether their capability to recognise the meaning of the act or to control their behaviour during the commission of the act was not disabled or severely limited) and Art. 79 § 1(4) (there is good reason to doubt whether their condition of mental health enables their participation in the proceedings or their defence of the case autonomously and sensibly). See R. Koper, 'Zgoda oskarżonego jako warunek skazania bez rozprawy,' *Palestra* 2001/5–6, pp. 12 ff.

existence of the prerequisites for the application in respect of such a juvenile of the regime of criminal liability. Within this context, an important question arises of whether a criminal court is able to make such an assessment without conducting evidentiary proceedings where one of the consensual procedures is used. In the opinion of the author, the answer to this question is positive. The assumption that in such a situation it is not possible not to conduct a trial would be contrary to the assumptions constituting the basis for consensual procedures.

In every situation, the shortening of the proceedings by carrying out a consensual procedure requires satisfaction of the prerequisite for the absence of doubt as to the circumstance of the commission of the crime by the accused and their guilt; furthermore, the attitude of the accused must indicate that the goals of the proceedings will be achieved despite not carrying out further acts, including the conduct of full court proceedings. These are prerequisites regarding circumstances whose establishment calls for specific evidentiary acts to be performed. A view that the court is unable to recognise without conducting a trial that such circumstances exist would negate the sense and expediency of the existence of the consensual procedures. In the same way, it must be accepted that the assessment of the prerequisites for a juvenile's criminal liability under Art. 10 § 2 CrC should be conducted on the same principles as the other grounds for passing a judgment of conviction within a consensual procedure. If the evidential material collected during the preparatory proceedings indicated the absence of any doubt as to the circumstances of the commission of the crime, the guilt and attitude of the accused, as well as the grounds for holding the juvenile criminally liable, there are no legal obstacles to the application of a consensual procedure also in the case of a juvenile. However, it must be stressed that in the Polish procedural criminal law each time the grounds for convicting the accused without conducting court proceedings in whole are assessed by an independent court, which in the event of entertaining any doubt as to the satisfaction of the conditions for a juvenile's criminal liability should not grant the motion for passing a sentence of conviction in a consensual procedure and should carry out full evidentiary proceedings aimed at dispelling all doubts. If this was not done during the preparatory proceedings, the court should in particular take evidence that will allow it to evaluate whether the circumstances of the case and the degree of the offender's development, their characteristics and personal conditions favour the holding of the juvenile criminally liable.

Considering the above, it should be concluded that where a juvenile offender is subject to the regime of the Code of Criminal Procedure, it is only in the case of the prerequisite under Art. 18 § 1(1) JJA, i.e. relating to the liability under Art. 10 § 2 CrC, that it is possible to use one of the available consensual procedures in respect of an accused juvenile, and because of the serious nature of the acts detailed to in the provision, a consensual procedure may only be applied in a few situations. The other prerequisites are procedural in nature and do not enable a penalty or another measure to be imposed on a juvenile under the substantive criminal regulations, which determines the inadmissibility of the use of a consensual procedure in such situations.

6. Selected issues related to the extinction of criminal liability

The Juvenile Justice Act does not on its own regulate the issue of a statute of limitations or extinction of criminal liability. This solution seems to comply with the general assumptions and grounds for proceedings in children's cases, based on the concept of the protective treatment of juveniles. Under Art. 3 § 1 JJA, in a juvenile case one should focus on the juvenile's welfare, aiming to achieve beneficial changes in their personality and behaviour, and to procure proper fulfilment by their parents or guardian of their obligations towards the juvenile, while taking account of the social interests. JJA is oriented on the protection against demoralisation, not on the holding of juveniles liable.[48] At the same time, the legislator avoids phrases typical of criminal liability, such as: "proceedings against,' 'liability,' 'sentences' or 'penalty.' It also seems appropriate that a corrective measure should not be regarded as a penalty or a kind of penalty.[49] However, despite some distinct differences in the treatment and conduct towards juveniles, JJA is undoubtedly on the borderline between substantive criminal law, fiscal criminal law and the law of misdemeanours.

Under Art. 14 JJA, in cases of juveniles who committed a punishable act, the provisions of the Criminal Code, the Fiscal Criminal Code and the Code of Misdemeanours apply accordingly, provided they are not inconsistent with the Juvenile Justice Act. On this basis, the Supreme Court pointed out that in respect of punishable acts the provisions of CrC regarding the statute of limitations for such acts apply, taking account of the time when they were committed and the designated periods of limitations.[50] This means that in respect of punishable acts

---

48 T. Bojarski in: T. Bojarski, E. Kruk, E. Skrętowicz (eds.), *Postępowanie w sprawach nieletnich. Komentarz,* Warsaw 2016, p. 25.

49 Judgment of the Supreme Court of 18 Sep 1984, III KR 237/84, *Orzecznictwo Sądu Najwyższego. Wydawnictwo Prokuratury Generalnej* 1985/2, item 29.

50 Judgment of the Supreme Court of 12 Jan 2011, III KK 260/19, Legalis No. 417449; also see judgment of the Supreme Court of 24 May 2012, V KK 49/12, Legalis No. 492220.

committed by juveniles the possibility of conducting proceedings in respect of them under JJA expires upon the expiry of the periods set out in the Criminal Code. Some comments are due, however, on the applicability of JJA, also where criminal proceedings are conducted in respect of a juvenile under the Code of Criminal Procedure.

Both Art. 18 and Art. 16 § 2 JJA have a procedural character,[51] which means that the hearing of a case by a court having territorial and substantive jurisdiction in accordance with the Code of Criminal Procedure does not release such court from taking account of the substantive criminal provisions of the Juvenile Justice Act. The wording of the provisions indicate unambiguously that in particular Art. 2, Art. 3 and Art. 5 JJA should be applied. The consequence of this is the applicability in such cases of educational and corrective measures. A penalty may only be imposed in exceptional situations, in the cases provided for in the Act, if other measures are not able to ensure the juvenile's social rehabilitation. Such a statutory exception is, above all, constituted by Art. 10 § 2 CrC, which provides for the possibility of holding a juvenile criminally liable, and thus imposing a penalty on them, if such a juvenile has attained the age of 15 years, but has not reached the age of 17 years and has committed one of the crimes listed in the provision.[52] In such cases, the imposed penalty may not exceed two thirds of the upper limit of the statutory threat connected with the crime that the offender is ascribed with. Furthermore, the court may also apply an extraordinary mitigation of the penalty. In such situations criminal liability expires on the general terms governing the periods of limitations in the Polish substantive criminal law.

In other cases, a juvenile is held criminally liable under the provisions of a procedural nature, not a substantive nature, which means that in respect of such a juvenile the educational and corrective measures specified in the Juvenile Justice Act should be applied. Thus, both in the case of a juvenile who committed a punishable act after attaining the age of 13 years and before reaching the age of 17 years and their proceedings were initiated after they turned 18 years, and in the case of a juvenile who committed a punishable act in a close relationship

---

51 See judgment of the Supreme Court of 3 Sep 1998, V KKN 301/98, Biul. Inf. Pr. 1999 No. 3, p. 26; judgment of the Supreme Court of 12 Oct 2010, II KK 86/10, *Orzecznitwo Sądu Najwyższego w Sprawach Karnych*, 2010/1, item 1917; judgment of the Supreme Court of 21 Sep 2011, III KK 234/11, Legalis No. 457366.

52 The second exception that enables a penalty to be imposed on a juvenile is provided for in Art. 94 JJA. Because the provision does not relate to juveniles in respect of whom criminal proceedings under CCP are conducted, this issue has been omitted here. More on the provision of Art. 94 JJA see the Chapter regarding JJA.

with an adult the application of the provisions of criminal procedure does not release the criminal court from the obligation to use the provisions on educational and corrective measures. Consequently, in such a situation, the final ruling confirming the commission of a punishable act by the juvenile is connected with the imposition of a specific educational or corrective measure, not a penalty or punitive measure known to the Criminal Code. At the same time, the adopted solution impacts the extinction of criminal liability.

The exercise of an educational or corrective measure is only possible in respect of a person on whom such a measure has been imposed, however no longer than until they reach the age of 21 years. JJA, when defining the notion of a 'juvenile,' refers to the age at which a given act was committed by the juvenile, and the very fact that the person has reached an age exceeding the limits designated in Art. 1 JJA does not deprive the person of the attribute 'juvenile' with reference to the proceedings in respect of the act in question. This means that if a person committed a punishable act in the period after they attained the age of 13 years and before they attained the age of 17 years, they will have the status of a juvenile, irrespective of when the proceedings in respect of them were commenced and when the final ruling is issued. The wording of Art. 1 § 1(3) 3 JJA indicates that if a court makes its ruling when the juvenile is at least 21 years old, it may not impose on them any of the educational or corrective measures provided for in the Act. In such a case there are no grounds for conducting proceedings in respect of the juvenile, because not only is the application of the measures specified in JJA inexpedient, but also impossible. Determination of the lack of any grounds for court intervention leads to the conclusion that any proceedings instituted in connection with the commission of a punishable act by a juvenile should (at any of its stages) be discontinued.[53] With regard to the rules of criminal procedure, discontinuation is effected in such a situation as a consequence of the occurrence of the negative procedural prerequisite referred to in Art. 17 § 1(11) CCP, and where proceedings are conducted by a family court – under Art. 21 § 2 JJA.

Until the coming into effect of the Act of 30 Aug 2013, there was in force Art. 13 JJA which enabled a penalty to be imposed on a juvenile, with an obligatory extraordinary mitigation if the court decided that the imposition of a corrective measure would no longer be expedient, where in respect of a juvenile who committed a punishable act as a juvenile, but had attained the age of 18 years by the moment of the ruling, there existed grounds for ordering the

---

53 Decision of the Supreme Court of 24 May 2005, I KZP 12/05, *Orzecznictwo Sądu Najwyższego Izby Karnej i Wojskowej* 2005/7–8, item 58, p. 1.

offender to be placed in a correctional facility. Disregarding any detailed deliberations concerning major controversy in respect of the said provision,[54] it is worth mentioning that it was frequently applied by courts where because of the attainment by the juvenile of the age of 21 years at the time of the ruling, it was not possible to impose on them any educational or corrective measure. Such a solution allowed for conducting proceedings and subsequently making a ruling as to the substance of a case and not leaving the perpetrator of a punishable act without any legal consequences, until the expiry of the statute of limitations. The provision of Art. 13 JJA was used both by family courts conducting proceedings under JJA, and by criminal courts conducting criminal proceedings against juveniles in the designated exceptional situations. At present, because of the derogation of Art. 13 JJA, there are no legal grounds for imposing on a juvenile any measures or penalties if by the time of the ruling they have reached the age of 21 years. This results in the need to discontinue proceedings in respect of a case, which in fact should be regarded as the extinction of the juvenile.

References

Bojańczyk A., 'Czy nieletni lub ubezwłasnowolniony mandant może cofnąć upoważnienie do obrony udzielone przez przedstawiciela ustawowego lub osobę, pod której pieczą pozostaje?,' *Palestra* 2011/7–8;

Bell E., 'Juvenile' in: Goldson B. (ed.), *Justice and Neoliberal Austerity in the European Union. Juvenile Justice in Europe: past, present and future*, Routledge Taylor & Francis Group 2019;

Bojarski T. in: Bojarski T, Kruk E., Skrętowicz E. (eds.), *Postępowanie w sprawach nieletnich. Komentarz*, Warsaw 2016;

Bratoszewski J in: J. Bratoszewski, L. Gardocki, Z. Gostyński, S.M. Przyjemski, R.A. Stefański, S. Zabłocki (eds.), *Kodeks postępowania karnego. Komentarz.* Vol. II, Warsaw 2003;

Choroszewski A., Starzyński P., 'Konsensualne zakończenie postępowania w przedmiocie odpowiedzialności prawnej nieletniego' in: Kulesza C. (ed.), *Ocena funkcjonowania porozumień procesowych w praktyce wymiaru sprawiedliwości*, Warsaw 2009;

---

54 See B. Stańdo-Kawecka, '"Zamiana" umieszczenia nieletniego w zakładzie poprawczym na karę. Uwagi na tle uchwały Sądu Najwyższego z 24 maja 2005 r.,' *Czasopismo Prawa Karnego i Nauk Penalnych* 2006/1, pp. 235 ff. and the literature listed there. See also V. Konarska-Wrzosek, *Prawny system postępowania z nieletnimi w Polsce*, Warsaw 2013, pp. 137–138 and the literature listed there.

Czarnecki P., 'Status nieletniego w postępowaniu w sprawach nieletnich,' *Przegląd Sądowy* 2016/9;

Doek J, 'The UN Convention on the Rights of the Child' in: Junger-Tas J., Dünkel F. (eds.), *Reforming Juvenile Justice*, Dordrecht-Heidelberg-London-New York, Springer 2009;

Drajewicz D. in: Drajewicz D. (ed.), *Kodeks postępowania karnego. Vol. I. Komentarz. Art. 1–424,* Warsaw 2020;

Drewicz M., 'A gloss to the Supreme Court judgment of 19 Jan 2012, court file No. I KZP 18/11,' *Czasopismo Prawa Karnego i Nauk Penalnych* 2012/3;

Dünkel F., 'Young People's Rights: The Role of the Council of Europe' in: Junger-Tas J., Dünkel F. (eds.), *Reforming Juvenile Justice*, Dordrecht-Heidelberg-London-New York, Springer 2009;

Dünkel F., Pruin I., 'Community Sanctions and the Sanctioning Practice in Juvenile Justice Systems in Europe' in: Junger-Tas J., Dünkel F. (eds.), *Reforming Juvenile Justice*, Dordrecht-Heidelberg-London-New York, Springer 2009;

Gaberle A., 'O wykładni i stosowaniu art. 16 u.p.n., czyli jak nie należy konstruować przepisów prawnych' in: Hofmański P. Waltoś S., *W kręgu prawa nieletnich. Księga pamiątkowa ku czci Profesor Marianny Korcyl-Wolskiej*, Warsaw 2009;

Goldson B., 'Reading the Present and Mapping the Future(s) of Juvenile Justice in Europe. Complexities and Challenges' in: Goldson B. (ed.), *Juvenile Justice in Europe: past, present and future*, Routledge Taylor & Francis Group 2019;

Górecki P., Stachowiak S., *Ustawa o postępowaniu w sprawach nieletnich. Komentarz,* edition 5, Warsaw 2010;

Gromek K., *Komentarz do ustawy o postępowaniu w sprawach nieletnich*, Warsaw 2001;

Grzegorczyk T., *Kodeks Postępowania Karnego*. Vol. 1, Warsaw 2014;

Grzegorczyk T., Tylman J., *Polskie postępowanie karne*, ed. 8, Warsaw 2011;

Grzeszczyk W., 'Właściwość sądu do stosowania tymczasowego aresztowania wobec nieletniego,' *Prokuratura i Prawo* 2002/7–8;

Gurgul J., 'A gloss to the Supreme Court judgment of 28 Aug 2002, court file No. II KKN 368/00,' *Prokuratura i Prawo* 2004/4;

Haak-Trzuskowska A., Haak H., *Ustawa o postępowaniu w sprawach nieletnich. Komentarz,* Warsaw 2015;

Hauser M., 'Odpowiednie stosowanie przepisów prawa – uwagi porządkujące,' *Przegląd Prawa i Administracji* Vol. LXV, Wroclaw 2005;

Herzog A., 'Prokurator a odpowiedzialność karna nieletnich,' *Prokuratura i Prawo* 2017/9;

Hodge R.D., 'Assessment in Juvenile Justice Systems' in: R.D. Hodge, N.G. Guerra, P. Boxer (eds.), *Treating the Juvenile Offender*, New York-London, The Guilford Press 2008;

Jaros P.J., Michalak M., *Prawa Dziecka. Dokumenty Organizacji Narodów Zjednoczonych*, Warsaw 2015;

Konarska-Wrzosek V., *Prawny system postępowania z nieletnimi w Polsce*, Warsaw 2013;

Koper R., 'Zgoda oskarżonego jako warunek skazania bez rozprawy,' *Palestra* 2001 5–6;

Liefaard T., Kilkelly U., 'Child-Friendly Justice. Past, present and future' in: B. Goldson (ed.), *Juvenile Justice in Europe: past, present and future*, Routledge Taylor & Francis Group 2019;

Marszał K., Zagrodnik J. (eds.), Koper R., *Proces karny*, Warsaw 2013;

Mazur P., Nowak W., 'Sytuacja prawna opiekuna oskarżonego ubezwłasnowolnionego całkowicie w polskim postępowaniu karnym przed sądem pierwszej instancji,' *Ruch Prawniczy Ekonomiczny i Socjologiczny* 2007/1;

Morawski L., *Wykładnia w orzecznictwie sądów. Komentarz*, Toruń 2002;

Nowacki J., '"Odpowiednie" stosowanie przepisów prawa,' Państwo i Prawo 1964/3;

Nowocień D., 'Instytucja "dobrowolnego poddania się karze" w kodeksie postępowania karnego z 1997 r.' in: L. Bogunia (ed.), *Nowa kodyfikacja prawa karnego*,Vol. VII, Wrocław 2001;

Siwik Z., '"Odpowiednie" stosowanie przepisów kodeksu karnego w prawie karnym skarbowym,' *Przegląd Prawa i Administracji*, Vol. XXIII, Wrocław 1987;

Stańdo-Kawecka B., '"Zamiana" umieszczenia nieletniego w zakładzie poprawczym na karę. Uwagi na tle uchwały Sądu Najwyższego z 24 maja 2005 r.,' *Czasopismo Prawa Karnego i Nauk Penalnych* 2006/1;

Stefański R.A., 'Skazanie bez rozprawy w znowelizowanym kodeksie postępowania karnego,' *Prokuratura i Prawo* 2003/6;

Steinborn S., *Porozumienia w polskim procesie karnym. Skazanie bez rozprawy i dobrowolne poddanie się odpowiedzialności karnej*, Cracow, Wolters Kluwer 2005;

Waltoś S., Hofmański P., *Proces karny. Zarys systemu*, Warsaw 2008;

Warchoł M., 'Domniemania przy tymczasowym aresztowaniu' in: T. Grzegorczyk (ed.), *Funkcje procesu karnego. Księga jubileuszowa Profesora Janusza Tylmana*, Warsaw 2011;

Wiśniewska K., Wolny M., 'Mój prawnik Moje prawa. Dostęp dzieci do pomocy obrońcy' in: *Raport Krajowy – Polska,* Warsaw 2017;

Witkowska K., 'Strony procesowe i ich reprezentanci w postępowaniu przygotowawczym,' *Prokuratura i Prawo* 2012/9;

Opinion of the Criminal Law Codification Committee on the implementation in Polish law of Directive 2013/48/EU of the European Parliament and of the Council of 22 October 2013 on the right of access to a lawyer in criminal proceedings and in European arrest warrant proceedings, and on the right to have a third party informed upon deprivation of liberty and to communicate with third persons and with consular authorities while deprived of liberty, available at: https://www.gov.pl/web/sprawiedliwosc/opinie-komisji-kodyfikacyjnej-prawa-karnego [access: Jan 14 2020].

Polish jurisprudence

Judgment of the Supreme Court of 18 Sep 1984, III KR 237/84, *Orzcznictwo Sądu Najwyższego. Wydawnictwo Prokuratury Generalnej* 1985/2, item 29;

Judgment of the Supreme Court of 19 Mar 1997, IV KKN 326/96, *Orzecznictwo Sądu Najwyższego Izby Karnej i Wojskowej* 1997/7–8, item 64;

Decision of the Supreme Court of 27 May 1997, V KKN 248/96, *Orzecznictwo Sądu Najwyższego Izby Karnej i Wojskowej* 1997/9–10, item 77;

Judgment of the Supreme Court of 3 Sep 1998, V KKN 301/98, *Biuletyn Informacji Prawnej* 1999/3;

Decision of the Supreme Court of 24 May 2005, I KZP 12/05, *Orzecznictwo Sądu Najwyższego Izby Karnej i Wojskowej* 2005/7–8, item 58;

Judgment of the Court of Appeal in Katowice of 24 Mar 2005, II AKa 4/05, *Krakowskie Zeszyty Sądowe* 2005/7–8, item 139;

Judgment of the Supreme Court of 14 Dec 2007, IV KK 285/07, Legalis No. 162856;

Judgment of the Supreme Court of 12 Oct 2010, II KK 86/10, *Orzecznictwo Sądu Najwyższego w Sprawach Karnych* 2010/1, item 1917;

Judgment of the Supreme Court of 12 Jan 2011, III KK 260/19, Legalis No. 417449;

Judgment of the Supreme Court of 21 Sep 2011, III KK 234/11, Legalis No. 457366;

Judgment of the Supreme Court of 24 May 2012, V KK 49/12, Legalis No. 492220.

European legal acts

Guidelines of the Committee of Ministers of the Council of Europe on child-friendly justice adopted by the Committee of Ministers on 17 November 2010 at the 1098th meeting of the Ministers' Deputies. Text available at: https://rm.coe.int/CoERMPublicCommonSearchServices/DisplayDCTMContent?documentId=09000016806b7c62 [access: Jan 9 2020];

Directive (EU) 2016/800 of the European Parliament and of the Council of 11 May 2016 on procedural safeguards for children who are suspects or accused persons in criminal proceedings, OJ L 132, 21.5.2016, v. 59, pp. 1–20. The deadline for the implementation of this Directive expired on 11 June 2019. Text available at: https://eur-lex.europa.eu/legal-content/EN/TXT/?uri=CELEX%3A32016L0800 [access: Jan 9 2020];

Directive 2013/48/EU of the European Parliament and of the Council of 22 October 2013 on the right of access to a lawyer in criminal proceedings and in European arrest warrant proceedings, and on the right to have a third party informed upon deprivation of liberty and to communicate with third persons and with consular authorities while deprived of liberty (OJ L 294, 6.11.2013, p. 1). Text available at: https://eur-lex.europa.eu/legal-content/EN/TXT/?uri=celex%3A32013L0048 [access: Jan 9 2020];

The European Court of Human Rights in Strasbourg points out that: 'However, "effective participation" in this context presupposes that the accused has a broad understanding of the nature of the trial process and of what is at stake for him or her, including the significance of any penalty which may be imposed.' See ECHR judgment of 15 June 2004 on S.C. v. UK, appl. No. 60958/00, item 29;

Recommendation Rec(2003)20 of the Committee of Ministers of the Council of Europe to member states concerning new ways of dealing with juvenile delinquency and the role of juvenile justice adopted by the Committee of Ministers on 24 September 2003 on 24 September 2003 at the 853th meeting of the Ministers' Deputies. P.J. Jaros, Prawa Dziecka. Dokumenty Rady Europy [The rights of the child. The Council of Europe documents], Warsaw 2012, pp. 516–522, text available at: https://brpd.gov.pl/sites/default/files/prawa_dziecka_dokumenty_rady_europy.pdf [access: Jan 9 2020];

European Parliament resolution of 21 June 2007 on juvenile delinquency, the role of women, the family and society (2007/2011(INI)), OJ C 146E, 12.6.2008, v. 51, p. 344–353. Text available at: https://www.europarl.europa.eu/sides/getDoc.do?pubRef=-//EP//TEXT+TA+P6-TA-2007-0283+0+DOC+XML+V0//EN [access: Jan 9 2020];

Recommendation CM/Rec(2008)11 of the Committee of Ministers of the Council of Europe to member states on the European Rules for juvenile offenders subject to sanctions or measures adopted by the Committee of Ministers on 5 November 2008 at the 1040th meeting of the Ministers' Deputies. P.J. Jaros, Prawa Dziecka. Dokumenty Rady Europy [The rights of the child.

The Council of Europe documents], Warsaw 2012, pp. 555–587, text available at: https://brpd.gov.pl/sites/default/files/prawa_dziecka_dokumenty_rady_europy.pdf [access: Jan. 9 2020].

Part III. Juvenile Delinquency: Comparative Perspective – Brazil

Denise Casanova Villela, Rodrigo da Silva Brandalise

Abstract: This part aims to present the Brazilian socio-educational system under the current Brazilian legislation and doctrine, addressing the historical aspects and the transition from the basic principles of minors' codes to the current doctrine relying on the Children and Adolescents Act. In this part, the socio-educational system is discussed, concerning both extrajudicial and judicial proceedings related to offences committed by adolescents aged 12 to 18 years and the review of socio-educational measures provided for in Brazilian law is undertaken.

Keywords: socio-educational system, National Brazilian Social-Educational Service System (SINASE), socio-educational measures, offence, adolescent offender, restorative justice.

1. General remarks

The Brazilian Child and Adolescent Act (hereinafter ECA) was first enacted in 1990,[1] as a result of the provisions of the 1988 Federal Constitution of Brazil (hereinafter referred to as CF/88), and the fact that the country became a signatory of the International Convention on the Rights of Children and Adolescents of 1989.[2]

The set of regulations mentioned above has guided the national socio-educational system for an extended period. However, the Brazilian National Socio-Educational Service System Act (hereinafter referred to as the SINASE

1 Law No. 8,069, of July 13, 1990. Children and Adolescents Act (ECA).

2 The Brazilian Government ratified the said Convention on September 24, 1990, and it entered into force in Brazil on October 23, 1990. Thus, the Convention started to be enforced and complied with as entirely as it contains, from the publication of the Decree of the Presidency of the Republic which so determined (Decree No. 17.943-A, of October 12, 1927. Consolidates the assistance and protection laws for minors, arts. 1 and 2).

Act)[3] was enacted in 2012. It amended the ECA and regulated measures aimed at the adolescents who committed offences.

An *offense* is any conduct defined as a crime or criminal offense in the ECA, Article 103. Under the law mentioned above, those who are not subject to indictment due to their age (under eighteen years old – ECA, Art. 104[4]), when they commit an offense, suffer the consequences according to the youth protection law.

However, it must be explained that when a child under 12 commits an offense, only the protection measures provided for in the ECA, Article 101, will be applied. The socio-educational measures themselves, which will be explained below, apply to *adolescents*, who are persons aged between 12 and 18 years.[5] The application and enforcement of the measures can be extended to persons up to 21 years old, according to the general rule in Article 2, a single clause of the ECA.

This system adopted by Brazilian legislation has as its primary goal the re-education of the adolescent who committed an offence without neglecting the offender's responsibility for the offense. However, it does not pursue this goal with a punitive intention, but keeping in mind the child and adolescent's peculiar condition as people whose development has not finished yet (ECA, Art. 6).

Based on these premises, the study addresses the incidence of offences and respective proceedings in the extrajudicial and judicial domains, as well as the socio-educational measures provided for by law, including historical digressions, and the transition from the Codes of Minors to the Child and Adolescent Act.

The methodology of the present study consists of qualitative exploratory, bibliographic and documentary research, in which books, articles, jurisprudence, public documents, and legislation relevant to the subject were used. Such a perspective provides a historical overview of the construction of the Brazilian socio-educational system and shows the principles and parameters that guide its applicability. In the same line, the study delves into the analysis of the procedure for investigating offences and discusses the socio-educational measures imposed by the legislation in force in Brazil.

---

3 Law No. 12,594 / 2012, of January 18, 2012. Established the National Social and Educational Service System – SINASE.

4 Despite simplifying the concept of *offense*, the ECA reiterated the criminal non-liability due to the age of the offender (A. Chaves, *Comentários ao Estatuto da Criança e do Adolescente*, 2 ed., São Paulo, LTr, 1997, p. 467).

5 The age limits that define who is a *child* and a *teenager* are given in the ECA, Art. 2.

2. The historical conception of the socio-educational system in Brazil

Historically, in Brazil, the legislation and policy on child and adolescent assistance has the Federal Constitution of Brazil, promulgated in 1988, as its turning point. Prior to the promulgation of the Constitution, the expression 'juvenile offenders,' currently called adolescent offenders, was marked by the concept of a 'minor,' which translated into the maintenance of order and the doctrine of an irregular situation, according to the foundation specified by the Codes of Minors of 1927 and 1979.

Specifically, concerning the first Code, which was enacted by Decree No. 17.943-A/1927,[6] M. F. Carmo and L. A. Bezerra observe that children and adolescents were *objects* of state intervention. Thus, the idea of institutionalization and the deprivation of minors of their liberty were considered ways to eliminate risks. Under this law, there was no proposal to strengthen the family and develop children and adolescents, which situation, they claim, still exists today. Therefore, minors were removed from their family nuclei, classified as *abandoned* or *delinquents* and were sent to institutions to ensure their social stabilization and education.[7]

The authors further explain that:

> (...) the Code of Minors of 1927 decreed that children under 14 years would have their degree of awareness assessed. For adolescents between 14 and 18 years, serious crimes would imply their admission to particular institutions. The mitigating age would range from 18 to 21 years.[8]

The second Code of Minors (published in 1979,[9] it amended the previous Code) reinforced the irregular situation ideology,[10] mainly by linking crime to poverty.

---

6 Decree No. 17.943-A, of October 12, 1927. **Consolidates the assistance and protection laws for minors.**

7 M.F. Carmo, L. A. Bezerra. 'Eixo 1: Medidas Socioeducativos: Aspectos Históricos e Conceituais' in: *Brasil, Ministério da Mulher, da Família e dos Direitos Humanos. Secretaria Nacional dos Direitos da Criança e do Adolescente, Escola Nacional de Socioeducação. Sistema Nacional de Atendimento Socioeducativo*, SINASE, pp. 11–13.

8 M.F. Carmo, L. A. Bezerra. 'Eixo 1...,' p. 13.

9 Law No. 6,697, of October 10, 1979. **Establishes the Code of Minors.**

10 Art. 2: For the purposes of this Code the minor is considered to be in an irregular situation: I – deprived of essential conditions for their subsistence, health and mandatory education, even if eventually, due to: a) absence, action or omission of the parents or guardian; b) it is impossible for the parents or guardian to provide them; II – victim of ill-treatment or immoderate punishment imposed by the parent or guardian; III – in

Regarding this Code, the authoritative juristic literature says that it had an even more *stigmatizing* and *discriminatory nature*, affecting poor children and adolescents, mostly black, with no schooling, who had been abandoned and were prone to delinquency. The National Foundation for Social Welfare of Minors (FUNABEM) and the State Foundation of Welfare for Minors (FEBEM) pursued the service policy of admission into institutions. Accordingly, judicial branch decisions were highly centralized with little or no opportunity to be heard for children and adolescents in an irregular situation.[11]

There was evidence of non-participatory situation of children and adolescents, with authority and repression prevailing, via centralized public policies and the reinforcement of their civil incapacitation. The judicial branch was omnipotent helped by the involvement of the police that focused on repression.[12]

A doctrine known as the *irregular situation doctrine* was effective at that time. The 1979 Code of Minors was thus seen as a criminal law for minors with a false protective system notion. There was no protection for children and adolescents but the application of effective penal sanctions.[13]

After the promulgation of the CF/88, the ECA was enacted to make Arts. 227[14] and 228[15] of the constitutional text operational. The ECA contains precepts and regulations aimed at ensuring integral protection[16] and fundamental

---

moral danger, due to: a) being, in a costumary way, in an environment contrary to good customs; b) exploitation in an activity contrary to good customs; IV – deprived of representation or legal assistance, due to the eventual absence of parents or guardians; V– With misconduct, due to serious family or community inadequacy; VI – perpetrator of a criminal offense.

11 MF. Carmo, L. A. Bezerra. 'Eixo 1...,' p. 15.

12 J.R.P. Veronese, A. V. Custódio, *Direito da Criança e do Adolescente: para concurso de juiz do trabalho*, São Paulo, Edipro, 2011, p. 26.

13 E.R. Meneses, *Medidas Socioeducativas: Uma reflexão jurídico-pedagógica*, 1st ed., Porto Alegre, Livraria do Advogado, 2008, p. 57.

14 CF/88, art. 227: It is the duty of the family, society and the State to guarantee to children, adolescents and young people, with absolute priority, the right to life, health, food, education, leisure, professionalization, culture, dignity, respect, freedom and family and community coexistence, in addition to putting them safe from all forms of negligence, discrimination, exploitation, violence, cruelty and oppression.

15 CF/88, art. 228: Minors under the age of eighteen are subject to criminal responsibility, subject to the rules of special legislation.

16 'What does "comprehensive protection" mean? It means the complete support, not only of the child and adolescent, from the material and spiritual point of view, but also their safeguard from the moment of conception, ensuring care for the health and

guarantees to children and adolescents, in contrast to the past of control and social exclusion, supported now, basically, by integral protection expressly provided for in the law.[17] The ECA, as it was conceived, grants broad rights and guarantees to the Brazilian child and adolescent population, who deserve to be given absolute priority by family, society, and the State.[18]

The adoption of this new perception in contrast to the old paradigm of the irregular situation established under the Code of Minors resulted in substantial changes to the rules that regulated compliance with socio-educational measures in Brazil. Technically, this new perception briefly envisaged the social inclusion of an offending adolescent who would no longer be considered a mere individual subject to State intervention.

According to W. D. Liberati, this constitutional change transformed children and adolescents into developing people, making them subjects with rights, despite their social condition. This new status forced the legislator to respect this in the provisions that gave rise to the ECA. Therefore, the idea that they were carriers of rights, but did not have the effective exercise thereof due to their little social inclusion and the complete submission to the family power,[19] as already described herein,[20] changed.

---

well-being of the pregnant woman and the family, natural or substitute of which you will be a part' (A. Chaves, *Comentários…*, p. 51).

17 ECA, art. 3: Children and adolescents enjoy all the fundamental rights inherent to the human person, without prejudice to *full protection* covered by this Law, assuring them, by law or by other means, of all opportunities and facilities, in order to provide them with physical, mental, moral, spiritual and social development, under conditions of freedom and dignity.

18 ECA, art. 4: It is the duty of the family, the community, society in general and the government to ensure, with *absolute priority*, the realization of the rights relating to life, health, food, education, sport, leisure, professionalization, culture, dignity, respect, freedom and family, and community coexistence.

19 W.D. Liberati, *Processo Penal Juvenil: a garantia da legalidade na execução de medida socioeducativa*, São Paulo, Malheiros, 2006, p. 27.

20 Brazil has also recognized the text of the Convention on the Rights of the Child that also establishes such consideration (art. 2, paragraph 1): 'States Parties shall respect the rights set out in this Convention and ensure that they are applied to each child subject to their jurisdiction, without distinction whatsoever, regardless of race, color, sex, language, belief, political or other opinion, national origin, ethnic or social status, economic status, physical disabilities, birth or any other condition of the child, parents or legal representatives' (Decree No. 17.943-A, of October 12, 1927. **Consolidates the assistance and protection laws for minors**).

3. Legislation applicable to the Socio-Educational System

The Children and Adolescents Act (Law 8069/90), although having undergone significant and essential changes and reflecting achievements related to children and adolescents' rights and guarantees, no longer expressly and objectively regulates matters directly related to the implementation of socio-educational measures at the national level.

According to E. R. Meneses, the ECA brought about three guarantee systems: the primary guarantee, focused on public policies and the care for children and adolescents; the secondary guarantee, intended for their protection; and the *tertiary* guarantee that focuses on socio-educational measures adopted in response to prohibited acts. The main factors of interpretation of each of these systems are the impossibility of distinguishing children and adolescents by race, colour or social class, consideration for people in development and the absolute priority they have received.[21]

With the complete protection legally established, children and adolescents began to enjoy the same rights that before had been recognized only for adults. Consequently, they gained special rights resulting from their condition as people in development, ceasing to be, from this historical landmark on, victims of society and becoming carriers of rights.

Thus, as for the socio-educational system, it moved away from the notion of coercibility to ensure that children and adolescents were guaranteed all opportunities and facilities that provide for an all-round development in agreement with the ECA, Art. 3: physical, mental, moral, spiritual and social, in conditions of freedom and dignity.[22]

For this reason (focusing on the advances contained in the legislation mentioned above), the National Council for the Rights of Children and Adolescents (hereinafter, CONANDA), the body responsible for deliberating on the policy of care for children and adolescents, came to contribute to the systematization of these gaps, proposing debates with the other actors of the Rights Guarantee System.

During 2002, CONANDA and the Special Secretariat for Human Rights, in partnership with the Brazilian Association of Magistrates and Promoters of Children and Youth and the National Forum of Governmental Organizations for Assistance to Children and Adolescents, held state meetings to debate and

21 E.R. Meneses, *Medidas Socioeducativas...*, p. 61.

22 W.D. Liberati, *Processo Penal Juvenil...*, p. 31.

evaluate the proposed law for implementing socio-educational measures and the pedagogical practice developed in socio-educational units. In the same year, they promoted a comprehensive national dialogue to discuss, deepen and contribute to the drafting of the document entitled National System of Social and Educational Assistance (hereinafter, SINASE), which became a guide in implementing socio-educational measures in Brazil.

The SINASE (approved by CONANDA, by Resolution No. 119/2006[23]) primarily aims to gather principles, rules and technical criteria that are primarily focused on the legal guarantee for the execution of socio-educational measures and assistance programs for adolescents aged 12 to 18 years and, exceptionally, young people up to 21 years old, who are responsible for offences.

Under the terms of the above Resolution, SINASE is a public policy aimed at the inclusion of adolescents in conflict with the law that correlates with and demands initiatives from various fields of public and social policies (Art. 2). It must operate according to the legal, political, pedagogical, financial and administrative criteria that govern the process of investigating an offence and affect the execution of socio-educational measures (Art. 3).

It is important to note that, until then, SINASE did not have legally established governance. In 2007, the discussion started to overcome this normative gap through the institution of such a system based on its coordination by the Union, with the participation of States, the Federal District and Municipalities.[24]

Given this, a debate began on the proposal for a law to implement socio-educational measures, which only came to fruition with the SINASE giving sanction to the law in January 2012. The purpose of the proposed and approved model was to establish an ordered set of principles, rules and criteria that must be observed in the process of investigating an offence and implementing socio-educational measures. They standardized the socio-educational service policy and laid down the central precepts to be followed by the entities of the Brazilian federation.

The public policy aims at implementing socio-educational measures through the enactment of regulations that aim at ensuring the rights and guarantees of adolescents in Brazil, based mainly on the Federal Constitution, Children and

---

23 NATIONAL COUNCIL ON THE RIGHTS OF THE CHILD AND ADOLESCENT. Resolution No. 119, of December 11, 2006. Provides for the National Socio-Educational Service System and other measures.

24 It is important to inform that the Federative Republic of Brazil is formed by the indissoluble Union of its States, Municipalities and the Federal District (CF / 88, art. 1).

Adolescents Act, Convention on the Rights of the Child and Global System and Inter-American Human Rights System (United Nations Minimum Rules for the Administration of Juvenile Justice – Beijing Rules; United Nations Minimum Rules for the Protection of Young People Deprived of Liberty).

With the function of qualifying and strengthening the rules laid down by the ECA, the SINASE Law objectively established some of the parameters that should guide the care institutions that apply socio-educational measures in Brazil. Primarily, it sought the development of socio-educational actions with a focus on human rights principles, expressly contemplated, such as exceptionality, brevity and respect for the peculiar condition of people in development, essential to guarantee and protect adolescents.[25]

First, the proposal provides for the rights of, and guarantees for, the adolescents who commit offenses, which are enshrined in the Convention on the Rights of the Child, to which we already referred.[26] In the second step, the proposal regulates the enforcement of socio-educational measures, eventually applied to the offending adolescent, and establishes a unique process for each kind of applied measure, taking into account the particularities of adolescents subjected to it. [27]

In short, the SINASE Law also instituted normative and explanatory rules of service programs, setting out precepts directed at governmental and non-governmental entities to enforce socio-educational measures. It also subdivided programs into open and custodial, with specific requirements for each type. The model creates an individual plan for compliance with socio-educational measures, which appears as a strong instrument of protection of the offending adolescent, insofar as it individualizes, to the maximum, the application of the measure, and takes into account the peculiarities of the adolescent.

The current individual plan is participated by several bodies in addition to the management of the assistance program: the body responsible for its preparation, Public Prosecution Office, defender of the adolescent and the judicial authority that, following its implementation, will take into account the opinion of the young person, as well as their parents and guardian.[28]

The SINASE Law also regulated the situation of adolescents who suffer mental illness, disability, or chemical dependence subjected to socio-educational

25 SINASE Law, art. 35 and subsections.

26 SINASE Law, art. 49 ff.

27 SINASE Law, art. 9 to 27, without prejudice to other provisions.

28 SINASE Law, art. 1, Paragraph 2, inc. II; art. 41, *caput*, e Paragraph 1; art. 43; arts. 52 a 59, without prejudice to other provisions.

measures.[29] It is worth mentioning, at this point, that the Children and Adolescents Act abstractly dealt with the issue, since it only prescribed that adolescents with mental illness or disability would receive individual and specialized treatment in a place appropriate to their conditions.

The legal text mentioned the need for an intersectoral group,[30] formed by technical teams from the care program and the health care network, to develop and carry out therapies, suitably to the peculiarities of the adolescent.

Without pretending to give an exhaustive analysis of the rules provided for in its nine chapters, the SINASE Law can be said to have focused on the implementation of human rights in favour of children and adolescents. Its *first chapter* focuses on the realities of the adolescents who come into conflict with the law; the *second chapter* deals with the characterization and integration of policies; the *third chapter* treats of the principles that govern the socio-educational system; the *fourth* and *fifth* chapters propose the organization and management of programs, with pedagogical management established in the *sixth chapter*. The *seventh*, *eighth* and *ninth* chapters deal with architectural parameters, management, financing, monitoring and evaluation.[31]

When setting the objectives of the socio-educational measures, the SINASE Law even sought to end doctrinal discussions about the sanctioning or pedagogical nature of these measures, finally giving expression to the legislator's conviction that they had a hybrid character: a socio-educational sanction with pedagogical purpose.

4. Application of the Socio-Educational System

After the introductory presentation of the socio-educational system, we must discuss how it is applied in the Brazilian context. Therefore, we will comment on the age of its recipients (and that will have a bearing on criminal responsibility), procedure for investigating offenses and the socio-educational measures themselves.

---

29 SINASE Law, art. 64 ff.

30 SINASE Law, art. 22, subsection IV.

31 M.C. Nunes, G. P. Bosco, *Sistema Nacional de Atendimento Socioeducativo (SINASE)*: Lei no. 12.594, de 18 de janeiro de 2012, no page number available.

4.1. The addressees of socio-educational measures: children and adolescents and the absence of responsibility under criminal law

CF / 88, in its Art. 228, clarifies that under Brazilian law, minors under 18 years of age are not accountable, subject to special legislation rules. This same wording is used in Art. 27 of the Brazilian Penal Code.[32] Therefore, as can be seen, Brazilian law provides for the so-called *criminal majority* at the age of 18.[33]

As is well known, *imputability* consists in the attribution of some conduct to a person, which is an efficient and voluntary cause of the fact has taken place. It is, therefore, the capacity that results in guilt. In other words, being the imputable agent, he or she may have to answer for the typical and illegal act committed, with the legal consequences being proportional to guilt.[34]

Therefore, imputability is the person's ability to determine what the legal duty imposes so that he or she can behave accordingly. It refers to the knowledge of the duty and the direction of the will with regard to it.[35] When talking about age, which is set according to a criterion owing much to convenience and criminal policy, it is necessary to work on the notion of individual maturity and consider a particular individual's development stage and life experiences.[36]

This notion works on the evident idea that the practice of crime is a cultural phenomenon and that people, at birth, do not bring with them the knowledge of

---

32 Brazilian Penal Code, art. 27: Minors under the age of 18 (eighteen) are not criminally liable and are subject to the rules established in the special legislation.

33 As stated in the Explanatory Memorandum of the current general part of the Brazilian Penal Code: 'The Project maintained the criminal responsibility against minors under eighteen years. This is an option supported by Criminal Policy criteria. Those who advocate reducing the limit, under the justification of increasing crime, which recruits a greater number of minors every day, do not consider the circumstance that the minor, being still incomplete, is naturally antisocial insofar as he is not socialized or instructed. The readjustment of the character formation process must be committed to education, not to criminal punishment. In addition, with the recently enacted legislation for minors, the State has the necessary instruments to remove the delinquent youth, under the age of eighteen, from social life, without his necessary submission to the treatment of the adult delinquent, exposing him to prison contamination' (item 23) (BRAZIL. Chamber of Deputies. Law No. 7,209, of July 11, 1984. **Explanatory Memorandum**).

34 F.A. Toledo, *Princípios básicos de direito penal*, 4 ed., São Paulo, Saraiva, 1991, pp. 312 ff.

35 J.F. Dias, *Liberdade, culpa e direito penal*, 3 ed., Coimbra 1995, pp. 65 ff.

36 J.F. Dias, *Liberdade...*, pp. 65–272.

the proper rules about human behaviour. They need to be acquired, learned and known. Therefore, a child needs to receive more attention to be able to control its most basic instincts and the freest thoughts of that age. More of this is needed in adolescence, when teaching is enhanced for the proper formation of the adult person.[37]

Since it is clear now that the age of 18 represents the moment of assuming criminal responsibility in Brazil, it remains to be explained what treatment is given to those who are under this age, which is regulated by a special law (under the constitutional mandate), namely the ECA that stipulates in Art. 104 that minors under the age of 18 do not bear criminal responsibility, subject to the measures provided for therein (the age will be verified on the date of committing an offence).

According to the ECA, Art. 2, for the purposes of this Act, a person up to twelve years old is considered a child and an adolescent is a person between twelve and eighteen years old.[38] This division also has a consequence when an offence is committed: when a child commits it, the measures to be applied are specific protection provided for in the ECA, Art. 101,[39] while to an adolescent socio-educational measures apply, to be discussed below.[40]

In line with what has been expressed by the authoritative juristic literature, what differentiates the treatment given to offenders under the ECA from that

37 F.A. Toledo, *Princípios...*, pp. 320 ff.

38 This age limitation was not subject to criticism. Among others: 'The establishment of the beginning of adolescence by the Statute at *twelve full years*, mainly to answer for an offence, through a contradictory process with wide defense, does not fail, except for better judgment, to be a recklessness, since at twelve years old the person still is a *child*. Thus, it seems to us that the establishment of adolescence at *twelve full years* even goes against the minimum United Nations rules for the Administration of the Justice of Minors (…)' (P.L. Nogueira, *Estatuto da Criança e do Adolescente comentado*, 4. ed., São Paulo, Saraiva, 1998, pp. 9 ff.).

39 Under the ECA, art. 101, are listed as a protective measure in favour of children and adolescents: I – referral to parents or guardian, through a term of responsibility; II – temporary guidance, support and monitoring; III – mandatory enrollment and attendance at an official elementary school; IV – inclusion in official or community services and programs for the protection, support and promotion of the family, children and adolescents; V – request for medical, psychological or psychiatric treatment, in hospital or outpatient regime; VI – inclusion in an official or community program of assistance, guidance and treatment for alcoholics and drug addicts; VII – institutional reception; VIII – inclusion in a family reception program; IX – placement in a substitute family.

40 P.L. Nogueira, *Estatuto da Criança e do Adolescente comentado...*, pp. 149 ff.

provided for in conventional criminal law is the fact that, in the former, the proceedings must initially analyse the person, and only then, the act committed. In criminal law, on the other hand, the analysis goes from the fact committed towards the person who committed it, that is, the appreciation is reversed.[41]

Note that, despite this age limitation, the ECA can be exceptionally applied to people between eighteen and twenty-one years old (Art. 2, sole paragraph). For example, this can happen when there is a need for commitment to an institution, as a socio-educational measure, for the maximum period (3 years – ECA, Art. 121(3)). After all, there may be an offence committed and, in the course of its investigation, the adolescent reaches the age of criminal responsibility. This is so true that there is a thesis formulated by the Brazilian Superior Court of Justice: [42]

> 2. THESIS: the attainment of the age of criminal responsibility does not interfere with the investigation of an offence nor the applicability of an ongoing socio-educational measure, including assisted liberty, until the age of 21 is reached.

The criminal statute of limitations applies to socio-educational measures under Precedent 338 of the Brazilian Superior Court of Justice.[43] The jurisprudence thus explains how the limitation period is counted when socio-educational treatment is involved:

1. Since there is no regulatory norm in the ECA, the Criminal Code rules are applied to assess the occurrence of prescription, regarding socio-educational measures. PRECEDENT 338/STJ.
2. Following the understanding signed within this Superior Court's scope, in the case of a socio-educational measure applied indefinitely, the limitation period must have as a parameter the maximum duration of commitment to an institution – 3 (three) years.
3. Thus, one must consider the prescriptive lapse of 8 (eight) years provided for in the Penal Code, Art. 109(IV), subsequently reduced by half due to the provision of the Penal Code, Article 115, as set on 4 (four) years.[44]

---

41 A. Chaves, *Comentários...*, p. 508.

42 BRAZIL. Superior Court of Justice. Special appeal No. 1.705.149-RJ. Furthermore: '1. The content of art. 121, Paragraph 5, of the Child and Adolescent Statute, the minor offender who reaches the age of 21 will be obligatorily released from the socio-educational measure he is eventually complying with' (Superior Court of Justice. Regulatory Appeal in Special Appeal No. 1.872.380-SC).

43 BRAZIL. Superior Court of Justice. Precedent 338.

44 BRAZIL. Superior Court of Justice. Regulatory Appeal in *Habeas corpus* No. 527.658-SP.

Finally, the age of criminal responsibility (18 years) in Brazil is controversial and debated.

Among the defenders of maintaining the current limit, there are those who claim that there is no evidence that there would be the necessary efficiency to confront, specifically, the problem of crime in the country. After all, there would be a lack of social, political, and even ethical projects that would support its correct implementation. The ideal would be to work on the Brazilian social situation[45]and take care of the proper application of the policies anticipated in the ECA in favour of children and adolescents.

Those who support the need to reduce the age of criminal responsibility point out that there is an increasing number of severe and violent crimes committed by adolescents, since the ECA would not be enough to suppress crime. Besides, today's teenagers are increasingly aware and developed owing to the technological revolution they experience.[46]

There is a proposal for a Constitutional Amendment (No. 4, 2019) to reduce the age of criminal responsibility to 16 years, the argument for being that '(…) it is common knowledge that criminal organizations, drug traffickers and drug factions use minors as mere instruments, after all they cannot be held legally responsible (…).' Besides, it would be an adaptation, since teenagers can already vote at this age.[47]

Therefore, we must wait for the opinion of the Brazilian Legislative Houses on this question.

4.2. Procedure for investigating a criminal act

According to the ECA, Arts. 171 to 190, applying socio-educational measures to adolescents accused of committing an offence is subject to a special procedure, expressly designed.

These rules stipulate specific norms and principles of Substantive and Procedural Civil and Criminal Law.[48] Specifically, it is important to verify the emphasis

---

45 For all: R. Roseno, *Sou contra a redução da maioridade penal*, 2003, no page number available.

46 For all: D.L. Célico, *A maioridade penal e suas implicações*, 2005, no page number available.

47 BRAZIL. Federal Senate. Proposed Amendment to Constitution No. 4, 2019.

48 ECA, art. 110: No teenager will be deprived of his or her freedom without due process of law; ECA, art. 152: To the procedures regulated in this Law, the general rules provided for in the relevant procedural legislation are subsidiarily applied.

on particular provisions that give differentiated guidelines in respect of childhood and youth, respecting the principles of absolute priority, full protection and best interest.

The procedure is governed by the idea of speed, despite its specific provisions. Insofar as it does not seek the application of criminal sanctions, procedural legislation and its possible complexity are only added to the procedure for investigating an offence in the absence of a specific provision in the ECA. However, even this application is linked to the principles indicated in the paragraph above. Concretely, the applicable appeals system is established only by civil procedural legislation, pursuant to the ECA, Art. 198.[49]

Under the ECA terms, the offender who is between 12 and 18 years old (with an exceptional application to persons up to 21 years old) can be apprehended, essentially, in two cases:

1. Art. 171: under a court order, when he or she must be first presented to the competent judicial authority;
2. Art. 172: apprehension in the act of committing an offence, when he or she should be immediately referred to the competent police authority.[50]

In the event of a flagrant offense aggravated by violence or a severe threat to the person, the police authority (under the terms of the Child and Adolescent Act) shall issue an arrest warrant, hear witnesses, seize the proceeds and instruments of the offence and request the necessary examinations or forensics to prove the commitment of the offense (ECA, Art. 173).[51] In other cases of *flagrante delicto*, the drafting of a record may be replaced by a detailed report (ECA, Art. 173).

---

49 M. J. Diácomo, *Procedimento para Apuração de Ato Infracional*, no page number available.

50 '1 – The adolescent caught in flagrante derelicto must be made aware of his rights (art.106, single paragraph of ECA) and forwarded to the competent police authority (art. 172 of ECA), with an INCONTINENTI communication to the Child Judge and Youth and his family or person indicated by him (art.107 of the ECA) (…)' (M.J. Diácomo, *Procedimento…*). It should be pointed out that, when apprehended in the act, the adolescent will be entitled to the identification of the person responsible for his arrest, to silence, to family assistance and to a lawyer (P.L. Nogueira, *Estatuto da Criança e do Adolescente comentado…*, p. 154).

51 In the doctrine: '(…) It is never necessary to lose sight of the fact that, in accordance with the provisions of art.114 of the ECA, the imposition of socio-educational measures is based on proof of the authorship and materiality of the offence' (M.J. Diácomo, *Procedimento…*).

In theory, if the release of the adolescent who has committed an offense is admissible, the ECA, Art. 174, expressly says that it will be mandatory for the adolescent to appear at a police station, accompanied by either a parent or guardian, at which time they must sign a commitment and a pledge to present themselves to the representative of the Public Prosecutor on the same day, or, that being impossible, on the first business day.[52]

Regarding the offenses committed with greater severity or violence to the person, the adolescent must remain under an order committing them to an institution, to guarantee their safety or maintenance of public order (ECA, Art. 174),[53] with due proof of authorship of the offence being essential. Through the proper institution of proceedings and production of evidence, the materiality of offence is established under the terms of Art. 114, with Art. 189, items I and IV, both from the ECA.[54]

The ECA, Article 183, says that the maximum and non-extendable period for concluding the proceedings (in cases in which the adolescent is in a pretrial commitment to an institution) shall be 45 days.[55] According to the sub-constitutional legislation, if the adolescent lives in a city where there is no detention establishment, the youth must remain at a police station separated from other prisoners for a maximum period of 5 days.

Regarding the Public Prosecution Office's performance in proceedings for investigating an offence, it is noteworthy that the ECA, Art. 179, provides that the Office, after the presentation of the adolescent offender, will proceed to their immediate and informal hearing and, if possible, of their parents or guardian, in

---

52 It is worth noting, in due course, that the Public Prosecutor's Office may order the surrender of the adolescent directly to the parents or guardian, by term, regardless of a court order, since the offense is nothing more than a risk situation created by the adolescent himself, which authorizes such measure (ECA, art. 98, inc. III, c / c art. 101, inc. I).

53 Under the terms of art. 178 of the ECA, the adolescent who committed an offense cannot be transported in a closed compartment of a police vehicle, under conditions that undermine his dignity or that imply a risk to his physical or mental integrity.

54 '4 – If the case demands the decree of provisional commitment into an institution of the adolescent (whose requirements are: a) severity of the act, b) social repercussion, c) need to guarantee the adolescent's personal safety or d) maintenance of the public order – art.174, in fine, of the ECA) or the parents or guardian does not appear, that immediately must be forwarded to the MP, with a copy of the arrest warrant' (M.J. Diácomo, *Procedimento*...).

55 In Brazilian case law: BRAZIL. Superior Court of Justice. *Habeas corpus* No. 580.480-SP.

addition to the victim and witnesses.[56] Said presentation may be due in view of the arrest warrant in *flagrante delicto*, a detailed police report or a police report.[57]

From then on, the representative of the Public Prosecutor's Office may, if he/she so wishes, promote the closing of the case file,[58] grant a remission, or petition the judicial authority for the possible application of the relevant socio-educational measure, as provided in the Child and Adolescent Act, Art. 180.

Specifically, concerning *remission*, it is worth mentioning that this is a kind of pardon granted by a prosecutor or a Judge of Law before the judicial procedure for investigating an offence begins. According to the ECA, art. 126, it is a hypothesis of exclusion from proceedings, taking into account the circumstances and consequences of the act, its social context and the personality of the adolescent and their greater or lesser participation in the offence. The provision mentioned above also adds that the judicial remission, that is, that offered by the judicial authority during the investigation of the offence, will result in the suspension or extinction of proceedings.[59]

The remission works thus as a *moderator*, insofar as it seeks to rationalize the progress of proceedings, which will only be initiated or continued when their need is demonstrated in a concrete plan.[60]

In judicial remission, in addition to the possibility that the socio-educational measure may be suspended or extinguished, there is also the opportunity that the remission may be accompanied by a socio-educational measure, except for

---

56 If the adolescent is presented after being caught in flagrante delicto, the Public Prosecutor will already receive the pieces with the questions basically performed (P.L. Nogueira, *Estatuto da Criança e do Adolescente comentado...*, p. 162).

57 '6.2 – The hearing before the MP will be held with the documents filed at the registry and with a background certificate. When the informal hearing takes place, both from the adolescent, as well as from their parents or guardian, information about their personal, family and social conduct (if they study, work, be obedient, respectful etc.), elements that will influence both in the decision-making about what action the MP should take in the case (act that must be substantiated – art.205, of the ECA), and, at the end of the procedure (if information is filed), in the indication of the measure (s) (s) to be applied' (M.J. Diácomo, *Procedimento...*).

58 Since the fact is nonexistent or atypical, or since the authorship is not of the adolescent, among others (M.J. Diácomo, *Procedimento...*).

59 Among others: P.J. Nogueira, *Estatuto da Criança e do Adolescente comentado...*, p. 206.

60 A. Chaves, *Comentários...*, p. 566.

semi-freedom and commitment to an institution, as provided for in the ECA, Art. 127.[61]

Art. 128 of the ECA, for its part, provides that the measure imposed by remission can be revised at any time, as long as there is an express request made by the adolescent, their legal representative or the Public Prosecution Office.

Once remission is granted, under the terms of the ECA, Art. 181, the Prosecutor, when deciding on the remission, must obligatorily refer the case to the judge so that the magistrate may approve or not the remission. If the decision is approved, proceedings[62]will be terminated. However, if it is not, the deed must be sent by the magistrate to the Attorney General of Justice under the ECA, Art. 181(2).[63]

Understanding that it is not a case of remission, the Public Prosecution Office, under the ECA, Art. 184, shall file information against the adolescent,[64] so the judicial authority will schedule the adolescent's presentation hearing, and decide, from the outset, on the decree or maintenance of provisional detention.

Then, the ECA provides that the adolescent and their parents or guardian will be informed of the content of the information filed against them, and notified to attend the hearing, accompanied by a lawyer (ECA, Art. 184(2)). If the adolescent is not found, the judicial authority shall assign a guardian to the adolescent and issue a search and seizure warrant, suspending the case until the adolescent's presentation (ECA, Art. 184(3)). If the adolescent who perpetrated an offence is in pretrial detention, their presentation will be requested, without prejudice to the notification of the parents or guardian (ECA, Art. 184(4)).

---

61 ECA, art. 127: The remission does not necessarily imply recognition or proof of responsibility, nor does it prevail for the purpose of antecedents, and may eventually include the application of any of the measures provided for in the law, except for the placement in a free regime and admission.

62 Having the judicial approval of the remission, compliance with any adjusted protective or socio-educational measure will be determined (M.J. Diácomo, *Procedimento...*).

63 ECA, art. 181, Paragraph 2: In disagreement, the judicial authority will forward the case file to the Attorney General, by reasoned order, and he will offer representation, designate another member of the Public Prosecutor to present it, or ratify the filing or remission, which will then be the authority judicial authority obliged to ratify.

64 It can be said that the representation formally resembles a criminal charge against adults, covering basic elements of the kind, such as addressing, the qualification of the parties, the narrative of the fact, the legal capitulation, among others. To give effect to the speed of the procedure, no pre-constituted proof of authorship and materiality is required when offering representation (ECA, art. 182, Paragraph 1 and 2).

When the offending adolescent appears at the court hearing, they will be heard, along with their parents or guardian. If deemed appropriate, the judicial authority may grant the remission after hearing the Public Prosecution Office.[65] If the act is serious, which allows the commitment to an institution or semi-freedom, the judicial authority will appoint a defender (if not yet appointed), schedule a subsequent hearing[66] and order a diligence and case study. The previous defence and the list of witnesses must be presented within three days by the adolescent's defence attorney (ECA, Art. 186(1–4).

After the presentation of evidence aimed at investigating the offence in the subsequent hearing, if the information filed by the legal authority against the adolescent is deemed valid, the relevant socio-educational measures shall be applied to the adolescent, suitable to the individual pedagogical needs of each adolescent, as recommended by the following articles: 112(1) and 113 (see next topic), jointly with Articles 99 and 100,[67] all of the ECA. In the absence of necessary elements in the case file, or in the case of unusual conduct or one covered by the exclusions of un-lawfulness, or the lack of evidence on the offender or even the inexistence of the act, the information is deemed groundless and prevents the application of any socio-educational measure to the adolescent.

If the judge orders a socio-educational measure of internment and/or semi-freedom, the notification of the decision, under the Child and Adolescent Act, Art. 190, shall be presented personally to the adolescent and their lawyer. If the adolescent is not found, the notification can be served on their parents or guardian, or through their lawyer (ECA, Art. 190, I and II). If the socio-educational measure applied is other than the penalty of incarceration (warning, obligation to repair the damage, provision of services to the community, assisted

65 In due course, the remission, as a form of extinction or suspension of the process, can be applied at any stage of the procedure, before the sentence (ECA, art. 188).

66 12 – In the ongoing hearing (true instructional and trial hearing), the witnesses of the representation, of the prior defence, a report (psychosocial study) of an interprofessional team are heard, and then the floor is given to the MP and to the lawyer for final oral reasons, for 20 minutes, extendable for another 10, then deciding the Magistrate (art. 186, §4° of the ECA) – see M.J. Diácomo, *Procedimento...*).

67 ECA, art. 99: The measures provided for in this Chapter may be applied alone or cumulatively, as well as replaced at any time. ECA, art. 100: When applying the measures, educational needs will be taken into account, with preference being given to those aimed at strengthening family and community ties.

freedom or protective measures), the notification may be served only to the lawyer (ECA, Art. 190).

If the notification is served on the adolescent, the adolescent *must state whether or not he/she wishes to appeal the decision* (ECA, Art. 190(2)). Even if the adolescent says he or she does not want to appeal, the lawyer is not prevented from doing so. However, if the adolescent's statement is in the affirmative, the lawyer shall be notified to file the reasons for the appeal.

Concerning resources, under the Child and Adolescent Act, Art. 198, in all procedures related to the Child and Youth Justice (including, of course, the procedures for investigating offences committed by adolescents), the court adopts the Brazilian Civil Procedure Code's appeals system, since the ECA does not provide for one.

However, even if the information against the adolescent is deemed groundless, the judicial authority, after analysing the concrete situation, may apply a protective measure to the adolescent, which shall not have a coercive nature, pursuant to the ECA, Art. 101, (see topic below).

We can conclude that there are adversary proceedings in place and ample opportunity for the adolescent to be heard in defence so the socio-educational measure can be applied to them.[68]

It is also worth highlighting that the judge assigned to the Child and Youth area at the location of the action or omission has jurisdiction to review and rule on the procedures for investigating an offence, as provided for in the ECA Art. 147(1), jointly with Art. 148, I and II, and Art. 152.

4.3. The socio-educational measures

Under ECA, Art. 112, the following measures may be applied in case of an offence:

I – Warning
II – Obligation to repair the damage
III – Provision of services to the community
IV – Assisted freedom
V – An institution under a semi-freedom regime
VI – Commitment to an educational establishment
VII – Any of those provided for in Art. 101, I to VI.[69]

68 P.L. Nogueira, *Estatuto da Criança e do Adolescente comentado...*, p. 149.

69 ECA, art. 101: Any of the cases provided for in art. 98, the competent authority may determine, among others, the following measures: I – referral to parents or guardian,

The provision of services to the community and assisted freedom shall be carried out in an open environment. The services are provided under the supervision of professionals who are aware of the justice system. Thus, these measures have a pedagogical intention, even though they carry the idea that the adolescent is somehow responsible. Above all, the vision of a social education policy (since there is a person subject to peculiar development) and protection in the childhood and youth area prevails. Semi-freedom and commitment to an institution, on the other hand, are exceptional measures, aimed at adolescents who have committed repeated offences or in the case of severe offences.[70]

Regarding the examination and study of socio-educational measures, the following are recommended objectives and principles:[71] (a) the adolescent's responsibility for the offence, with the consequent disapproval of its practice; (b) the social integration of adolescents and the guarantee of their individual and social rights; (c) the need to respect human rights; (d) the realization that an adolescent is a person in a peculiar situation of growth and development; (e) absolute priority, particularly according to CF/88, Art. 227; (f) respect for due legal process; (g) the exceptional and brief character,[72] respecting the peculiar condition of a person who is at the growth and development stage; (h) respect for the adolescent's ability to comply with the measure, after checking the circumstances, the severity of the offence and the pedagogical needs of the adolescent upon defining them.

Based on the above, each of the socio-educational measures can be summarized as follows:[73]

---

through a term of responsibility; II – temporary guidance, support and monitoring; III – mandatory enrollment and attendance at an official elementary school; IV – inclusion in official or community services and programs for the protection, support and promotion of the family, children and adolescents; V – request for medical, psychological or psychiatric treatment, in hospital or outpatient settings; VI – inclusion in an official or community program of assistance, guidance and treatment for alcoholics and drug addicts.

70 M.F. Carmo; L.A. Bezerra, 'Eixo 1…,' p. 35.

71 M.F. Carmo; L.A. Bezerra, 'Eixo 1…,' pp. 66 ff.

72 Exceptionality, especially commitment to an institution, should only be applied when there is no other more beneficial measure applicable to the determined offense (P.L. Nogueira, *Estatuto da Criança e do Adolescente comentado*..., p. 179).

73 As extracted from: M.F. Carmo; L. A. Bezerra, *'Eixo 1...,'* pp. 37–40; T.A.P. Castro, A. A. Soares, A. C. Barroso, *O Sistema Socioeducativo no Brasil…*, pp. 9–14.

a) *warning*: provided for in the ECA, Art. 115, consists of a verbal admonition, reduced to a signed document and depends on proof of materiality and sufficient evidence of authorship (ECA, Art. 114, sole paragraph). The warning goes beyond the verbal intimidation that is intended to threaten with likely more severe measures in the future. The warning is meant for offending acts without violence or serious threat, and first offenses perpetrated by adolescent offenders; for these reasons the warning is simple;[74]
b) *obligation to repair the damage*: is intended for offences with an impact on property; in involves the return of the property, the indemnity of the harm or other compensation for the damage suffered by the victim (ECA, art. 116). This measure is little applied, since there is no adequate planning and monitoring. Its main objective is to provide the adolescent with a sense of responsibility for the quantifiable losses caused to third parties;[75]
c) *provision of services to the community*: consists of carrying out free tasks of general interest for a period not exceeding six months with assistance entities, hospitals, schools and other similar establishments and community or government programs. Adolescents work a maximum of 8 hours per week and the work must be carried out in a way that does not affect school attendance (such as on Saturdays, Sundays and holidays) (ECA, Art. 117, *caput* and single paragraph). The work is carried out in places such as schools and hospitals in such a way that dignity, citizenship, work, community relations and social justice are valued, in addition to strengthening the public good;
d) *assisted freedom:* is intended to accompany, assist and guide the adolescent who has committed an offence (ECA, Art. 118), in an open environment. Assisted freedom lasts at least 6 months and may be revoked, extended or replaced by another measure, after hearing the advisor, the Public Prosecution Office and the lawyer (ECA, Art. 118(2)). The measure does not aim to separate adolescents from their family or community, but instead, it is geared to social promotion, including inclusion in aid and assistance programs. as

74 'Measure to be applied, mainly to adolescents *primary*, the *warning* does not require further formalities, although it constitutes an effective and educational means, capable of producing the desired effects, when the offence resulted from unthinking, hasty conduct arising from acts specific to youth' (P.L. Nogueira, *Estatuto da Criança e do Adolescente comentado...*, p. 176).

75 'It is to be seen that the Statute provides for the repair of the damage caused only by the *adolescent*, since, if it is *child*, for which the parent or guardian responds exclusively, the victim will have to file a reparation action for the damage to *common justice*' (P.L. Nogueira, *Estatuto da Criança e do Adolescente comentado...*, p. 179).

well as school supervision, seeking professionalization and introduction into the job market (ECA, Art. 119, items I to III). The measure intends to give the adolescent a new meaning in life, breaking their ties with crime. The measure is aimed at the adolescent's improved performance;

e) *semi-freedom*: This measure can be ordered from the beginning of compliance with socio-educational measures but also as a way of transition from incarceration in an institution to the open environment. The measure allows external activities, regardless of judicial authorization, without a determined term and is governed under the institution commitment rules (ECA, Art. 120(2)).[76] The measure requires schooling and professionalization (ECA, Art. 120(1)). As can be seen, it is intended for more serious offenses, with restrictions on freedom, since the measure requires the adolescent to come to the institution at night and on weekends, being able to return to the parents' house during the fulfilment of the sentence, which shall not exceed three years;

f) *incarceration*: there is an effective deprivation of the freedom of the offending adolescent, with the possibility of carrying out external activities at the discretion of the technical team of the institution to which they are committed, unless there is a court order to the contrary (ECA, Art. 121(1)). The measure does not have a fixed term, but it must be reasonably reassessed every 6 months, and cannot exceed 3 years. When the measure reaches 3 years, the adolescent shall be placed in a semi-freedom or assisted freedom regime (ECA, Art. 121(2–4). The incarcerated adolescent shall be released when he or she attains 21 years of age (ECA, Art. 121(5)). In addition, the adolescent is required to participate in schooling and educational activities to be away from crime and no longer be in conflict with the law. This measure is similar to the most serious measure of the criminal enforcement systems for adults, namely the closed-prison regime, and the idea of the *dangerousness* of the person involved is considered in both systems.[77]

In addition to what was indicated regarding commitment to an institution, the commitment applies when the offence is committed through a serious threat[78]

76 Unlike an institution, semi-freedom does not have fixed and definitive case of application, and can be applied according to the peculiarities of the case in other case that, by themselves, would not give rise to commitment to an institution (among other decisions in this sense, it is cited: BRAZIL. Superior Court of Justice. Regulatory Appeal in *Habeas corpus* No. 600.021-SC).

77 P.L. Nogueira, *Estatuto da Criança e do Adolescente comentado...*, p. 190.

78 (BRAZIL. Superior Court of Justice. *Habeas Corpus* No. 338.517-SP).

or violence to the person,[79] by reiterating[80] other serious offences[81] and also by non-compliance in the commission of other serious violations (ECA, art. 122, items I to III).[82]

Summing up, we can conclude that there is a provision for adopting a system that is not penalty-oriented, but comprises retributions for the offences committed, with some of them being treated similarly to real criminal-law penalties.[83]

5. Restorative Justice in the Socio-Educational System

Although there is no exact, closed and/or fully defined concept of the subject, Restorative Justice can be conceptualized as an understanding that there is an individual and social damage that need accountability and resolution, beginning with the definition of the people involved in a non-formal manner.[84] This is a new model of justice, based on a critical analysis of the current punitive system in force. The justice is enforced based on others' ethics, in which, above all, dialogue and respect are sought vis-à-vis the autonomy of the parties through the solutions that effectively provide the empowerment of those involved and social conciliation.[85]

---

79 Here, it is worth pointing out Precedent 492 of the Brazilian Superior Court of Justice, which states that 'the offense analogous to drug trafficking, by itself, does not necessarily lead to the imposition of a socio-educational measure of the adolescent's commitment to an institution' (BRAZIL. Superior Court of Justice. Precedent 492).

80 The reiteration has the same meaning as the recurrence provided for in Criminal Law (P.L. Nogueira, *Estatuto da Criança e do Adolescente comentado...*, p. 193).

81 In this case, the commitment to an institution cannot be longer than 3 months, under the terms of ECA, art. 122, Paragraph 1. In this same sense, in Brazilian jurisprudence: BRAZIL. Superior Court of Justice. Regulatory Appeal in *Habeas corpus* No. 469.391-DF.

82 Brazilian jurisprudence enshrined that the case provided for in art. 122 of the ECA as justification for commitment to an institution are exhaustive, do not accept expansion by analogy or extensive interpretation, as well as that the reiteration of serious justifying offenses is the practice of new conduct after previous application of a socio-educational measure, except for lack of contemporaneity or less relevance of the antecedent infraction practice (We cite the following among others: BRAZIL. Superior Court of Justice. Regulatory Appeal in *Habeas corpus* No. 598.030-AL).

83 P.L. Nogueira, *Estatuto da Criança e do Adolescente comentado...*, p. 154.

84 R.S. Brandalise, 'Algumas observações sobre a justiça restaurativa e a mediação penal de adultos portuguesa,' *Revista de Derecho* 2016/13, p. 14.

85 R.S. Brandalise, *Algumas observações sobre a justiça restaurativa...*, pp. 18 ff. Still on restorative justice, it is reiterated, it is said that it seeks respect for the sanctions provided

The mediation of conflicts under Law 8.069/90, as pointed out by M. J. Diácomo, aims at the encouragement, coordinated action and integration of the bodies and other parties responsible for the care of children, adolescents and their respective families. This is also accomplished by inserting public policies into the institution that encompasses the most varied judicial interventions limited to what is absolutely necessary.[86]

As to the legal foundations that promoted the institution of mechanisms aimed at mediating conflicts in the Childhood and Youth field, we refer to those introduced in the ECA, through Laws 12.010 / 2009 and, more recently, Law 13.010 / 2014, which established, among other points, the need to create extrajudicial mechanisms for conflict resolution (ECA, Art. 70-A, inc. IV).[87] Likewise, the publication of the SINASE Law, setting parameters to be observed in the care of adolescents who have committed an offence, also included mechanisms and

---

for by law, respectful listening, equality among all, the exercise of the will with the acceptance of withdrawal at any time and respect for rights humans. As there is no pre-determined procedure, several restorative practices are accepted, such as victim support, victim-offender mediation, restorative conference, sentence and healing circles, among others (D.S. Achutti, 'Justiça restaurativa e abolicionismo penal' in: *Contribuições para um novo modelo de administração de conflitos no Brasil*, São Paulo, Saraiva, 2014, p. 68). As for the methodology of this conflict resolution system, V. H. P. Erlich states that, in restorative justice, the work takes place '(…) with the insertion of beacons for the transformation of conflicts, such as non-violent communication, listening qualified, confidentiality and consensus building (…). In restorative justice, feelings are explored based on the consequences of the fact, with the recovery of values, with some pillars: empowerment and care for the victim; accountability of the offender and reparation of the damage (in a broad sense); construction, by all those directly and indirectly affected by the damage, including the community, of a new path to be followed.' V.H.P. Erlich, *Justiça Restaurativa na Socioeducação*, no page number available.

86 M.J. Diácomo, *A mediação e o Direito da Criança e do Adolescente no Brasil: construindo alternativas para a desjudicialização do atendimento*, no page number available.

87 M. J. Diácomo adds that: '(…) Law No. 8,069 / 1990 started to include more explicit references to the need to create extrajudicial conflict resolution mechanisms, starting with the inclusion, among the principles that should guide state intervention in matters of childhood and youth (listed in its article 100, single paragraph), included those related to "minimal intervention", "early intervention" and "mandatory listening and participation", which clearly point for the need to find 'alternative paths' for the full realization of the rights of children and adolescents, recognizing more clearly the right to express their will and to participate in the solution of the problems they face.' M.J. Diácomo, *A mediação e o Direito…*

guidelines related to the self-resolution of conflicts (art. 35, inc. II), as is the case with mediation.

Among other innovations, the SINASE Law, in an unprecedented way, brought restorative principles that encourage, as a priority, '(...) the use of practices or measures that are restorative and, whenever possible, meet the needs of victims' (Article 35, item III, of the SINASE Law).[88] These principles are in harmony with the legal objectives of the socio-educational measure, as they emphasize its pedagogical character, aiming at the adolescent's responsibility regarding the harmful consequences of the offence committed, always encouraging its repair, the social integration of the adolescent and the guarantee of their individual and social rights. The aforementioned legal provision also refers to the offence, rendering the provisions of the sentence effective as the maximum parameter of deprivation of liberty or restriction of rights, subject to the limits provided for in law (SINASE Law Art. 1(2), items I to III,).

Accordingly, even within the ECA program, restorative practices focus on the idea of the consequence of acts, based on the joint responsibility of the adolescent, family, community, society and the government for bringing about the recovery of ties, and the idea of non-violence.[89]

Still in Brazil, particularly in the State of Rio Grande do Sul, it is worth highlighting the recent renewal of the Cooperation Protocol for a State Policy of Restorative Justice and Peacebuilding, originally signed in 2016, which provides for collaborative actions between the State, Public Prosecution Office, Public Defender's Office, Court of Justice and Legislative Assembly.[90] This instrument was proposed by the Court of Justice of the State of Rio Grande do Sul

---

88 In this sense, in 2014, the National Council of the Public Prosecution Office (CNMP), through Resolution 118, created, within the scope of the Public Prosecution Office, the National Policy of Incentive to Self-composition, starting from that to the Brazilian Public Ministries in accordance with the guidelines set by the CNMP, it was tasked with implementing and adopting mechanisms for the proper treatment of conflicts, controversies and problems, especially the so-called self-composition mechanisms, such as negotiation, mediation and the restorative process, including the provision of assistance and guidance to citizens on such mechanisms (art. 1, sole paragraph) (BRAZIL. National Council of the Public Prosecutor's Office. Resolution No. 118, of December 1, 2014).

89 BRAZIL. State of Paraná. Justiça Restaurativa e Socioeducação. Cadernos de Socioeducação, p. 18.

90 BRAZIL. State of Rio Grande do Sul. Public Prosecutor's Office. Instituições renovam protocolo para política de Estado de justiça restaurativa.

to strengthen and promote the inter-institutional expansion of the actions of the *Restorative Justice Program for the 21st Century.*[91] The Protocol's signatories undertook to use their best efforts to promote social conciliation strategies, based on the dissemination of principles and the development of restorative practices for the prevention and constructive transformation of conflicts in the judicial and extrajudicial spheres, including the children and youth area.[92]

As a result, and as an example, the Court of Justice of Rio Grande do Sul issued Resolution No. 1219 / 2018 (COMAG) and created the Center of Restorative Justice as an integral part of the Program mentioned above,[93] aimed to mitigate violence involving children and adolescents in Porto Alegre. The technique also involved the restorative circle, and can occur in two ways: (a) before the start of trial, as an alternative to the traditional justice system; (b) during the trial, as a complementary activity to the traditional justice system. The procedure is carried out by coaches from the Judicial Branch.

According to the authoritative juristic literature and other informative materials, there is a range of restorative practices to encourage the participation of those involved and decrease the participation of the legal operators. The following list includes some practices that are consistent with the ECA and the SINASE Law:[94]

a) *support to the victim*: to reduce the consequences of the action suffered by the victim, even without the presence of the offender;
b) *victim-offender mediation*: the mediator, who is unaware of discussions between the victim and the offender, will work towards possible remediation, compensation, restitution or minimization of the damage suffered. For this purpose, mediation can occur directly or indirectly, depending on whether the victim and offender participate in face-to-face meetings or they are mediated;
c) *restorative circle*: is characterized as a conference of family groups, and is quite common within the Child and Youth Justice. The victim, the offender, other community members are present. Other members of the Judiciary Branch, Public Prosecutor's Office, Public Defender's Office and other people

---

91 State of Rio Grande do Sul. Court of Appeal. *Programa Justiça Restaurativa para o século XXI, passim.*

92 State of Rio Grande do Sul. Court of Appeal. *Programa Justiça Restaurativa para o século XXI*, pp. 23–24.

93 State of Rio Grande do Sul. Court of Appeal. Resolution No. 1.219/2018- COMAG.

94 State of Paraná, *Justiça Restaurativa e Socioeducação...*, pp. 24–26.

deemed important for the case's solution may also be present. This aims to make parties perceive how the acts committed affect not only the person who committed them but also third parties, based on an exchange of experiences, reports, and sharing of responsibilities;

d) *community service*: Community Service may be the result of a restorative process or a judicial decision, so there is a discussion about whether there is any restorative character in this practice, although it may result from the concerned parties' resolution.

In the light of these considerations, the idea of restorative justice has been developed to break the rule of force and imposition determined by the Judicial Branch, but exalting conciliation and care for the victim of the offense.[95] This reorientation hinges on the view according to which conventional justice would not be qualified to respond adequately to conflicts, to meet the needs that arise from them, and to properly promote accountability for offences.[96]

Finally, we shall briefly refer to the essential restorative work to be carried out in schools that provides teachers and employees of educational institutions with training to hold restorative workshops in the classroom, aiming to improve relationships and solve conflicts of small offensive potential.[97]

Therefore, we can conclude that Restorative Justice currently seeks a new way of resolving conflicts and allows all institutions that make up the Justice System to assume their role as main players by granting an efficient and simplified justice

---

95 A.A. Konzen, 'Justiça juvenil restaurativa na comunidade: A prática do encontro antes de sua conformação jurídica' in: A. C. C. Petrucci et al. (eds.), *Justiça juvenil restaurativa na comunidade: uma experiência possível*, Porto Alegre, Procuradoria-Geral de Justiça, 2012, p. 35.

96 L. Brancher, 'Justiça, responsabilidade e coesão social. Reflexões sobre a implementação na Justiça da Infância e da Juventude em Porto Alegre' in: C. Slakmon; M. Machado; P. Bottini (eds.), *Novas direções na governança da justiça e da segurança*, Brasil, Ministério da Justiça, 2006, pp. 672–673.

97 'The application of restorative practices in the school environment, insofar as it will send everyone involved to a network of belonging, will make a total difference to achieve the result we all hope for: the school as a stronghold for the formation of conscious, responsible, prepared citizens to live and that incorporate human rights in daily life. The role of the Public Prosecutor in initiatives for the application of restorative practices in the school environment, both as prevention and treatment of school offenses, can contribute to the solution of many problems related to violence, with an impact on school offenses' (V.H.P. Erlich, *Justiça Restaurativa na Socioeducação*, no page number available).

system, based, in particular, on a cooperation of the State, community, and the parties for the resolution of disputes.[98]

Based on the guidelines outlined here, Restorative Justice primarily aims to change the prevailing culture of pure and simple segregation in the criminal system. The principles of minimum intervention and that of the revision of a socio-educational measure, at any time, emphasize the non-retributive pedagogical nature of the socio-educational measures to be enforced with respect to adolescents. Still, the norm referred to herein encourages the strengthening of family and community bonds, making the adolescent's values and relationships superimposed on the retributive criminal trajectory of deprivation or restriction of freedom.

6. Conclusion

The Federal Constitution of 1988 is a historic milestone for social policies in Brazil. As a result, it is also called *Citizen Constitution*. Owing to this Constitution, several human needs that had been ignored until then were acknowledged, such as the citizen's rights and the duty of the State, ensuring, in the legal field, the right to have access to social services hitherto never provided by the Brazilian government.

One of these acknowledged treatments is the treatment given to children and adolescents, which forced Brazil to adapt its legal policies in this area, which engendered the ECA.

Particularly within the scope of socio-education, the ECA and SINASE models propose interdepartmental management, in which the compliance with the

98 V. H. P. Erlich provides that: 'In this scenario, of a perfect legal outline that does not transfer to practice, based on a retributive paradigm in a global crisis, it is necessary to recognize the very important role of treating the infraction in order to provide the protagonism of each one involved or interested in search for solutions to the damage and its consequence, with accountability and awareness formation in the adolescent, restoring relationship bonds and social reliability broken with the infraction. The abolitionism of the retributive model is not advocated here, nor the abandonment of the struggle for the constitutional command to be obeyed and actually implemented, but the possibility of restorative justice being applied, in the infraction area, to the greatest number of possible cases, as more adequate to achieve the objectives of socio-education. Still, if the retributive paradigm proves to be the most appropriate for the case, that the socio-educational measure can be carried out under a restorative approach, as for example, with the preparation of the Individual Service Plan through a restorative circle' (V.H.P. Erlich, *Justiça Restaurativa* ...).

demands of the segment under discussion aims at integrated actions among all social policies under the Government's responsibility. The basis for all socio-educational action must aim to prevent the offending practice, considering the adolescent's ability to comply with the measure ordered by justice.

Therefore, socio-education has become a public social policy aimed at assisting the adolescents and young people who commit crimes and their families, based essentially on institutional incompleteness. Therefore, the socio-educational action must respect the adolescent's integral development phases, taking into account their capabilities, subjectivity, and limitations, thus guaranteeing individual monitoring.

Thus, based on this new legal framework established by the SINASE Law, new and essential legal models of execution and socio-educational policy have been added to the ECA. Children and adolescents are individually viewed as developing people and subjects of complete protection and priority care.

References

Achutti D.S., *Justiça restaurativa e abolicionismo penal: Contribuições para um novo modelo de administração de conflitos no Brasil*, São Paulo, Saraiva, 2014;

Brancher L., 'Justiça, responsabilidade e coesão social. Reflexões sobre a implementação na Justiça da Infância e da Juventude em Porto Alegre' in: C. Slakmon; M. Machado, P. Bottini (eds.), *Novas direções na governança da justiça e da segurança*, Brasil, Ministério da Justiça, 2006, Available at https://biblioteca.cejamericas.org/bitstream/handle/2015/2908/governanca.pdf?sequence=1&isAllowed=y [access: Nov. 20 2020];

Brandalise R.S., 'Algumas observações sobre a justiça restaurativa e a mediação penal de adultos portuguesa,' *Revista de Derecho*, 2016/13;

Carmo M. F.; L. A. Bezerra, 'Eixo 1: Medidas Socioeducativos: Aspectos Históricos e Conceituais' in: *Ministério da Mulher, da Família e dos Direitos Humanos. Secretaria Nacional dos Direitos da Criança e do Adolescente, Escola Nacional de Socioeducação. Sistema Nacional de A tendimento Socioeducativo* – SINASE, available at: http://ens.ceag.unb.br/sinase/ens2/images/Biblioteca/modulos_dos_cursos/MedidasSUAS/Eixo1-SUAS.pdf [access: Nov. 20 2020]

Castro T. A. P., Soares A.A., Barroso A.S., *O Sistema Socioeducativo no Brasil*, available at: <https://semanaacademica.org.br/system/files/artigos/artigo_26.06.pdf> [access: Nov. 20 2020]

Célico D.L., *A maioridade penal e suas implicações*; available at: https://crianca.mppr.mp.br/modules/conteudo/conteudo.php?conteudo=275 [access: Nov. 20 2020]

Chaves A., *Comentários ao Estatuto da Criança e do Adolescente*, 2 ed., São Paulo, LTr, 1997;

Diácomo M.J., *A mediação e o Direito da Criança e do Adolescente no Brasil: construindo alternativas para a desjudicialização do atendimento*, available at: <https://crianca.mppr.mp.br/arquivos/File/doutrina/justica_restaurativa/mediacao_e_o_direito_da_crianca_e_adolescente.pdf> [access: Nov. 20 2020]

Diácomo M.J., *Procedimento para Apuração de Ato Infracional*, available at: <http://crianca.mppr.mp.br/pagina-1661.html> [access: Nov. 20 2020];

Dias J. F., *Liberdade, culpa e direito penal*, 3 ed., Coimbra,1995;

Erlich V. H. P., *Justiça Restaurativa na Socioeducação*, available at: <https://congressonacional2017.ammp.org.br/public/arquivos/teses/45.pdf.> [access: Nov. 20 2020]

Konzen A.A., 'Justiça juvenil restaurativa na comunidade: A prática do encontro antes de sua conformação jurídica' in: A. C. C. Petrucci et al. (eds.), *Justiça juvenil restaurativa na comunidade: uma experiência possível*, Porto Alegre, Procuradoria-Geral de Justiça, available at: [access: Nov. 20 2020];

Liberati W.D., *Processo Penal Juvenil: a garantia da legalidade na execução de medida socioeducativa*, São Paulo, Malheiros, 2006;

Meneses E.R., *Medidas Socioeducativas: Uma reflexão jurídico-pedagógica*, 1. ed., Porto Alegre, Livraria do Advogado, 2008;

Nogueira P.L., *Estatuto da Criança e do Adolescente comentado*, 4 ed., São Paulo, Saraiva, 1998;

Nunes M.C., Bosco G.P., *Sistema Nacional de Atendimento Socioeducativo (SINASE): Lei no. 12.594, de 18 de janeiro de 2012*, available at: <https://jus.com.br/artigos/51212/sistema-nacional-de-atendimento-socioeducativo-sinase-lei-n-12-594-de-18-de-janeiro-de-2012> [access: Nov. 20 2020];

Roseno R., *Sou contra a redução da maioridade penal*, 2003, available at: https://crianca.mppr.mp.br/modules/conteudo/conteudo.php?conteudo=373 [access: Nov. 20 2020];

Toledo F. A., *Princípios básicos de direito penal*, 4 ed., São Paulo, Saraiva, 1991;

Veronese J. R. P., Custódio A.V., *Direito da Criança e do Adolescente: para concurso de juiz do trabalho*, São Paulo, Edipro, 2011.

Brazilian legal acts and selected jurisprudence

Federal Constitution. Available at: <http://www.planalto.gov.br/ccivil_03/constituicao/constituicao.htm> [access: Nov. 20 2020];

National Council of the Public Prosecutor's Office. Resolution No. 118, of December 1, 2014. Available at: https://www.cnmp.mp.br/portal/images/Resolucoes/Resolu%C3%A7%C3%A3o-118.pdf [access: Nov. 20 2020]

State of Paraná. Justiça Restaurativa e Socioeducação. Cadernos de Socioeducação. Curitiba, 2015. Available at: https://crianca.mppr.mp.br/arquivos/File/publi/justica_restaurativa/justica_restaurativa_e_a_socioeducacao_2015.pdf [access: Nov. 20 2020]

State of Rio Grande do Sul. Court of Appeal. Programa Justiça Restaurativa para o século XXI. Available at: https://www.tjrs.jus.br/export/poder_judiciario/tribunal_de_justica/corregedoria_geral_da_justica/projetos/projetos/justica_sec_21/J21_TJRS_P_e_B.pdf [access: Nov. 20 2020]

State of Rio Grande do Sul. Court of Appeal. Resolution nº 1.219/2018- COMAG. Available at: https://www.tjrs.jus.br/novo/jurisprudencia-e-legislacao/publicacoes-administrativas-do-tjrs/ [access: Nov. 20 2020]

State of Rio Grande do Sul. Public Prosecutor's Office. Instituições renovam protocolo para política de Estado de justiça restaurativa. Porto Alegre: Ministério Público, 2019. Available at: https://www.mprs.mp.br/noticias/infancia/50000/ [access: Nov. 20 2020];

Superior Court of Justice. *Habeas Corpus* No. 338.517-SP. Brasília: STJ, 2016. Available at: <https://processo.stj.jus.br/processo/revista/documento/mediado/?componente=ITA&sequencial=1480281&num_registro=201502570598&data=20160205&formato=PDF>. [access: 20 nov. 2020];

Superior Court of Justice. *Habeas Corpus* No. 339.439-SP. Brasília: STJ, 2016. Available at: <https://processo.stj.jus.br/processo/revista/documento/mediado/?componente=ITA&sequencial=1477663&num_registro=201502676329&data=20160215&formato=PDF>. [access: Nov. 20 2020];

Superior Court of Justice. *Habeas corpus* No. 580.480-SP. Brasília: STJ, 2020. Available at: https://processo.stj.jus.br/processo/revista/documento/mediado/?componente=ITA&sequencial=1955404&num_registro=202001105781&data=20200623&formato=PDF [access: 20 nov. 2020];

BRAZIL. Superior Court of Justice. Precedent 338. Brasília: STJ, 2007. Available at: <https://scon.stj.jus.br/SCON/sumanot/toc.jsp#TIT4TEMA0>. Access: 24 nov. 2020. [access: 20 nov. 2020];

Superior Court of Justice. Precedent 492. Brasília: STJ, 2012. Available at: <https://www.stj.jus.br/internet_docs/biblioteca/clippinglegislacao/S%C3%BAmulas_491a493_STJ.pdf>[access: 20 nov. 2020];

Superior Court of Justice. Regulatory Appeal in *Habeas corpus* nº 598.030-AL. Brasília: STJ, 2020. Available at: https://ww2.stj.jus.br/websecstj/cgi/revista/REJ.cgi/ITA?seq=2003991&tipo=0&nreg=202001762122&SeqCgrmaSes

sao=&CodOrgaoJgdr=&dt=20201120&formato=PDF&salvar=false [access: Nov. 20 2020]

Superior Court of Justice. Regulatory Appeal in *Habeas corpus* nº 600.021-SC. Brasília: STJ, 2020. Available at: https://processo.stj.jus.br/processo/julgamento/eletronico/documento/mediado/?documento_tipo=integra&documento_sequencial=115612783&registro_numero=202001840796&peticao_numero=202000570262&publicacao_data=20200929&peticao_numero=202000570262&ejulgpres=true&formato=PDF [access: Nov. 20 2020]

Superior Court of Justice. Regulatory Appeal in *Habeas corpus* nº 469.391-DF. Brasília: STJ, 2019. Available at: https://processo.stj.jus.br/processo/revista/documento/mediado/?componente=ITA&sequencial=1794731&num_registro=201802406023&data=20190308&formato=PDF [access: Nov. 20 2020]

Superior Court of Justice. Regulatory Appeal in *Habeas corpus* nº 527.658-SP. Brasília: STJ, 2020. Available at: https://scon.stj.jus.br/SCON/GetInteiroTeorDoAcordao?num_registro=201902434438&dt_publicacao=16/03/2020 [access: Nov. 20 2020]

Superior Court of Justice. Regulatory Appeal in Special Appeal nº 1.872.380-SC. Brasília: STJ, 2020. Available at: https://processo.stj.jus.br/processo/revista/documento/mediado/?componente=ITA&sequencial=1974149&num_registro=202001015086&data=20200904&formato=PDF [access: Nov. 20 2020]

Superior Court of Justice. Special appeal nº 1.705.149-RJ. Brasília: STJ, 2018. Available at: https://scon.stj.jus.br/SCON/GetInteiroTeorDoAcordao?num_registro=201702692923&dt_publicacao=13/08/2018 [access: Nov. 20 2020]

NATIONAL COUNCIL ON THE RIGHTS OF THE CHILD AND ADOLESCENT. Resolution No. 119, of December 11, 2006. Available at: https://www.legisweb.com.br/legislacao/?id=104396 [access: Nov. 20 2020];

Decree No. 17.943-A, of October 12, 1927. Consolidates the assistance and protection laws for minors. Available at: http://www.planalto.gov.br/ccivil_03/decreto/1990-1994/d99710.htm [access: Nov. 20 2020];

Decree No. 17.943-A, of October 12, 1927. Consolidates the assistance and protection laws for minors. Available at: http://www.planalto.gov.br/ccivil_03/decreto/1910-1929/D17943A.htm [access: Nov. 20 2020];

Law No. 6,697, of October 10, 1979. Establishes the Code of Minors. Available at: http://www.planalto.gov.br/ccivil_03/LEIS/1970-1979/L6697.htm#art123 [access: Nov. 20 2020];

Chamber of Deputies. Law No. 7,209, of July 11, 1984. Explanatory Memorandum. Brasília: Chamber of Deputies, 1983. Available at: https://www2.camara.leg.br/legin/fed/lei/1980-1987/lei-7209-11-julho-1984-356852-expo

sicaodemotivos-148879-pl.html#:~:text=A%20culpabilidade%2C%20os%20antecedentes%2C%20a,medida%20de%20conveni%C3%AAncia%20da%20substitui%C3%A7%C3%A3o. [access: Nov. 20 2020];

Law No. 8,069, of July 13, 1990. Statute for Children and Adolescents (ECA). Available at: <http://www.planalto.gov.br/ccivil_03/leis/l8069.htm> [access: Nov. 20 2020]

Law No. 12,594 / 2012, of January 18, 2012. Established the National Social and Educational Service System – SINASE. Brasília, 2012. Available at: <http://www.planalto.gov.br/ccivil_03/_Ato2011-2014/2012/Lei/L12594.htm> [access: Nov. 20 2020];

Federal Senate. Proposed Amendment to Constitution No. 4, 2019. Available at: https://legis.senado.leg.br/sdleg-getter/documento?dm=7916543&ts=1594003104347&disposition=inline [access: Nov. 20 2020].

Part IV. Juvenile Delinquency: Comparative Perspective – Portugal

Vanessa Pelerigo

Abstract: The article deals with the issue of criminal responsibility of juveniles in Portugal criminal law. Specifically, it analyses the question of the age limit of criminal liability and the prerequisites of juvenile criminal responsibility. The article also discusses the problematic relationship between the offender's age and the attribution of guilt, and the issues related to the severity of penalty for a juvenile offender.

Keywords: juvenile, age of criminal responsibility, Portuguese juvenile justice system, age of majority, guilt in criminal law.

1. General remarks

With the densification and great importance of the development of universal rights – human rights – the need to establish adequate guarantee mechanisms to enforce them has arisen.

The United Nations established a common standard of human rights, grounded in the principle of respect for the human person's dignity, with the adoption of the Universal Declaration of Human Rights in 1948.

In particular, after the Second World War, it became imperative to confer on children the role of autonomous carriers of rights, given the peculiarities resulting from the stages of their development. Therefore, child rights started to be acknowledged in the Declaration of the Rights of the Child, adopted by the League of Nations in 1924 and proclaimed by Resolution 1386 (XIV) of the United Nations General Assembly on November 20, 1959.

Although this instrument was of great importance, the Declaration was not binding on States, which made it necessary to adopt the Convention on the Rights of the Child, approved by the United Nations in 1989, and ratified by Portugal on 12 September 1990.

This was followed by the European Convention on the Exercise of Children's Rights, adopted in Strasbourg on 25 January 1996, approved by Portuguese Parliament and ratified by the President of the Republic. This Convention is highly important as an international legal instrument and binds Portugal to ensure the exercise of the rights of children under eighteen years of age: 'The object of the present Convention is, in the best interests of children, to promote their rights, to grant them procedural rights and to facilitate the exercise of these rights by ensuring that children are, themselves or through other persons or bodies, informed and allowed to participate in proceedings affecting them before a judicial authority.'[1]

There are also international declarations of principles for the defence of the different rights of the child that we must take into account.[2]

Directive (EU) 2016/800 of the European Parliament and of the Council of 11 May 2016, on procedural safeguards for children who are suspects or accused persons in criminal proceedings stresses the importance of considering the best interests of the child, the minor, and their degree of maturity before deciding to subject them to the law, which means that the child is deemed an agent of the fact and not as a victim.

It is not only the criterion of age that is taken into account here since, in this case, the child would lack criminal responsibility. In other words, the degree of maturity may determine the suitability of a criminal-law censure.[53]

Revolutions at various levels that led to a new social reorganization marked the 1960s and 1970s. Since the beginning of the 20th century, there have been several social, economic and cultural transformations. In fact, children and young people are particularly vulnerable to all such changes, especially when they find themselves in harmful environments, characterised by unemployment

---

1 See Article 1(2).

2 See the United Nations Minimum Rules for the Administration of the Justice of Minors (Beijing Rules); the United Nations Guiding Principles for the Prevention of Juvenile Delinquency (Riyadh Guiding Principles); the standard United Nations Minimum Rules for the Elaboration of Non-custodial Measures (Tokyo Rules); the United Nations Rules for the Protection of Youth Deprived of Liberty; see also the European Pact for Youth and the Promotion of Active Citizenship, the European Social Agenda and the European Employment Strategy.

3 In the same line of thought, A.R. Alfalate, 'O artigo 19. do Código Penal Português à luz de uma nova visão sobre a (in)imputabilidade penal em razão da idade,' *Revista do Centro de Estudos Judiciários*, 2017/1, p. 158: 'Actually, since this is still a stigmatizing proceeding, the young people who do not have the essential characteristics to be subject to the criminal law must be withdrawn from the proceeding. This is also a way to respect the particularities of the criminal law. Taking this into account, the subrogation of the sanctioning conditions is no longer sufficient, which prevailed regarding our perception of the problem, concerning the current development of the (criminal) law of children and young people, which is an actual lengthy alternative.'

or alcoholism, among other issues. Young people try to break down the paradigms of old-fashioned society. They long for a distinctive freedom and that is when 'modern tribes' or gangs appear.

The increase in juvenile delinquency is a challenge for the security forces and for the judicial system itself. The growing number of acts of aggression committed by young people, the increase in reoffending and the relationship between juvenile delinquency and adult criminality requires the response of States to juvenile crime.

International regulations on juvenile crime accelerated the entire reforming process of the Minors' Law in Portugal.[4]

2. Minors: Law on the protection of children and young people in danger, Child Education and Protection Act, and Extraordinary Criminal Regime for Young Adults

From what moment can a minor be considered an adult? When they reach the age of majority or adulthood? What are the characteristics of this development until we can assume the minor has the psychological, moral and civic maturity of an adult? Do the two events occur in parallel? When does a minor reach a sufficient level of maturity to be held responsible for their actions?

In Portugal, the responses to juvenile delinquency vary according to the offender's age. If the offender is under 12, he/she will always be treated as a child in danger, and protection measures will be applied. Thus, below the age of 12 years, there is no responsibility, so a minor shall not be subject to any sanction or penalty for the commission of a crime. Therefore, a child will always be a victim. These measures are enshrined in the Law on the protection of children and young people in danger[5] and aim to protect children, as well as promote

4 See L. Furtado, 'A responsabilização do jovem infractor e o seu tratamento processual' in: *Estudos em Homenagem a Rui Epifânio,* Almedina, 2010, *passim.*

5 Law No. 147/99 (1 IX), amended by Law No. 31/2003 (22 VIII), namely No. 2 of art. 3rd: 'The child or juvenile is considered to be in danger when, in particular, they experience one of the following situations: a) He/she is abandoned or lives alone; b) he/she suffers physical or psychological abuse or is the victim of sexual abuse; c) he/she does not receive the care or affection appropriate to his/her age and personal situation; d) he/she is being cared for by third parties, for a period of time in which the establishment of a strong bonding relationship was observed and at the same time the parents did not exercise their parental functions; e) he/she is obliged to perform activities or work that are excessive or inappropriate to their age, dignity and personal situation or that are harmful to their growth or development; f) he/she is subject, directly or

their education and safety, which may require family support or even an institutional framework to guarantee children's interests.

The development of children's cognitive ability, their capacity for abstraction, and their psychological foundations are very different from adults' since they are only rudimentary. This unfledged condition is a specific characteristic of childhood.

To respond to situations of children in danger, we now have the Law on the protection of children and young people in danger, and for situations of juvenile delinquency, the Child Education and Protection Act provides. Although these laws have different approaches, they are also complementary since a child in danger can grow into a young delinquent.

If a person belongs to the age group of 12–16 years old and commits an act described as a crime, the authorities may apply an educational protective measure, as defined in the Child Education and Protection Act.[6]

If the offender is over 14 years old, this measure may result in a custodial regime.[7] This regime is not to be equated with a prison sentence since these measures 'aim at the education of minors concerning their rights and their introduction, in a dignified and responsible manner, in community life.' In other words, they try to raise awareness and instil accountability in young people, encouraging their development.[8] Thus, the Child Education and Protection Act aimed to limit the State's intervention in minors' education, only contributing to their integration.

The Supreme Court of Justice has come to understand that, under the Child Education and Protection Act, a minor under 16 years old shall not be held criminally and legally accountable because their personality is not yet fully developed. However, the Public Prosecution Office advocates otherwise.

---

indirectly, to behaviours that seriously affect his/her security or emotional balance; g) he/she shows a behaviour or engages in activities or consumption that seriously affect his/her health, safety, training, education or development without the parents, the legal representative or whoever has the de facto custody adequately that fail to terminate situation. h) he/she has foreign nationality and is hosted in a public, cooperative, social or private institution that has a cooperation agreement with the State, without authorization to reside in the national territory.'

6 Thus, Law 166/99 (14 IX).

7 See Guimarães Court Appeal, dated May 15, 2006 (case 719/05-1).

8 In this regard, see P. Guerra, 'Medidas tutelares educativas institucionais e não institucionais – execução e acompanhamento' in: *Direito Tutelar de Menores – O Sistema em Mudança*, Coimbra Editora, 2002, *passim*.

Majority does not exclude the minority age regime. It just provides the minor with a full capacity to exercise rights, enabling them to decide for themselves and freely dispose of assets as if they were of legal age (Civil Code, Articles 132–133).

Hence, there is a certain discrepancy in Portugal between the age at which minors are deemed capable of self-determination and that when they are held responsible for their actions. In fact, an offender under the age of 18 cannot vote, but can be held responsible for any offence he or she commits.

The age of majority is 18. We could reasonably expect that it is also at this age that young people start answering criminally for crimes they may commit. However, this is not so simple. Criminal responsibility is borne from the age of 16 years.

From the age of 16, the offender is considered imputable unless they suffer from a mental abnormality, which means that the criminal capacity to be held responsible for an offence is a presupposition of guilt,[9] which arises with the acquisition of maturity. However, does the cognitive development of all minor offenders reach its peak when they are 16 years old? Alternatively, is the assessment of abilities at a certain age reliable? Has the development of minor been completed at 16 years of age, or are we considering just the probabilistic statistical data? Although a 16-year-old offender can understand the distinction between right and wrong, between good and evil, and even if, in some way, they have some kind of discernment, they will not have the necessary strength to control their emotions, which is an ability required of an adult.

There are minors between 16 and 18 years old. However, there is an Extraordinary Criminal Regime for Young Adults,[10] which has been created to be applied (or withdrawn) when young people between 16 and 21 years old are convicted, since they are on the threshold of maturity, of an act qualified as a crime.

This criminal law for young offenders should 'come close to the principles and rules of the law to re-educate minors (…). It is a question, in short, of enacting a law which is more re-educational than punitive,'[11] given the vulnerability of young people at this stage.

The law says that only a corrective measure may be applied to young offenders up to the age of 21 and provides that, in case of a prison sentence, the judge must extraordinarily mitigate the sentence, under the Criminal Code, Articles 73 and

---

9 In this respect, F. Dias, *Direito Penal, Parte Geral – Questões fundamentais, A doutrina geral do crime*, Vol. I, 2 ed., Coimbra Editora, 2007, pp. 568 ff.

10 Decree-Law No. 401/82 (23 IX).

11 Thus, points 3 and 4 of the Preamble to Decree-Law No. 401/82 (23· IX).

74, when the judge has serious reasons to believe that the mitigation will result in advantages for the social reintegration of the convicted youth (*see* Article 4).[12] This regime involves a reduction by one-third of the maximum limit of the penal sanction provided for the type of offence and a reduction of the minimum limit to one fifth if it is equal to or greater than 3 years and to the legal minimum if it is shorter.

However, it is important to note that before proceeding to special mitigation, the court shall seek to encourage the rehabilitation of the offender, taking into account the interests of society and the proposed measures that do not rule out the imposition of a prison sentence on those young people who are capable of crime and are above 16 years old, when it becomes necessary. The judge shall assess, on a case-by-case basis, the young person's personality as well as their usual conduct.[13]

Therefore, the young person's introduction into society will be crucial for applying the regime, namely their family stability, economic situation, and more importantly, if they sought to mitigate somehow the consequences of their unlawful behaviour. If there are no reasons that preclude rehabilitation, the application of the special regime will act as a stimulus for eradicating the offender's wrong behaviour. Moreover, it will avoid a stigmatizing effect.

It is clear that, from the age of 16 onwards, some criminal capacity elements can already be noticed since there is a significant cognitive development. The

12 However, the jurisprudence has considered that the Judge cannot fail to expressly assess whether this regime should be applied, when the young defendant's age ranges between 16 and 21 years old. In this regard, see the STJ Decision dated March 3, 2005 (Case 04P4706), establishing that the application of this special criminal regime: '(…) is not granted at Judge's discretion, but is rather an *associated power-duty* that the judge shall (must) use whenever the respective assumptions are proven; the application in such circumstances is both mandatory and compulsory.'

13 In this regard, see Case law decision (Case 75 / 05.6TACPV): 'A preventive action must be taken under the general positive or integration framework: the positive function of socialization must be performed, or any of the subordinate negative functions of individual warning or safety or imprisonment. The extent of need for offender's socialization is, however, in principle, the decisive criterion, of the requirements of special prevention. This is only considered, however, if the offender proves he/she lacks socialization. If such a deficiency is not found, the penalty shall be deemed a sufficient warning in terms of special prevention: This will allow the penalty to go close to the minimum limit of the prevention framework or even a limit that coincides with the sentence.'

offender should already understand well what crime is and conform their conduct to the social order.

It must be ascertained then whether the offender had the capacity to know the characteristics of their behaviour as well as its consequences at the moment they committed the offence. This question is quite controversial since the definition of the age at which a minor can understand their actions and be held responsible is not linear. The time when a minor enters adulthood is not the same for all individuals but takes into account the peculiarities of each one.

Even with special mitigation of sentences, keeping the enforcement regime equal to that designed for adults results occasionally in minor offenders serving time in prison together with adults. With their personality not yet fully formed, a child inmate will be forced to adopt certain 'types' of behaviour prevailing in the prison milieu in which they are placed. Thus, a minor offender is likely to assimilate a moral code that is not compliant with the law. However, this regime is not automatic or mandatory and has a very limited scope.

Thirty-eight years after the enactment of this law, the regime has not been reviewed, nor has it taken into account contributions of psychology or neuroscience to the understanding of the brain structure of children and young people. If these sciences have any information that may help the law to arrive at a different interpretation of the phenomena that it should regulate, the inaction of the legislator does not seem justified.

Therefore, we need a robust internal regulatory development, as this instrument is not sufficiently capable of fulfilling the international recommendations either because it does not consider social evolution.

3. The lack of criminal responsibility due to age

We usually associate children and young people's lack of criminal responsibility with their minority and treat them differently from adults.

Immunity from prosecution owing to age is defined exclusively by a formal criterion in Portugal. Is age, however, a sufficient criterion to allow us to say that a person should be subject to a criminal penalty? Despite its randomness, the criterion tries to encompass the transition between childhood and adolescence – a significant period in personality formation.

It is clear that age, while being a crucial factor, is not the only requirement, for it is often the case that people of the same age do not have the same maturity, just as women and men do not have the same maturity levels. Therefore, there is a deficiency in the delimitation of immunity from prosecution. This exemption from criminal responsibility should be dependent not only on age, but also on the mental and psychological development of a person who is still considered a child or a young person.

Even if we objectively consider that an offence committed is the same regardless of whether its perpetrator is a young person or an adult, their maturity will surely not be the same because only experience gained with the passing of years brings a different assessment of various situations. This means that there are special personality traits of the individual consistent with their age. Hence, we recognize the need for an additional subjective criterion: the maturity (emotional, ethical, social) of the offender, that is, the consideration of biological and cerebral elements, and knowledge of value structures in the development process. In short, if the development of the cognitive system is incomplete, the limbic system will prevail and will impair the ability to judge.

Thus, the criminal dogmatic framework of immunity from prosecution owing to age must be developed in order to understand fully the general regime of imputability.

It should be noted that this problem does not arise only in Portugal. In fact, there is no international consensus on an equal age of criminal responsibility for all countries, particularly when crime coverage in the media increases. A short tour around various countries is enough to find different solutions. Even then, the prevalent position is that which makes the age of majority coincide with criminal imputability.

Portugal adopted an age below the world average as an overall criterion, which is not consensual. While some maintain that the age should be raised to 18 years, others argue that it should be lowered to 14 years.[14] We consider, however, such a decrease a serious violation of child protection.

On the one hand, there is a certain sense of impunity in committing offences by juveniles under 16 years old, especially when, in many cases, the background is characterised by violence (homicide, rape, serious offences against physical integrity), which society cannot disregard. On the other hand, there is the principle of child's best interest that must be respected.

14 Different Law proposals have already been submitted but have not been upheld. See, by way of example, Law Project 295 /VIII (available at http://app.parlamento.pt/webutils/docs/doc.pdf?path=6148523063446f764c324679595842774f6a63334e7a637664326c756157357059326c6864476c3259584d76566b6c4a535339305a58683062334d76634770734d6a6b314c565a4a53556b755a47396a&fich=pjl295-VIII.doc&Inline=true) [access: Jan. 20 2021].

Even if we consider that the age should be raised to 18 years to harmonise the Portuguese legal system with other legal systems, because a full integration of the person should be achieved,[15] we do not argue that the age of criminal responsibility should coincide with 18 years since this would constitute a legal fiction.

The truth is that we cannot consider only bio-psychological reasons, but first and foremost – criminal policy ones.

If the age of minority does mean an absolute immunity from prosecution, if we consider biological and moral criteria, then raising the age of criminal responsibility will not automatically mean extending incapacity of crime. Actually, there are individuals who show an early development, while others just the opposite. How can this disparity be balanced?

Knowing when young people reach the maturity and development necessary to be held responsible for their actions, knowing what characterises adolescence and how it influences a young person's behaviour is extremely important to Criminal Law.

Criminal Law will have the task of assessing the cognitive and moral characteristics of the offender to define whether they should be submitted to Criminal Law, despite their age (equal to or above 16). Thus, we must also take into account subjective elements, namely a biological criterion, and assess the differences in the brain structures of young people and adults.

We cannot fail, however, to notice that there must be a 'clear separation between legal criminal dogma and criminal policy.'[16] Criminal Law cannot play the role of social policy, compromising its real task and threatening its own autonomy. This is not to say that Criminal Law must entirely disregard investigations into the determination of children and adolescents' will.

In fact, law must not define imputability in terms of an abstract capacity for determination what the rule is, but must take into account the processes of maturation of intelligence, abstract thinking, and ethical judgment, among others, the knowledge of which only psychology and neurosciences can provide. However, even development psychiatry does not establish its categories nor does it undertake its analysis of the stages and development factors of the person deconditioned by law.[17]

---

15 See A. Rodrigues, 'Repensar o Direito de Menores em Portugal- Utopia ou Realidade?,' *Revista Portuguesa de Ciência Criminal* 2007/3, p. 374.

16 Thus, J. De Faria Costa, 'O princípio da igualdade, o direito penal e a constituição,' *Revista de Legislação e Jurisprudência* 2012/3974, p. 285.

17 According to M. F. Palma, 'Desenvolvimento da pessoa e imputabilidade: no Código Penal Português,' *Sub-Judice* 1996/11, pp. 61–64; cf. H. Per-Oler, H. Wikström, R.

Thus, the offender who, due to his biological, neuro-intellectual, ethical and social conditioning, is unable to understand the facts and rules and, therefore, cannot adapt his behaviour to the normative framework, will not be considered guilty. If there is no legal-penal configuration, there will be no guilt.

A fact can only be classified as a crime and the offender be criminally responsible if the offender's action is criminally relevant, typical, illicit and culpable. There is a censure judgment regarding the offender, who may have acted intentionally or negligently.

It is thus important to know, taking into account the specific situation in which the offence occurred, whether or not the action is objectionable. We have to understand whether the offender had sufficient capacity for self-determination and discernment upon committing the offence. Moreover, if they recognised the offence as illicit, punishable and contrary to the law, but nevertheless committed it.

As a result, the capacity for guilt is assigned to the offender who, knowing the legal framework, guided their behaviour in a manner entirely inconsistent with it. Thus, the offender can be blamed for an action when they are imputable. That is, when their personality is fully formed and developed.

Suppose a minor offender cannot be held criminally responsible. In that case, the minor should be considered outside Criminal Law, following the principle of minimum intervention,[18] under the Child Education and Protection Act.

Is anyone really free? Alternatively, on the contrary, deterministically, would anyone placed in the offender's situation/position adopt identical conduct – based on the principle that everyone should be treated as free,[19] except for particular cases of imputability.

A penalty cannot be imposed on a person immune from prosecution since they cannot be held responsible. However, we can apply security measures,[20] taking into account the special dangerousness of the offender, as well as the protection of society itself.

There are two categories of immunity from prosecution: a lack of criminal responsibility due to psychic abnormality and due to age. The immunity from prosecution regime is provided for in the Criminal Code, Articles 19 and 20.

Svensson, 'When does self-control matter? The interaction between morality and self-control in crime causation,' *European Journal of Criminology* 2010/7 (5), pp. 395–410.

18 Confront Decision of the Supreme Court of Justice, AUJ 3/2009 (17 II).

19 See M. F. Palma, *O Princípio da Desculpa em Direito Penal*, Almedina, 2005, pp. 42 ff.

20 See A. S. Cabral *et. al.*, 'Da Psiquiatria ao Direito,' *Revista Julgar* 2000/7, pp. 185–196.

Article 19 provides for absolute immunity due to age: 'minors under 16 are not imputable.' There is thus the definition of a limit below which Criminal Law does not apply. As argued so far, this article must be amended and considered more than just a formal criterion, that of age, but also a subjective criterion, to determine criminal imputability.

In turn, Article 20 enshrines the immunity from prosecution due to a psychic abnormality. It has to prevent the offender from 'assessing the unlawfulness of the act or determining his own actions according to that assessment,' which means that we cannot have a conviction against the offender, as they were not guilty of their actions, but we can hold them responsible. The consequence will not be a penalty, but a security measure, after verifying the offender's dangerous nature.

Well, if we take into account bio-psychological considerations in the case of a psychic abnormality, why can we not consider them in respect of the lack of criminal responsibility due to age, given the randomness of the criterion?

4. Conclusion

The research carried out in this work contributed to an interdisciplinary discussion of the matter, more than answering questions.

If, on the one hand, there is an increasingly significant movement towards child protection (especially to provide guarantees for their personal growth and development), on the other hand, we cannot ignore the increasingly frequent and violent events of juvenile delinquency.

The lack of homogeneous criteria among countries means that the age limits of legal and criminal responsibility are different. Thus, different criminal policies are adopted, taking into account the background in which violence occurs. This could result not only in an international, European disagreement, but also within the Portuguese legal system itself. The scenario is one of discord. From what age should young people be punished by Criminal Law?

As demonstrated throughout this work, neuroscience and psychology may help us in this matter. Although, their researches are mainly focused on psychic abnormalities and significant neurological alterations, understanding these mechanisms and the respective brain processes casts new light on the immunity from prosecution regime.

Neuroscience, for example, does not intend to change the concept of guilt in Criminal Law, but rather points out what should be valued in a young delinquent's behaviour.

We must realize whether the offender, taking into account their bio-psychological development stage, would be in a position to meet the objective requirements of the law. That is, would they abide by the legal system if they met the intellectual requirements of maturity?

Thus, if we should not hold young people responsible for law-breaking behaviour, in many situations, we will also not be able to equate them with adults. We cannot require that children and adolescents' behaviour have the same level of control as expected from adults. Thus, we cannot have a similar conviction judgment.

This situation leads to two scenarios: on the one hand, we may be faced with people who have no criminal capacity by reason of their age, but may be held criminally responsible, given the high level of maturity; there will be others who, given their incomplete development, cannot be subject to judgments of criminal-law guilt. Hence, we must establish differentiating objective and subjective criteria in order to grade various types of behaviour by adolescents.

It will be up to the State, in the first instance, to adopt purely preventive conduct. Then, the family, school and different aggregating groups of society shall contribute to the effective integration of young people. If this is unlikely to occur, they should call attention to them when their behaviour does not comply with the legal order.

The State should assume its role and punitive character when the preventive function is clearly insufficient, and attempt to provide an adequate response to the problem of juvenile delinquency.

Even so, we point out that the submission of a young person to a protective rather than punitive regime is always beneficial since the former aims to educate, while the latter – to censor and punish.

References

Alfaiate, A.R., 'O artigo 19. do Código Penal Português à luz de uma nova visão sobre a (in)imputabilidade penal em razão da idade,' *Revista do Centro de Estudos Judiciários* 2017/1;

CabralL, A.S. *et. al.*, 'Da Psiquiatria ao Direito,' *Revista Julgar* 2009/7;

Figueiredo Dias, *Direito Penal, Parte Geral – Questões fundamentais, A doutrina geral do Crime,* Vol. I, 2 ed., Coimbra Editora, 2007;

de Faria Costa J., 'O princípio da igualdade, o direito penal e a constituição,' *Revista de Legislação e Jurisprudência* 2012/3974;

Furtado L., 'A responsabilização do jovem infractor e o seu tratamento processual' in: *Estudos em Homenagem a Rui Epifânio*, Almedina, 2010;

Guerra P., 'Medidas tutelares educativas institucionais e não institucionais – execução e acompanhamento' in: *Direito Tutelar de Menores – O Sistema em Mudança*, Coimbra Editora, 2002;

Palma M.F., 'Desenvolvimento da pessoa e imputabilidade: no Código Penal Português,' *Sub-Judice* 1996/11;

Palma, M.F., *O Princípio da Desculpa em Direito Penal*, Almedina, 2005;

Rodriques A., 'Repensar o Direito de Menores em Portugal – Utopia ou Realidade?,' *Revista Portuguesa de Ciência Criminal* 2007/3;

Wikström, Per-Olof H., Svensson R., 'When does self-control matter? The interaction between morality and self-control in crime causation,' *European Journal of Criminology*, 2010/7 (5).

Lex et Res Publica

Polish Legal and Political Studies

Edited by

Anna Jaroń

Vol. 1 Anna Jaroń: Socio-Economic Constitutional Rights in Democratisation Processes. An Account of the Constitutional Dialogue Theory. 2012.

Vol. 2 Stanisław Filipowicz: Democracy – The Power of Illusion. 2013.

Vol. 3 Teresa Dukiet-Nagórska (ed.): The Postulates of Restorative Justice and the Continental Model of Criminal Law. As Illustrated by Polish Criminal Law 2014.

Vol. 4 Agnieszka Kupzok: Enforcement of Patents on Geographically Divisible Inventions. An Inquiry into the Standard of Substantive Patent Law Infringement in Cross-Border Constellations. 2015.

Vol. 5 Alicja Jagielska-Burduk / Wojciech Szafrański: Legal Issues in Cultural Heritage Management. A Polish Perspective. 2016.

Vol. 6 Maciej Mataczyński (ed.): The Takeover of Public Companies as a Mode of Exercising EU Treaty Freedoms. 2017.

Vol. 7 Maciej Barczewski (ed.): Value of Information. Intellectual Property, Privacy and Big Data. 2018.

Vol. 8 Pawel Smoleń, Marcin Burzec: Introduction to Polish Tax Law. 2018.

Vol. 9 Łukasz Pohl, Konrad Burdziak: Judicial Interpretation of the 1997 Criminal Code Provisions on Self-Defence. 2019.

Vol. 10 Adam Szot: Judicial Review of Administrative Discretion. The Influence of Court Decisions on Administrative Actions. 2019.

Vol. 11 Michał Peno / Konrad Burdziak (eds.): The Concept of Modern Law. Polish and Central European Tradition. 2019.

Vol. 12 Leszek Leszczyński / Bartosz Liżewski / Adam Szot (eds.): Potential of Precedent in the Statutory Legal Order. 2019.

Vol. 13 Łukasz Bolesta: In Search of a Model for the Legal Protection of a Whistleblower in the Workplace in Poland. A legal and comparative study. 2020.

Vol. 14 Paweł Chmielnicki / Adam Sulikowski (eds.): New Perspectives on Legislation. A Comparative Approach. 2020.

Vol. 15 Marcin Burzec / Beata Kucia-Guściora / Paweł Smoleń: Agricultural Activity in Poland: A Fiscal and Legal Study. 2020.

Vol. 16 Magdalena Półtorak / Ilona Topa (eds.): Women, Children and (Other) Vulnerable Groups. Standards of Protection and Challenges for International Law. 2021.

Vol. 17 Josef Albert Fox: Die polnische Verfassung vom 3. Mai 1791. Hintergründe der Entstehung und der Außerkraftsetzung. Stellung Polens im Zeitalter der Aufklärung. 2021.

Vol. 18 Barbara Janusz-Pohl (ed.): Juvenile Justice Systems: Poland-Brazil-Portugal. 2021

www.peterlang.com

www.ingramcontent.com/pod-product-compliance
Ingram Content Group UK Ltd.
Pitfield, Milton Keynes, MK11 3LW, UK
UKHW021833100926
8556IPUK00004B/307

9 783631 855843